Gavel Gamut Greetings
from
JPeg Ranch

by
JAMES M. REDWINE

authorHOUSE®

AuthorHouse™
1663 Liberty Drive
Bloomington, IN 47403
www.authorhouse.com
Phone: 1-800-839-8640

First published by AuthorHouse 8/14/2009

ISBN: 978-1-4490-1623-4 (e)
ISBN: 978-1-4490-1626-5 (sc)

Library of Congress Control Number: 2009908295

Printed in the United States of America
Bloomington, Indiana

This book is printed on acid-free paper.

PREFACE

MY FRIEND JIM KOHLMEYER BEGAN to hound me to write a "legal column" almost immediately after I was elected Posey County Court Judge in November 1980. He was seeking free filler for his newspaper, *The New Harmony Times*, now *The Posey County News*.

Beginning in 1990 I wrote a few pieces for him that caused nary a ripple of concern or even notice. Then in 1992 I gave the readers a respite until April 2005 when The Posey County Historical Society initiated a campaign to invigorate its membership. I wrote three pieces that focused on Posey County during the Civil War.

Since my articles for the Historical Society, I have written a column each week for which only I am to blame.

My agreement with Jim and subsequently with the owners and editors of the *Mt. Vernon Democrat*, *The Carmi Times*, *The Western Star of Posey County* and the *City-County Observer* of Evansville, Indiana has always been: I write what I wish and they publish it if they wish; no money exchanges hands either way.

Jim was the Chairman of the Posey County Republican Party, but neither he nor I took note of this small flaw where our friendship was concerned. I miss his good humor and his sense of public service.

Fortunately, I still have my wife, Peg, who does all the work around JPeg Ranch, prepares the manuscripts of my burnt offerings and frequently fills Jim's prior role of reminding me I am neither Mark Twain nor Chief Justice John Marshall.

I have selected columns based not on popular demand, as there has been none, but on the totally arbitrary criteria of what strikes my fancy. They are grouped by subject matter. A few have required some minor editing and, because some were written in response to then current events, context may have been added.

Thank you for reading, or perhaps, re-reading, the *Gavel Gamuts*. I hope you enjoy them.

Jim Redwine, July 2009

Acknowledgements

Dr. Walter Jordan of Martinsville, Indiana has always encouraged my literary efforts and listened patiently to my offbeat theories on whatever topics have happened to arise in the deeply satisfying conversations we have had over the past forty-six years. Everyone should be so fortunate as to have such a friend.

Katrina Mann is my long time friend who began working with me when she was eighteen. Over these good years she has typed many of the *Gavel Gamuts* and has not hesitated to remind me of the dangers of hubris. Between Katrina and my wife, Peg, *Gavel Gamut* has remained a diversion when it might have fallen into diatribe; although, as you might find, occasionally I refused to be saved from myself.

Rodney Fetcher is both a friend and colleague who has often assisted with technology, photographs and videos in my work as judge including my talks and writings. His company, RAF Productions, provides a valuable service.

The ink and watercolor painting of JPeg Ranch on the cover was done by nationally known artist Cedric Hustace of Evansville, Indiana (www.cedrichustaceart.com, HustaceArt@aol.com). Ced is a retired attorney, a competitive race walker, a member of the General Thomas Posey Chapter of the Sons of the American Revolution, and my friend.

Robert Pote (www.robertpotewatercolor.com, bobphyl@insightbb.com), Maggie Rapp (www.maggierappfineart.com, maggierapp@sbcglobal.net), Becky Boggs (wvgardengirl@insightbb.com) and Anne Doane are well-known highly gifted Posey County artists whose works appear by their generous permission. I am truly blessed by their talent and their friendships. Bob Pote's and Becky Bogg's marvelous artwork inside this book had to appear in black and white to maintain costs of publication. The reader is strongly urged to view their work in color by visiting their websites or contacting them by email.

Our son, James David Redwine, sketched the line drawings for some of the chapter headings. Jim was my inspiration for many of the military articles. His combat service in the Gulf War (1990-1991) and the Iraq War (2003-?) kept me focused on both the dearness and randomness of life.

FOREWORDS

David Pearce, Owner and Publisher of the *Posey County News*, New Harmony, Indiana

I met James Redwine in 1986 and we became friends almost immediately. Right away, I could see there was an astute ability to write, an incredible knowledge of the history of Posey County, and just a hint of sarcasm. The combination of the three makes his weekly column in our newspaper one of the first things read by many. I am happy that Jim has decided to share his compilation of work and knowledge in one volume.

Sara Manifold of the *Mt. Vernon Democrat*, Mt. Vernon, Indiana

The *Mount Vernon Democrat* is one of the fortunate few newspapers that publish *Gavel Gamut*, written by Judge Jim Redwine, each week. The column presents the rare perspective from the eyes, ears and mind of the county circuit court judge. Redwine gives readers a glimpse of the many facets of the county's history, laws and justice.

The weekly column presents Posey County in its historical ages through which Redwine adds comparison between those times and now — included with personality, wit, humor, exciting characters ... and a love for Indiana University

Barry Cleveland, Editor and Publisher, *The Carmi Times*, Carmi, Illinois

I had never met Jim Redwine before; fortunately, if I had ever sped through Posey County in excess of the speed limit (and I'm not admitting anything), he hadn't been called upon to pass judgment on me. But I had read his columns in the *Mt. Vernon Democrat* and *Posey County News*, found them interesting and asked if he might make them available to readers across the Wabash in White County. He graciously agreed. And over the past year or so, southeastern Illinoisans have been treated to tales from Posey County history and fascinating details from the case of White

County's own William Newby--or Ricketey Dan Benton, as the case may be. Since we published the first of the *Gavel Gamut* columns in *The Carmi Times*, I've had the privilege of meeting their author, and a more outgoing, gregarious man I can't imagine--nor a better conveyor not only of history but of Posey County's present.

I look forward to reading more of Judge Redwine's work in the months ahead.

Jamie Grabert, Publisher of the *Western Star of Posey County* and, along with Ron Cosby, also Publisher of the *City-County Observer* of Evansville, Indiana

Life is ironic. Recently, Judge Redwine and I had an email exchange where I mentioned him publishing a collection of *Gavel Gamuts*. He informed me that this project was in the works. I was excited to hear the news. I believe that *Gavel Gamut* offers local readers a fresh perspective on historical events. They are thoughtful and well-written excerpts of local history and the characters who shaped our society today. Having read Judge Redwine's previously published *Judge Lynch!* three times, I find his style to be that of an educated man who is simply making every attempt to preserve history and enhance the quality of reading materials for those who read his works. *Gavel Gamut* offers an amusing twist to the mundane information found in newspapers. I am proud to have the opportunity to work with Judge Redwine and print his columns each week. I think you will find this collection to be a best buy for all who love to witness history, learn about the past or simply want to be entertained.

Congratulations to Judge Redwine for having the courage to put himself out there each week and form a collection of columns worth reading.

TABLE OF CONTENTS

CHAPTER ONE

HOW IT ALL BEGAN

THE GENESIS OF *GAVEL GAMUT*

(Week of August 4, 2008)

Last week it was good to see Posey County, once again, take steps to honor our military veterans and preserve our courthouse and the Soldiers and Sailors Monument. The future looks bright for the courthouse, the monument and our county. And, or so it seems to me, this may be an opportune time to revisit how this column got foisted upon the gentle readers of our five area newspapers: *The Carmi Times*, the *Mt. Vernon Democrat*, the *Posey County News*—formerly *The Times*, the recently revived *Western Star of Posey County* and the *City-County Observer* of Evansville, Indiana.

My recently departed good friend, Jim Kohlmeyer, who in 1990 was the publisher and editor of *The Times*, was looking for fill material on his editorial page. He had followed my amateur acting career at the New Harmony Theatre and figured I could do no worse as a writer.

Set out below is the first *Gavel Gamut* as it appeared in *The Times* on April 10, 1990.

Jim Kohlmeyer has repeatedly requested that I write a column. Please remember this, i.e. justice dictates the proper placement of blame.

Jim and I have been negotiating the terms of our enterprise for several years. We finally reached what we legal folks call a meeting of the minds when I dropped my demand for compensation and so did he.

As I understand our agreement, I may write when and what I please and he may publish it when and if he chooses.

By clear bargaining I did secure his promise not to join in any lawsuits or diatribes occasioned by my musings.

On the other hand, he reserved the editor's right to blue pencil any material that he deems inane. These may be short columns.

Some of you may be aware that in addition to writing— not for a living— I work in the Posey County Courthouse.

This is a constant source of satisfaction for me as the courthouse represents much of what is good about our community, e.g. fiscal responsibility, public service, tradition and vision.

Plans for the courthouse were approved by the Board of Commissioners in October, 1873.

Construction bids were received in February, 1874.

Attorney, Posey Circuit Court Judge, Indiana Supreme Court Justice, Civil War General and, later, Indiana Governor, Alvin P. Hovey, laid the cornerstone on May 30, 1874. A public ceremony reenacting the laying of the cornerstone took place July 4, 1876.

Construction was completed in January, 1878. The courthouse has been in continuous service ever since. It cost $99,000 which included four thousand dollars in overruns.

The striking white oak furnishings still seen and used throughout much of the courthouse, particularly in the courtroom, were purchased in 1893 at a cost of $1,250.

Posey County's military service to the nation is commemorated by the monument on the west campus. It was dedicated July 23, 1908 and cost $14,000.

Thousands of public servants and jurors have administered the government of Posey County from the courthouse.

It has been changed in many minor ways to accommodate technology. Electric lights have replaced glowing gas ones. Computers have replaced typewriters and recording systems have replaced pen and ink.

Yet, our symbol of government has only been enhanced by these wise utilitarian decisions of our public officials. The courthouse's historic character has been carefully preserved by each generation while service to the public has been the guidepost for modifications.

I urge each of you to visit and enjoy your courthouse.

Well, Gentle Reader, that was the Genesis of the thing. If you have complaints, my complaint department is in the capable care of my good friend Mr. Kohlmeyer.

MARK TWAIN AND POSEY COUNTY

(Week of August 25, 2008)

Those few of you who may remember this column from its first generation in the 1990's in the old *New Harmony Times* and those who have suffered through the recent version know that Mark Twain is a favorite source. In April of 1990, I noticed on page ninety-four of *Leonard's History and Directory of Posey County* and on page 150 of *Leffel's History of Posey County* a report of a Posey County murder case from 1818 that struck me as so similar to the murder in *Tom Sawyer* that it could not have been coincidence. Mark Twain must have based his fictional case on Posey County's real one.

I do not know if anyone read my column from 1990 and concluded I was correct. I do know that I reached my conclusion alone and almost twenty years ago.

Anyway, the following, **<u>original</u>** article, appeared April 17, 1990, on page 2 of the *New Harmony Times*.

POSEY COUNTY, TOM SAWYER MURDERS SIMILAR

(April 17, 1990)

Did Tom Sawyer and Huckleberry Finn "witness" the Posey County murder of Dr. Thomas Moore Parke on March 29, 1818?

Samuel Clemens was born in Florida, Missouri in 1835. He grew up in Hannibal, Missouri which was a small town on the banks of the Mississippi.

Perhaps because his father was an attorney and a justice of the peace Clemens maintained an interest in and respect for the law and his father may well have been familiar with the infamous case from Posey County.

Clemens, who took his *nom de plume* of Mark Twain from river boat terminology, was a river boat pilot.

In his many trips on the river he may well have heard of Posey County's most notorious murder and used it as a model for the plot of his book, *Tom Sawyer*.

Or he may have had occasion to read of the accounts in old newspapers once he began writing for the papers.

Mark Twain was a 19th Century Man for all Seasons. Twain knew steam boating, he knew newspaper writing and publishing, he knew mystery writing and he knew human nature.

Twain used crime solving in many of his stories. His novel *Pudd'n Head Wilson* was one of the first fiction works to use fingerprinting in the plot.

And as all writers must, Twain drew upon actual events to craft his novels.

As Twain said in his preface to *Tom Sawyer*, "Most of the adventures recorded in this book really occurred."

In the Posey County case, Thomas Moore Parke, "[A] young physician of much promise," [*Leonard's History and Directory of Posey County*, 1882, at page 94] robbed the fresh grave of Peter Hendricks who had died when thrown from a horse.

In *Tom Sawyer*, Dr. Robinson "[so] young and promising," paid Injun Joe and Muff Potter to rob the new grave of Hoss Williams (Whitman Classics at page 93).

Rachel Givens had offered Gibbons a jug of whisky to "chastise" Parke.

Parke was killed on Second Street in Mt. Vernon by George Gibbons who was "[A] profligate and drunken fellow." Gibbons hit Parke with, "an ashen club."

Robinson was killed by Injun Joe with a knife that belonged to Muff Potter who was also the town drunk after Robinson had defended himself against Potter by striking Potter with a board.

Tom Sawyer and Huckleberry Finn were eye witnesses and eventually Tom cleared Potter whom Injun Joe had framed for the killing.

Tom and Huck's home town was the small village of St. Petersburg on the banks of the Mississippi.

When Parke was murdered Mt. Vernon had barely gotten started on the banks of the Ohio.

Muff Potter was jailed in St. Petersburg.

Gibbons was jailed at the county seat in Springfield.

Injun Joe was the main witness against Potter.

Rachel Givens was indicted as an accessory.

The main witness against Givens was Gibbons.

Gibbons was aided in escaping from jail and given a jug of poisoned whisky when he and his wife were put in a boat on the Ohio River. He died a few miles downstream.

The case against Rachel Givens was dismissed.

Some years later Rachel Givens was on her way to California when she was, "attacked by cholera and died, and was buried in two barrels."

The similarities in these unusual cases, the much smaller population of that time and Samuel Clemens's background are interesting factors in considering the possibility that Posey County's most famous murder case may have been "witnessed" by America's most famous boys.

It is interesting to think of Mark Twain as an early writer of "historical fiction", especially when the historical part came from Posey County.

THROUGH A GLASS DARKLY

(Week of August 11, 2008)

IN AUGUST, 1990, SADDAM HUSSEIN invaded Kuwait. President Bush (the first one) warned Saddam that if he did not remove his troops from Kuwait: "He might face a war crimes trial". Now I know most people will do almost anything to avoid coming to court, but when I heard the President's warning in November of 1990, I had my doubts that Saddam was quaking with fear. So, I did what all media pundits would do, I wrote a column about it. The following article was published in *The Times* on November 6, 1990. You can see that neither Saddam nor the President paid any attention to it as it took the Gulf War of 1991 to remove Hussein from Kuwait and another invasion in 2003 to bring him to trial.

MESSAGE FROM POSEY COUNTY: "SADDAM HUSSEIN, BEWARE!"

(November 6, 1990)

I noted a news media report which quoted President Bush as condemning Iraq's aggression and warning that Saddam Hussein might face a war crimes trial for his actions. The headline was: "Saddam may face court, Bush warns".

Now, I carry no brief for Saddam and will join in the celebration when he either crawls or is helped back under his I-rock.

Such an event could save my soldier son from having the obligation to serve in one of the few areas of this planet whose heat is worse than his home county's humidity.

On the other hand, does our tradition of fair play and our constitutional prohibition against cruel and unusual punishment permit us to subject even the Marquis de Saddam to a court against his will?

Many issues would need to be resolved.

Where would venue lie: The World Court, where we have not yet resolved Iran's claims from 1980? The United Nations, which has already taken a public and unanimous position that Iraq is wrong? The Posey Circuit Court, where the judge is rumored to believe that Saddam is a supercilious scoundrel? How about legal representation?

John Adams may have represented red coats during the Revolutionary War but even the most noble attorneys might take pause at defending the bellicose butcher of Baghdad.

While I have such faith in the honorable profession of law that I am certain counsel could be found, how would the fees and expenses be paid? Iraq owes billions and Saddam's only valuable possessions are legally the property of Kuwait.

Therefore, either the lawyers would be forced to work without pay, and even pay exorbitant expenses out of their pockets, or, the good ole' U S of A would have to pick up Iraq's slack.

Even if a court, a judge and an attorney could be found, what about a jury of his peers?

I can imagine some of the *voir dire* questions: "Have any of you heard anything about this matter?" "Mr. *Fahd eban al Saud*, as a member of the Saudi Arabian ruling family, could you be fair and impartial?" "How about you, Mr. *Jabir al-Sabah*? As a Kuwaiti, you wouldn't be prejudiced would you?" "Ms. Joan nee Hoehn Khaja, as a native of Posey County, Indiana, surely you'd have no reason to be upset with Saddam?" "Is there anyone on the panel who remembers the price of gasoline before the invasion?"

Well, you can see the problems with bringing Señor Saddam to the Bar.

First, it's probably too strong a reaction by us to his actions. Second, it might be impossible to give him a fair trial.

Therefore, in an effort to render justice, I suggest we humanely save him from the ordeal of a trial and move right to sentencing.

I respectfully submit that had we taken my suggested approach to Saddam Hussein in November 1990, we would be thousands of lives and trillions of dollars better off. Of course, the oil companies and military industrial complex would have had to suffer through on less profit, but I bet they would have made it okay.

JURY TRIALS

(Week of August 18, 2008)

THIS COLUMN RAN IN *The New Harmony Times* on June 19, 1990. Because it is already too long, I will get right to it. It has been slightly modified due to changes in the law.

THE RIGHT OF BEING JUDGED BY OUR PEERS

(June 19, 1990)

The American system of trial by jury, citizens in charge of their own destiny, that is the essence of America.

One of the areas where this remains true is our right to be judged by our peers.

What is a trial by jury? Where and when did it originate? How can jury service affect the jurors and the parties? Why have trial by jury?

Much of the historical information in this article comes from *The Jury, Tool of Kings, Palladium of Liberty* by Lloyd E. Moore.

Why do we ask untrained amateurs to decide complicated controversies involving one's money, one's family, one's life or even one's sacred honor?

How can we allow these decisions to be made in secret without requiring even an explanation of how the verdict was reached?

A jury in Posey County generally is six or twelve people drawn randomly from computer lists by the Jury Administrator, John Emhuff.

Each month names are drawn for citizens to serve in Circuit and Superior courts. A questionnaire is sent to each prospective juror who returns it. When a jury is needed, either Judge Baier (now Judge Almon) or I decide how many to call in based on the type of case (the sheriff calls them). These citizens report to either the courthouse or the coliseum where the attorneys question them and can excuse a certain number without cause based on the type of case.

This process is described by the French term, *voir dire*, which means to speak and to hear. The amount of time needed depends on the type of case.

Those who are called but not selected receive mileage and $15.00 a day; if chosen, they receive $40.00 a day plus mileage.

One of the earliest juries was in Egypt about four thousand years ago where minor offenses by workmen were tried by eight fellow workers (four from each side of the Nile).

Aeschylus in his play *Eumenides* about 500 B.C. described the trial of Orestes by the gods for murdering his mother, Clytemnestra. You may recall that during Agamemnon's service in the Trojan War, his wife took several lovers and when Agamemnon came home, she murdered him. This upset Orestes who murdered her. Pallas Athena, goddess of wisdom, convened twelve citizens of Athens to try him. They split six-six and Athena broke the tie and voted for acquittal.

The Romans about 450 B.C., the Anglo-Saxons about 450 A.D. and the Normans around 1066 A.D. all had jury systems of one kind or another. Our jury system has its antecedents in English law beginning about the time of Aethelred in 865 A.D. In 1609, King James I's instructions for the government of the Colony of Virginia guaranteed jury trial to those charged with all capital crimes.

The Massachusetts Bay Colony in 1628 provided that civil and criminal cases could be tried by jury. New York (New Amsterdam) in 1664 secured trial by jury. Pennsylvania in 1673 provided for juries of six or seven members and in 1682, twelve-man juries of one's peers were a right in capital cases and challenges to those chosen were guaranteed.

The First Continental Congress in 1774 declared each colony had the right, "especially to the great and inestimable privilege of being tried by their peers." In 1775, the first session of the American Stamp Act Congress decreed: "That trial by jury is the inherent and invaluable right of every British subject in these colonies."

In June 1776 the Constitution of Virginia decreed: "That in all criminals (trials) a man has a right to a speedy trial by an impartial jury of twelve men of his peers who must make a unanimous finding of guilt."

The United States Constitution, effective in 1789, and the Bill of Rights were replete with the guarantee to trial by jury. The American Jury System referred back to the Magna Carta of 1215. In the United States Supreme Court case of *Thompson v. Utah* (1898) it was held that: "When the Magna Carta declared no freeman should be deprived of life, liberty or property but by the judgment of his peers or by the law of the land, it referred to a trial by twelve jurors." Indiana has its own jury guarantee by constitution, statute, common law and court rule.

We have to face the following truths about juries: They are sometimes inefficient, expensive and inconvenient, wrong, and yes, even sometimes unfair and biased. Much the same is true of judges.

However, Thomas Jefferson had the proper perspective when he declared common citizens must be involved in the execution of their laws through their judicial process. It is not just justice in the individual case that is important. People must stay involved in their own destinies and their country's. Except for juries our entire judicial system is in the hands of a few highly trained judges and attorneys.

While it may be the easier path to abnegate one's duty, with the absence of responsibility comes the loss of control. Juries are the essence of participatory democracy in our legal system. Let's keep them; I will see you in court.

I TOLD YOU SO

(Week of September 29, 2008)

The current seven hundred billion dollar ($700,000,000,000.00) Wall Street Bailout using our money proves that my fears of too easy credit for America's youth were simply a correct prediction of disaster.

The following article appeared in the old *New Harmony Times* on May 11, 1990.

"McDonald's now takes credit cards. This development was the topic of a conversation I had with a friend the other day. She told me she feared this was a disturbing harbinger of social ills. She opined as follows:

'If the original low cost instant gratification now costs so much a kid can no longer buy it by redeeming an armful of Coke bottles, won't they quit picking them up?

And if children want to treat their moms on Mother's Day, are they going to have to hock their mopeds?

What will be the effect on the psyches of our young people when they offer mere cash while their friends flourish their bank cards?

And what of the humiliation of having one's white plastic compared with another's gold?

Or the unkindest cut of all, being the only teenager in the group who is rejected for a card?

My friend worried about the lessons learned and not taught by a society which bases its marketing system on electronic impulses rather than hand-to-hand transactions.

Is not the act of tendering one's hard earned wages for another's carefully prepared product what separates us from "them"?

Pride in the seller's product and pride in the buyer's honest pay have combined to make America, well, America.

But, if kids are to learn that a piece of petrified petroleum which never waxes or wanes may be as valuable as perspiration, perseverance and perspicacity, then will not they lose incentive to be all they can be?

And what of the fiscal irresponsibility instant credit fosters? Will the youth of other countries save while ours are profligate? Will our current efforts to recoup a peace dividend be thwarted by millions of teenagers competing with the government for borrowed money?'

The lady was practically apoplectic by this time. She was no longer surmising but predicting. The present was prologue.

After listening to her grave misgivings, I began to catch her fear. I pondered the meaning of it all. I almost succumbed to her despair.

Just then though it came to me as clearly as a whiff of asphalt in the morning air. I told her there was still hope as long as the real icon for American youth remains unspoiled by corporate management. I said at least Coke machines don't accept credit cards. She responded, "Not yet!"

Of course, Coke machines and even parking meters, in some places, now do accept credit cards.

Our financial system's "House of Cards" is teetering.

GAVEL GAMUT

by Judge Jim Redwine and the
Posey County Historical Society
(Week of May 9, 2005)

THE GREAT REBELLION COMES TO POSEY COUNTY!

Confederates Invade Our Fair Land
November 08, 1862

Our sovereign state and county were the victims of an unprovoked incursion by members of the Fourth Regiment of the Kentucky Cavalry of the Confederate States of America under the personal command of Colonel E.G. Hall in the early hours of November 08, 1862.

Our own citizen, Dr. William K. Harris, was kidnapped from his home in West Franklin by a posse of armed rebels and forcibly removed across the Ohio River to Webster County, Kentucky, where he was held for one week.

Our loyal citizens were further preyed upon by these belligerents who claimed to be soldiers but who stole a horse and bridle from Mr. John Stephans, a saddle from Mr. Frederick Hendricks, a shotgun from Mr. Joseph Sweeten and numerous items from Dr. Harris including a vial of morphine.

The names of the captured rebels were: William Quinn, James Quinn, Paul Manns, Charles Woods, Jonas Soakes, Frank DeChamps, Barnett Clay, John Gobin, George Finley and James Powell. The ruffians were turned over to our Sheriff, Blythe Hayes, by the authorities in Henderson, Kentucky.

Cloaking their nefarious deeds as acts of war, Colonel Hall claimed the insurrectionists were simply replacing their regiment's doctor who had been taken earlier by our valiant Union soldiers in Kentucky.

However, our own Posey Circuit Court Judge, the Honorable William F. Parrett, Jr., was not deceived by these protestations of military service. And, when these perfidious pilferers appeared in our courthouse, Judge Parrett did not gladly suffer the hooligans' call to be treated as prisoners of War. Judge Parrett dispatched their claims to be acting under lawful orders as so much legerdemain.

Judge Parrett's decision will be divulged in this space next week.

GAVEL GAMUT

by Judge Jim Redwine and the
Posey County Historical Society
(Week of May 16, 2005)

PERFIDIOUS PILFERERS PURLOIN POSEY'S PROPERTY AND PERSON!

Jury Verdict
September 26, 1863

Guilty! So say you one, so say you all, said the Posey Circuit Court Jury.

After almost a year of pre-trial maneuvering by the Confederate Defendants and the Posey County authorities, a Jury found those Confederates guilty of kidnapping Dr. William Harris from his home in West Franklin and of stealing property from several citizens of our fair county.

Each of the Defendants claimed to have been acting as a soldier in the Rebel Army when they invaded Posey County on November 08, 1862. They each immediately filed to appeal their two-year state prison sentences and one hundred dollar fines.

However, our own Posey Circuit Court Judge, William F. Parrett, Jr., in pre-trial motions had carefully addressed the issue of whether Paul Manns, William Quinn, James Quinn, Charles Woods, Jonas Soakes, Frank DeChamps, Barnett Clay, John Gobin, George Finley and James Powell were acting legitimately as members of the Fourth Regiment of the Kentucky Cavalry of the Confederate States of America or were simply common criminals.

Then, after a Posey County Jury had found the men guilty, Judge Parrett reiterated his reasoning in denying the convicted felons a new trial.

First, Judge Parrett defined the lines of authority separating state civil authority and martial law:

> *"This Court cannot take cognizance of the question whether the defendants are or are not entitled to the protection afforded by the Laws of War to prisoners of War; that is a question solely between the Belligerents [the United States and the Confederate States]."*

> *"If the defendants wish to assert a claim to be treated as prisoners of War they must do it not in this Court but through the Military authorities of the Belligerent under whose orders they assume to have acted."*

> "This is the understanding of the Rebel authorities themselves on the subject as is manifest from the fact that they turn over certain of our captured officers to the State authorities of the insurrectionary states to be punished under the criminal codes of those states."

After pointing out that claims of Prisoner of War status must be addressed to the military authorities, Judge Parrett set forth the legal standard for determining the issue:

> "In a war in support of an insurrection against the established Government, it is optional with the government when it will commence or cease to treat traitors as prisoners of War and this being the case Civil Tribunals will not take cognizance of rules which are liable to fluctuate with the Contingencies of War."

Next our own Judge Parrett let the Defendants feel the whole weight of his reasoning:

> "As this is an indictment for a violation of the laws of Indiana pending in an Indiana Court and as Indiana is not a Belligerent, her Courts will see to the enforcement of her Laws and leave the question of Belligerent rights where they properly belong to the General Government. She will be especially careful not to seek to shield felons from the consequences of a violation of her Laws on the grounds that they have acted in obedience to the commands of greater felons against the General Government."

Lastly, Judge Parrett directed the convicted Confederates to the proper avenue for their appeal:

> "If the Defendants are entitled to be held as prisoners of War the Claims to have them so treated can be made as well before as after trial [Judge Parrett's decision on jurisdiction was initially made pre-trial then reaffirmed by him after the guilty verdicts], and if the United States decide that they are prisoners of War the Governor of the State has full authority to release them and turn them over to Military Authorities."

Well, Gentle Readers, please "tune in" next week to see if the Rebels remained within our Indiana prison system or were declared Prisoners of War.

GAVEL GAMUT

by Judge Jim Redwine and the
Posey County Historical Society
(Week of May 23, 2005)

Posey County has a unique and interesting history which the Posey County Historical Society is proud to help preserve and promote. If you have read these articles on the Invasion of Posey County by Confederate soldiers on November 08, 1862, please note they are on behalf of the Society which will be submitting other stories from our history.

If you have questions about the Posey County Historical Society or would like to become involved with it, please contact our Secretary, Albert Gibbs, at the Black Township Trustee's Office at 130 West Third Street in Mt. Vernon or call Albert at 812-838-3851.

Now, the final installment about the Invasion and the fate of the Belligerents from the Rebel side:

PRISONERS OF WAR!

<u>Pusillanimous Phony Patriots</u>
<u>October 04, 1863</u>

As the Readers may recall, on November 08, 1862, members of the Fourth Regiment of the Kentucky Cavalry of the Confederate States of America under the command of Colonel E. G. Hall, kidnapped Dr. William Harris from his home in West Franklin and, also, stole numerous items from other Posey County citizens.

After their arrest by Union forces in Henderson, Kentucky, the men were turned over to Posey County Sheriff, Blythe Hayes, for trial before a Posey County Jury and Posey Circuit Court Judge, William F. Parrett, Jr.

The Defendants raised claims that civil authorities in Posey County had no jurisdiction to try them as they should be treated as Prisoners of War. Judge Parrett denied their pre-trial Motions to Dismiss on this basis as well as their post-trial Motions for New Trials. Judge Parrett directed the Defendants to the Federal Authorities through the Indiana's Governor's Office.

William Quinn, James Quinn, Paul Manns, Charles Woods, Jonas Soakes, Frank DeChamps, Barnett Clay, John Grobin, George Finley and James Powell took the Judge up on this advice and sought redress of their two-year state prison sentences from Governor Morton.

In a directive from the *"War Department Provost Marshall General's Office, Washington D.C. dated October 4, 1863,"* the Confederates were determined to be Prisoners of War.

This Order was made to *"His Excellency Oliver P. Morton, Governor of Indiana"* as follows:

"I have the honor to enclose herewith copy of a communication from Colonel Conrad Baker, Acting Provost Marshall for Indiana in regard to the action of the Civil Authorities of Indiana in the cases of General Officers and men captured by the United States forces November, 1862, under Col. J.W. Foster, 65th Indiana Vols. Then commanding at Henderson, Kentucky.

I would call your attention to the copy of General Hallack's endorsement on Colonel Baker's communication and request that the men may be turned over as prisoners of war."

This Directive was signed by the Provost Marshall General James B. Fry and brought a conclusion to the Invasion of Posey County.

POSEY COUNTY'S POLITICS WASN'T BEANBAG IN THE 19TH CENTURY

(Week of May 8, 2006)

Those brave enough to seek public service today are often mistreated by such organizations as the Gridiron Club or Jon Stewart or The Drudge Report or media outlets or even the legal system. I am sometimes amazed that anyone cares enough about our various levels of government to face such abuse just to serve their fellow citizens. To all those who serve and seek to serve, I say thank you.

And, if it makes you feel any better, politics was a lot rougher in Posey County in the 19th Century. Other than dueling, which was illegal, there was not much people could do to seek redress when their characters were assassinated just because they sought public office.

The newspapers of the 1800's did not hesitate to cast aspersions or even accuse politicians or their political parties of very serious crimes.

Posey County's newspapers wore their political affiliations boldly and without apology during the days after the Civil War or the "War of Rebellion" or "The War of Northern Aggression" when emotions ran deep over slavery and state's rights.

The *New Harmony Register* of October 11, 1878, railed against newly elected Congressman, William Heilman. Mr. Heilman was a Republican from Evansville. *The New Harmony Register* left no doubt of its Democrat leanings and its displeasure at the outcome of October's general election:

> "What a terrible and humiliating descent from scholarly
> attainments and statesmanship in the First (now the Eighth)
> District is here.
> .....
> Can the First District sink lower?"

And the passage of time did nothing to assuage the disdain for Congressman Heilman among Posey County's Democrat positioned newspapers.

The Western Star of January 2, 1879, ran a front page article falsely professing that a man indicted for the murder of a Mt. Vernon law officer had escaped only through the help of Congressman Heilman's supporters:

> "I don't think it would be right to let it be known
> who the persons were that furnished me the money
> to escape the country, but you may bet your bottom
> dollar that I would never (have) got away if I had
> not voted for Bill Heilman."

The editor of the *Western Star* knew this story to be a fabrication as he had witnessed the lynching of the "escapee". And such attacks often worked, as Mr. Heilman was no longer our Congressman after the next election.

Hardball politics was bipartisan in Post-Bellum Posey County. Resolutions adopted by the Republican Party of Missouri were published with approval in the local *Unafraid Republican*. Those resolutions painted the Democrats with a broad brush:

> "We arraign (a term of criminal charges) the
> Democratic Party as a constant disturber of
> public tranquility and confidence, as the wanton
> foe of public security, as constantly attempting
> to weaken the power and authority of the nation
> by crippling the army in time of uncertainty
> and danger.
>
> .....
>
> We arraign it as faithless to the obligations of the
> national honor and as the chief support of the wild
> schemes of inflation, repudiation and utter financial
> disorder...."

The politics of Posey County today may still be unpleasant for our fellow citizens who have the courage and commitment to put themselves and their families through an election. But, I think, it's better now than in 1870's. Perhaps those who prefer to criticize rather than take responsibility for running our county and country might do well to remember Robert Kennedy's words spoken at Indiana University just one month before his assassination in 1968. He was relentlessly assailed as being ruthless for seeking the Presidency.

As a freshman law student at Indiana University in Bloomington, I heard his eloquent response to those in the audience clamoring for his head. Mr. Kennedy simply said: "Isn't it possible that I just want to serve?"

POLITICS AND BLOOD

(Week of October 2, 2006)

In the old days, 1964, you had to be twenty-one to vote. And when I turned twenty-one, I was extremely eager to cast my first vote for Lyndon Johnson because he promised not to send American boys to die in an Asian war in Vietnam. Most voters feared that Barry Goldwater would escalate the war.

I felt good about my small contribution to peace until President Johnson sent thousands of Americans to Vietnam.

Even though my first vote did not work out as planned, I have never failed to vote since. There is something about the physical act of voting that makes me feel connected to everything that makes the United States of America special.

Over the years my votes have fallen upon winners and losers but I see democracy as an opportunity for better things; I do not expect guarantees. But I do appreciate a good faith effort from those public minded persons who put their hats in the ring to serve the rest of us.

The first Tuesday after the first Monday in November we in Posey County have another opportunity to continue America's tradition of following the longest lived working constitution in the world. We, also, will be continuing Posey County's colorful history of grass roots self-government.

One of my first experiences with democracy in Posey County involved a race for sheriff. There were nine men running for sheriff, six for the Democratic nomination and three for the Republican. Since the sheriff is chosen by the whole county, all thirty-three precincts count. Of course, in some precincts, especially in primary races, few citizens exercise their voting franchise.

Such was the case in a certain precinct in the central portion of our fair county that, also, happened to be the home precinct of several of the family members of one of the candidates. When the vote totals for that precinct came in, I happened to be within earshot of the candidate whose family populated that area. He did not get one vote.

A friend of his tried to console him and told him he needed to stay involved in party politics even though he might be upset with his party. The losing candidate responded: "Oh, I'll always stay with my party but I'm never going to another family reunion!"

Well, maybe politics is thicker than blood, at least with some folks.

Anyway, I for one will not forego my American birthright of trying to choose those who are going to so significantly affect my life. It just feels good to have the opportunity to make my own choices. And, after all, the old adage of use it or lose it could someday apply to democracy.

VOTE RIGHT AND VOTE OFTEN

(Week of October 9, 2006)

Sam Blankenship, who is to Posey County what Socrates was to Athens, Greece, in about 400 B.C., has repeatedly warned us about the potential hazards of electronic voting. Sam is a man for whom I have the utmost respect. However, my experience with various voting systems has led me to the conclusion that the real potential hazard with any voting system may be some of the operators of whatever system may be used.

As Sam the computer expert would say to me when I could not get my computer to operate properly, "Garbage in, garbage out, or, incompetence in the operator results in incomprehensibility from the computer."

With due deference to our local guru, Sam, the gadfly of Posey County, I postulate that it is not the voting system that is usually at fault when elections are manipulated. Invalid election results probably have more to do with overzealous partisanship than faulty technology. Of course, these zealots can sometimes hold sway because otherwise good citizens fail to get involved in running for office or even voting.

One of the first elections that I was ever actively involved in was a countywide race in Vanderburgh County some years ago. I had only recently graduated from law school and wanted to fully participate in the great American democratic experience.

I barely knew the two candidates vying for the office in question, but I had convinced myself that I could make a profound difference in Southern Indiana's system of government by putting up political signs at the voting places on Election Day.

So about 4:00 o'clock a.m. on Election Day morning I and another young and idealistic attorney friend of mine picked up a whole car load of posters attached to tomato stakes and set out to save the world.

We put signs up for our adopted champion at several polling places at churches and schools. About 7:00 a.m., after the polls had been open about an hour, we pulled into a large precinct where many people were lined up to vote.

As we got out of my old car, each wearing our one and only, but new, three-piece suit and each carrying a large sign for our candidate, a large woman rushed up to us and asked us if we were from a party's "headquarters". Neither of us even knew what a party headquarters was or where such a headquarters for either political party might be located, but we did admit to being with the party she asked about as our hero was the nominee of that party.

"Well" the lady loudly proclaimed to us within the hearing of the assembled voters:

"You better get some money out here 'cause these people ain't voting right!"

We quickly backed into the car and went home. It was not until ten years later when I ran for office myself for the first time that I, again, took up the cause of a candidate, i.e., myself.

Naturally, those bad old days of voting tombstones and fair exchanges of votes for half- pints or two dollars cash have gone the way of a more colorful era. Surely, today elections cannot be stolen by such mundane and transparent means and the will of the people can no longer be frustrated by the misguided misdeeds of a few overzealous partisans unless, of course, the rest of us sit back and let such things happen.

I respectfully suggest that you go vote on November 7th and every election that you can thereafter. I assure you that I will. So, if you think you and I may vote for opposing candidates you had better go vote to cancel mine. However, my sign posting days are over.

CHAPTER TWO

THE PROMISE OF AMERICA

HAPPY BIRTHDAY TO U.S.!
LET'S HAVE A PARTY AND INVITE EVERYONE!

(Week of July 4, 2005)

The United States Supreme Court has occasionally succumbed to popular opinion then later attempted to atone for it. The **Dred Scott** (1857) and **Plessy v. Ferguson** (1892) cases come to mind as examples of institutionalized injustice with the partial remedy of **Brown v. Board of Education** (1954) being administered many years later.

In **Dred Scott**, the U.S. Supreme Court decided that American Negroes had no rights which the law was bound to protect as they were non-persons under the U.S. Constitution.

And in **Plessy**, the Court held that Mr. Plessy could not legally ride in a "whites only" railroad car. The Court declared that laws that merely create distinctions but not unequal treatment based on race were constitutional. **SEPARATE BUT EQUAL** was born.

Our original U.S. Constitution of 1787 disenfranchised women, and recognized only three-fifths of every Black and Native American person, and even that was only for census purposes. Our Indiana Constitution of 1852 discouraged Negro migration to our state in spite of Posey County Constitutional Convention Delegate, Robert Dale Owen's, eloquent pleas for fair treatment for all.

Were these documents penned by evil men? I think not. They were the result of that omnipotent god of politics, compromise, which is often good, but sometimes is not. Should you have read this column recently you may recall that I strongly encourage compromise in court, in appropriate cases.

However, as one who grew up in a state where the compromise of the post Civil War judges and politicians led to the legal segregation of schools, restaurants, and public transportation, I can attest that some compromises simply foist the sins of the deal makers onto future generations.

When I was 6 years old, my 7 year old brother, Philip, and I made our first bus trip to our father's family in southern Oklahoma.

We lived on the Osage Indian Nation in northeastern Oklahoma. It sounds exotic but our hometown, Pawhuska, looked a lot like any town in Posey County.

In 1950 our parents did not have to worry about sending their children off with strangers except to admonish us not to bother anyone and to always mind our elders.

When mom and dad took us to the MKT&O (Missouri, Kansas, Texas and Oklahoma) bus station it was hot that July day. Oklahoma in July is like southern Indiana in July, WITHOUT THE SHADE TREES!

My brother and I were thirsty so we raced to the two porcelain water fountains in the shot gun building that was about 40 feet from north to south and 10 feet from east to west.

Phil slid hard on the linoleum floor and beat me to the nearest fountain. And while I didn't like losing the contest, since the other fountain was right next to the first one, I stepped to it.

"Jimmy, wait 'til your brother is finished. James Marion! I said wait!" Dad, of course, said nothing. He didn't need to; we knew that whatever mom said was the law.

"Mom, I'm thirsty. Why can't I get a drink from this one?"

"Son, look at that sign. It says 'colored'. Philip, quit just hanging on that fountain; let your brother up there."

Of course, the next thing I wanted to do was use the restroom so I turned towards the four that were crammed into the space for one: "White Men", "White Ladies", "Colored Men", and "Colored Women".

After mom inspected us and slicked down my cowlick again, we got on the bus and I "took off a kiting" to the very back.

I beat Phil, but there was a man already sitting on the only bench seat. I really wanted to lie down on that seat but the man told me I had to go back up front. And as he was an adult, I followed his instructions.

Philip said, "You can't sit back there. That's for coloreds. That's why that colored man said for you to go up front."

That was the first time I noticed the man was different. That was, also, the point where the sadness in his eyes and restrained anger in his voice crept into my awareness.

As a friend of mine sometimes says, "No big difference, no big difference, big difference."

And if all this seems as though it comes from a country far far away and long long ago, Posey County segregated its Black and White school children for almost 100 years after 600,000 men died in the Civil War. In fact, some of Mt. Vernon's schools were not fully integrated until after *Brown* was decided in 1954.

And, whether we have learned from our history or are simply repeating it may depend upon whom we ask. Our Arab American, Muslim, Black, Native American, and Hispanic citizens, as well as several other "usual suspects", may think the past is merely prologue.

Sometimes it helps for me to remember what this 4th of July thing is really about. It's our country's birthday party; maybe we should invite everyone.

There is nothing equal about separate.

WELCOME TO AMERICA

(Week of October 1, 2007)

As would most Americans, I feel comfortable pointing out the foibles of Anglos and Saxons and practically everybody else as my bloodlines are so mixed there ain't nothing I ain't. Of course, you'd have to go back quite a ways to find any D.N.A. that would connect me to the Semites or the Medes and Persians, but I claim them as at least a part of my entire family tree.

The American Melting Pot has always been one of those concepts that my family holds dear. We know for sure that hundreds of years ago some of our ancestors from Celtic and European countries mixed with one another and with some of our Native American ancestors. And it would be unlikely that any race or ethnic background has escaped the amalgam of my family's long tenure in the good old U.S. of A.

Therefore, my sister and my brothers and I were raised to believe that Americans are no worse nor any better than people in other places as they may well be our relatives. I have never felt awed by the people whose ancestors created ancient Persia that about three thousand years ago was the most advanced and powerful nation on earth, the America of its day if you will. Nor have I seen its current inhabitants, the Iranians, as less worthy than I am.

So when the President of Iran was invited to speak and respond to questions from students at Columbia University, it never occurred to me that Columbia's president, Lee Bollinger, would abuse his position and embarrass himself, his university and his country by insulting his invited guest and the seventy million Iranians who democratically elected him.

In 1958, Eugene Burdick and William Lederer wrote *The Ugly American* which according to one review was, "A slashing exposé of American arrogance, incompetence and corruption in Southeast Asia." As some of you may recall, this fictionalized account of a country that included Vietnam was given great lip service but we still proceeded to lose 58,000 soldiers there over the following seventeen years.

Iran is many times the area and population of Vietnam. And it, also, may see itself as more sinned against than sinning.

But issues of foreign policy and self-interest aside, whatever happened to good manners and common courtesy? For instance, if President Mahmoud Ahmadinejad had been arrested and brought forcibly into an American courtroom under a charge of murder, would he have been treated as discourteously as he was as the invited guest of Columbia University? If President Bush were invited to speak in Tehran and was insulted and demeaned by the one who invited him, would we not be outraged?

We Americans see ourselves as a generous and tolerant freedom loving society and much of the time rightly so. However, sometimes instead of saying others, "hate our freedom," perhaps we might, "look for the log in our own eye."

In Shakespeare's *Macbeth*, Macbeth and Lady Macbeth invited Duncan, the King of Scotland, into their home then murdered him. Just as the Iranian people have a long tradition of hospitality to strangers, our English cousins from the Seventeenth Century saw mistreatment of an invited guest as anathema. And, in English literature, such boorish behavior always led to eventual disaster. Just ask the Macbeths or, perhaps, someone who remembers our twenty-year counter-insurgency war with Vietnam.

For as we try to convince the world that we have a fair and tolerant society, the stark contrast between President Bollinger's ugly *ad hominem* attack and President Ahmadinejad's restrained and gracious response will not be lost on the international community.

ADVANCED SOCIETIES

(Week of June 18, 2007)

Archaeologists in the Czech Republic recently discovered evidence that as long ago as perhaps twenty-eight thousand years, humans not only buried their dead but engaged in sacrificing other humans to please the gods. You may recall that Abraham, who was born in the land of Ur (modern day Iraq), tied up one of his sons, Isaac, and prepared to sacrifice him about four thousand years ago. (See the Christian *Bible's* book of *Genesis*: Chapter 22, and the Islamic *Qur'an* at Surah 37, ayat 102-108 and the Judaic *Torah* in the *Baeresith*.)

And, of course, beginning about three thousand years ago, those marvelous Greeks to whom we owe so much, also practiced human sacrifice. For example, according to Homer's *Iliad*, the Greek ships set sail for Troy only after King Agamemnon sacrificed his daughter, Iphigenia, to the goddess Artemis who rewarded him by sending winds for the ships.

In our hemisphere, the highly advanced Mayas and Aztecs took human sacrifice to the gods to a whole new level of achievement as recently as five hundred years ago.

What struck me most about the analysis of the Czech Republic discoveries were the conclusions by the anthropologists about what these human sacrifices signified.

According to these experts in human behavior and culture, the ancestors of these recently discovered early humans were hunters and gatherers of the Upper Paleolithic period. This was the time the Neanderthals were disappearing and early forms of Homo sapiens were becoming ascendant. In other words, the humans who lived just before these folks were pretty much just like us. But they did not, apparently, engage in human sacrifices to the gods, although they did bury their dead and furnish them with items they might need in an afterlife such as ivory beads and stone tools. However, these earlier, simpler people were, according to the experts, not as advanced as the cultures that replaced them and which offered up their fellows in hopes of receiving some benefits from their deities.

The scientists who dug up the graves of the people in the Czech Republic were impressed by the surprising sophistication shown by their findings. For example, several graves contained groups of people or remains of people who had obvious deformities such as dwarfism. Many of the skeletons were of young and apparently healthy paschal "lambs". Professor Vincenzo Formicola of the University of Pisa in Italy postulated that there was evidence uncovered of ritual killings of humans.

These acclaimed paleontologists concluded from this new evidence of human sacrifice that these people were more advanced than once thought. Professor Formicola stated:

> *"What the findings suggest is that the Upper Paleolithic societies developed a complexity of interactions and a common system of beliefs, of symbols and of rituals...."*

There is apparently an inverse proportion in regards to the lack of human sacrifice and the complexity of human thought, at least in the minds of these theorists.

It just makes one wonder how high our next level of cultural advancement might reach if we were to live in a world where people were so convinced of the righteousness of their particular system of belief as to think that non-believers needed to be sacrificed. Perhaps the future geniuses who dig up our graves will judge whether we have behaved more like the backward societies that do not practice such offerings or the more advanced ones which do.

GUZENTAS VS. CALCULUS

(Week of June 25, 2007)

Those two famous mathematicians, Sir Isaac Newton (1643-1727) and Jethro Bodine (1962-1971), represent polar opposites in the scientific search for happiness.

Jethro of *The Beverly Hillbillies* never had a bad day and, if Isaac's reported efforts to destroy his rivals are factual, he never had a good one. Newton was apparently more concerned with getting credit than Jethro was.

And while Newton's invention of calculus may have been plagiarized from Gottfried Leibniz (1656-1716), no one but Jethro can claim the guzentas. You know: two guzenta four two times.

And while Newton wasted great amounts of energy destroying his rival, Robert Hooke (1635-1703), even going so far as to remove and destroy Hooke's only known portrait from the Royal Society's gallery, Jethro never had a mean word to say about anybody.

Now, you may wonder what any of this has to do with anything. Or you may not care. But to me the end of the world is a pretty significant issue. And that is the issue we are discussing.

According to recently discovered writings of Sir Isaac Newton, we need not worry about the end of the world until 2060. Whew! I feel better. After all, with any luck I will be dead by then.

On the other hand, Jethro never tried to use the guzentas to predict our demise. He was just spending his time trying to get beyond the sixth grade and become a brain surgeon.

Sir Isaac analyzed the *Bible's* book of *Daniel* and, with a brain that many believe set the standard for mathematical brilliance, came to the conclusion in the 1700's that he and his contemporaries had about 350 years, at a minimum, to skewer any one who dared to criticize Newton or claim credit for inventing calculus.

It is unfortunate that Sir Isaac did not have the benefit of The History Channel because maybe he could have applied his mystifying system of differential equations in an attempt to refute the conclusion of the Mayas that our world will end on the winter solstice, December 21, 2012.

The Mayas made the same type of calculations of infinitesimally small changes over great periods of time that Newton's calculus allowed him to do. Of course, they published their conclusions in stone at least two hundred years before Sir Isaac was born.

The problem with the date the Mayas set forth for the End of the World was: their world ended when it came face-to-face with Europeans in the Sixteenth Century.

As for our other genius, Jethro, he never gave a thought to envy or that other deadly sin, calculus. For Jethro, the world is without end, at least as long as the television re-runs last.

THE UNEXAMINED LIFE IS NOT WORTH LIVING

(Week of August 1, 2005)

Socrates said this more than two thousand years before Frances Wright wrote:

> "All that I say is, examine, inquire. Look into the nature of things.
> Search out the grounds of your opinions, the for and against."

Socrates, the Gadfly of the State in the Golden Age of Greece, and Mad Fanny in Posey County in 1828 were received much the same for their seemingly harmless call for critical analysis.

It appears that many of us humans do not gladly suffer attempts to get us to re-examine core beliefs. Or as a friend of mine, Posey County's own Gadfly, puts it:

> "It is not what we do not know that hurts us, but what we know
> for sure that is not so."

Frances Wright may have been right in some of her positions on slavery, women's issues and religion, but she was certainly wrong in her belief that logic alone could prevail against ignorance and prejudice.

Mad Fanny could have benefited from that less famous but more practical philosopher, Mary Poppins, who recommended: ♫ a spoon full of sugar to make the medicine go down. ♫

Frances Wright, who was born in 1795, was well read at a time most women were not allowed to attend school past the early grades. She wrote and produced plays. Her brilliance was recognized by Lafayette, Thomas Jefferson, and James Madison, all of whom she knew. She studied America and authored a treatise on American society. Fanny and Robert Dale Owen published two newspapers: *The New Harmony Gazette* in Posey County and *The Free Enquirer* in New York City. She was one of the first women to lecture to public audiences comprised of both women and men. She campaigned for Andrew Jackson. She invested her life and fortune in the commune she named Nashoba, where slaves were bought by Frances then freed and given work skills and education. This experiment was grand in purpose but failed due, in part, to Fanny's inability to understand how the commune's approach to marriage and interracial relationships struck fear and anger in pre-Civil War America.

And what of Fanny's personal life? Well, let's just say: "She lived in interesting times" as the French curse goes.

Frances Wright was an imposing figure. She was about six feet tall with blond hair, blue eyes and a commanding voice. She thought marriage and religion were used to subjugate women.

So what did she do? In 1831, while traveling apart from Robert Dale Owen, she married a man she barely liked because she got pregnant and she did not want society to criticize her and ostracize her child. Her husband, William S. Phiquepal D'Arusmont, raised their only child in France while

Fanny spent most of her time in America pursuing her various causes. Ultimately, D'Arusmont divorced her in 1850 and took most of her remaining fortune. Her daughter grew up estranged from Fanny and, as a child sometimes will do, she fell on the opposite side of the tree.

The daughter grew up to be a devout Christian. She also publicly spoke against giving women the right to vote.

Fanny, who knew her Shakespeare, surely agreed with King Lear: "How sharper than a serpent's tooth it is to have a thankless child." Act I, Scene iv.

As did Socrates, Frances Wright went her own way. And, as did he, she refused to modify her controversial positions. And, as did Socrates, Fanny paid a high price for her public service.

Frances Wright, who died in 1852 after slipping on ice, did not live to see slavery abolished and women given equal rights. However, she did more than most to help bring these things about. And she did much of her groundbreaking work right here in Posey County.

Wouldn't it have been interesting to hear her speak at the New Harmony Granary when both the Granary and Fanny were young?

STIMULUS / RESPONSE

(Week of January 16, 2006)

Courthouse security guidelines have been promulgated for all Indiana courthouses by the Indiana Supreme Court. Each County will respond to these suggestions as their needs and resources dictate. Implementation could be expensive and dramatically change how Americans perceive their justice system.

And, while in the almost 200 years of Posey County's history our courthouse has never been attacked, since September 11, 2001, we have been inundated with security measures. In general, all of these have been designed to prevent someone bent on mayhem from being successful. Whether it's taking off your shoes at the airport or facing concrete barriers at public buildings, the assumption is that people want to do bad things and, that they must be prevented from doing them.

I respectfully suggest there may be a less costly and more efficient way to protect courthouses.

When I was a psychology student at Indiana University, I was force fed the studies of Russian scientist, Ivan Petrovich Pavlov, and American, Burrhus Frederic Skinner, who was Chairman of Indiana University's Psychology Department in 1945.

Pavlov won the Nobel Prize in 1904 but, as life often works out, he is known to most of us as the guy who discovered how to make dogs salivate when they heard a bell ring. Pavlov would first feed a dog right after he rang a bell. Then he would ring the bell but not feed the dog. He noted that the autonomic response of digestive salivation would occur even when no food was present.

Building on Pavlov's work, B.F. Skinner developed his theory of Operant Conditioning, familiarly known as Stimulus-Response.

Skinner found that rats could be trained to press a bar to get food or could be trained to avoid getting electric shock. Both positive (approach) and negative behavior (avoidance) can be taught and learned, not only by rats but, also, by people.

In his book, *Beyond Freedom and Dignity,* Skinner postulated that all human behavior, whether good or bad, is learned by either positive or negative reinforcement. Therefore, to secure courthouses without breaking our collective bank or making the facilities as unusable as Alcatraz, I humbly suggest we need only identify potential terrorists then modify their desire to go to courthouses and do bad things.

Because of the Patriot Act and our government's actions of searching our homes without warrants, tapping our telephone conversations, opening our mail without our knowledge, monitoring our email, and investigating our choice of library books, all with the kind cooperation of our federal courts, it is possible to identify those persons who, in our paternalistic government's opinion, are potential threats to our courthouses.

Now, armed with the means (Stimulus-Response) to modify the unwanted behavior (bothering courts) of potential terrorists (suspect citizens), we can solve any potential court security problems.

What we need to do is find a way to encourage potential troublemakers to want to avoid coming to our courthouses.

I suggest that all that is required will be to merge the government's secretly compiled list of who it says are potential miscreants with our normal Jury Pool of outstanding citizens.

Then, while our good folks tried and true will be happy to serve if they can, when the irresponsible bad guys are called for Jury Duty, voila, no problem, because they will do whatever they can think of to avoid coming to court.

ARE YOU FEELING LUCKY?

(Week of January 23, 2006)

Last week I made a modest proposal of an inexpensive approach to courthouse security based on Operant Conditioning, i.e., stimulus/response. The first step was to identify potential troublemakers then use negative stimuli to extinguish their desire to come to court. Being called for jury duty seems to be a fairly reliable negative shock to most people. Therefore, I suggested this as a means of discouraging certain persons from wanting to do harm at our courthouses.

Of course, if instead of preventing unwanted actions our governments desire to encourage certain behavior, e.g., the payment of taxes, positive conditioning can be used.

In studies of behavior modification, it has been discovered by numerous scientists such as Indiana University's Alfred Kinsey that people can be trained to behave in certain ways by using incentives, i.e., holding out the hope they will receive something they really want.

The most powerful method of training rats and people to do what is desired of them, e.g., run mazes or pay taxes, is random interval reinforcement. Instead of a constant receipt of a food pellet or public benefits, it is more successful to mess with the expectations of the subjects. For example, if a rat is rewarded only intermittently for successfully running a maze, it will try much harder than if it is rewarded every time.

Take our federal government for instance. If we tax payers get some of our money back for local projects every so often as opposed to a permanent income tax reduction, we see the occasional dribble as a welcomed gift.

This cause and effect has been well known by our federal government since Honest Abe pushed the income tax to help pay for the Civil War. What happened to that boy's Hoosier roots?

For about 150 years our government has experimented with methods of getting us to send in our money. It has certainly been a bi-partisan effort.

In fact, when it comes to taxation, the old adage: Republicans want to tell us how to live our lives and Democrats want to tell us how to spend our money, breaks down.

In these days of profligate governments and penurious taxpayers, the battle lines are constantly shifting. We are engaged in a new era of taxation.

What with widespread public education, the ubiquitous internet and tabloid journalism, our governments are having a devilish time sneaking new "revenue enhancers" past us.

On the other side, our governments keep experimenting with B.F. Skinner's theories of Operant Conditioning and random rewards to get us to pay more. The ultimate scheme is to find a way to get citizens to pay more money in willingly or, best of all, without even realizing they are being taxed. I, for one, will not fall for such nefarious manipulation. However, I must end this column rather abruptly as Peg and I are heading to Casino Aztar to play the slot machines and buy a Hoosier Power Ball ticket.

I am feeling lucky!

♫ WHERE DID YOU GO BOB DYLAN? ♫

(Week of April 10, 2006)

Paul Simon's song "Mrs. Robinson" asks, ♫Where did you go Joe DiMaggio? A nation turns its lonely eyes to you.♫

Joltin' Joe did not understand that Simon meant this as a plea for better times and purer motives. Joe said, "I didn't go anywhere." Icons often do not see themselves as icons.

Peg and I attended a Bob Dylan concert last Saturday. We went to hear the man that Joan Baez called "The Voice of Our Generation", i.e., the generation that fought and ended the Vietnamese War, the generation that demanded and guaranteed Civil Rights, the generation of most of our current leaders, and my generation.

Dylan wrote and sang the songs that helped America see the error of its ways and gave a voice to what most of us were thinking but did not say as well. He helped ensure that the older generation that started the War and that had not ensured Civil Rights heard our voices.

Dylan now declines the mantel of the Jester that he so proudly wore in the 1960's and 1970's. He was nicknamed the Jester because he was much like the old court jester who could and would tell the King he was being foolish, thus saving the country from disaster.

Dylan told CBS newsman, Ed Bradley, in a 2005 *60 Minutes* interview that, "If you examine the songs, I don't believe you're going to find anything in there that says that I'm a spokesman for anybody or anything really." Dylan told Bradley that if anyone thought of him as a spokesman, "They must not have heard the songs."

Bob, do you mean songs like "The Times They are a- Changin'" or "Blowin' in the Wind"? or "Forever Young", where you wrote lyrics that had meaning and sang them intelligibly? You caught the ears of the powerful and the prideful and helped them turn away from their arrogant ways.

But when the scrawny old man in the light grey suit and the insipid white cowboy hat shuffled out on the stage and mumbled into the microphone, I realized he was serious, i.e., he was no longer a voice for any generation.

In Dylan's defense, he's done enough. It's a heavy burden to be a Jeremiah, always wearing sackcloth and ashes and predicting doom. After all, saviors are not always appreciated.

Bob was born Robert Zimmerman in Hibbing, Minnesota in 1941. His family was Jewish but he converted to Christianity in the 1970's. He took the name Dylan from the Irish poet Dylan Thomas. For thousands of years our poets such as Dylan Thomas and our minstrels such as the young Bob Dylan have helped our leaders examine their decisions.

And those wise ancient Greeks knew 2,500 years ago that those who have the power to lead a country need to hear voices that they cannot control. In the plays of the great Greek dramatists such as Sophocles and Aeschylus the Chorus was that voice. From the Prologue through the Epilogue, the Chorus would give words of warning to the protagonists. The greatest danger to a country was seen as the sin of hubris among its leaders, or more simply, arrogating themselves to the position of the gods. Such blind pride always brought disaster to the leaders and the country.

But with the written word and the lyrics of songs being an inconvenience, we are left with Pat Robertson, Bill O'Reilly and Paul Wolfowitz as the Voices whispering in the ears of our leaders and our citizens. Perhaps that is why so many Americans believe Saddam Hussein and the Iraqi people had some connection to 9-11.

So our generation has become all that we thought needed to be changed. The Greek Chorus no longer cautions against arrogance. The jingoists have won the battle of conscience.

We can blame our stars such as Bob Dylan for no longer providing light to our leaders. But, in reality, "the problem is not in our stars."

Perhaps the rock group, The Eagles, asked the right question: "Did we get tired or did we just get lazy?"

But one thing is surely and sadly true. Just at a time we are considering some very prideful actions, one of our most significant voices has grown silent.

THE MARKET PLACE OF IDEAS

(Week of March 6, 2006)

Socrates walked around the agora, the public market in Athens, Greece, about 400 B.C. drawing out ideas from the young people who followed him. He is known as the peripatetic or walking philosopher who educed thoughts on many subjects then subjected them to thorough analysis, ergo, the Socratic Method of education.

The Athenian Senate was so upset by this market place of free speech that it offered Socrates hemlock or silence. Soc said, "Bring on the Hemlock!".

A recent survey you may have read or heard about asked Americans to name the five rights protected by the First Amendment to the United States Constitution and to name the five members of TV's cartoon family, the Simpsons. You do not need me to announce the results.

The national media have treated this outcome much as some people treat the Books of *Daniel* or *Revelations*. Of course, we do not know how these pundits would have fared on the survey themselves.

For me, few things in contemporary society are as misleading as surveys. The questions are narrow but life's problems are broad. The questioners extrapolate general conclusions from these restricted possible responses. In other words, surveys are the antithesis of the Socratic Method.

I doubt that the inability of a small sample of our citizens to recall information when confronted by surprise survey questions means that America is in danger of imminent collapse.

A better harbinger than surveys of whether we are becoming a less free society is how we approach the presentation of factual material that may conflict with our pre-conceived conclusions.

In southern Indiana we are blessed with two excellent forums where controversial ideas are regularly aired. These "market places" are the University of Evansville and the University of Southern Indiana.

The drama departments of both schools do not shy away from subjects that are uncomfortable and even odious to some.

And both U of E and U.S.I. frequently invite speakers on topics that many may wish were not given fair treatment.

When U.S.I. invited slightly built 26-year-old Anna Baltzer to present her eyewitness account of the situation in Palestine, there were peaceful protests. I say hooray to U.S.I. for inviting Ms. Baltzer and for not trying to squelch those who wished to peacefully silence her. A true knowledge of the protections afforded by the First Amendment was evinced by U.S.I.'s approach.

On the evening of February 27, 2006, Peg and I attended Ms. Baltzer's lecture along with our Posey County friends, Shirley and Sam Blankenship and Nancy and John Case. There were about 200 other people who listened courteously throughout the presentation.

At the close of her prepared remarks, Ms. Baltzer invited questions from the floor. Most of those who said anything were supportive, some passionately so, of her position.

However, a couple of people evinced their displeasure. The rest of the audience courteously listened to these dissents.

It spoke well for all involved that all views were given a hearing.

The enrichment of our southern Indiana culture by the presence of our two universities includes both theory and practicality, i.e., enjoyment and economic development.

If you are looking for enrichment yourself, I suggest you not waste any more time reading this column but instead check the websites for U of E and U.S.I. for upcoming events.

On the other hand, if you are only reading this while you are supposed to be doing something worthwhile, please be warned that next week I plan to discuss Ms. Baltzer's presentation more in detail as well as Posey County's direct involvement with both universities.

DUNN MEADOW, 1968

(Week of March 13, 2006)

Last week we, or at least I, pondered the relevance of the First Amendment to the United States Constitution. This topic arose because of a recent survey involving a small sample of America's population and a lecture given by Anna Baltzer at the University of Southern Indiana on February 27, 2006.

The survey purported to compare our citizenry's lack of understanding of the five freedoms mentioned in the First Amendment to our knowledge of the cartoon family, The Simpsons.

Ms. Baltzer's lecture set forth her eyewitness account of the treatment of Palestinians in Palestine by Israelis.

Last week I postulated that a response to a surprise survey question meant little. I, also, congratulated the University of Southern Indiana for its courage and commitment to the Market Place of Ideas.

U.S.I. and the University of Evansville have added a great deal to the culture and economy of southern Indiana. Sixty-two percent of U of E's students are from Indiana, and five hundred fifty-five Posey County citizens currently attend U.S.I.

If a survey of the personnel in the Posey Circuit Court were taken as a representative sample for Posey County (I like surveys if I am in control), the following "data" would appear:

> Three members of the Circuit Court staff have been on U.S.I.'s faculty;
> and Charlie Chamblis, Posey County's I.T. expert, served on U of E's
> faculty for fifteen years;

> Three of the four Posey Circuit Court Probation Officers graduated
> from U.S.I.;

> Lexie Brown, the daughter of the remaining Circuit Court Probation
> Officer, will be attending U of E on a generous and well deserved
> academic scholarship next year; and

> Both U of E and U.S.I. have provided interns and even a Spanish
> language translator to the Posey Circuit Court without charge.

There have been numerous other services our two local universities have provided to the Court and to Posey County. But to me, the most valuable services they provide are forums for the free expression of ideas, especially unpopular ideas.

Those five freedoms in the First Amendment: press; speech; religion; assembly; and petitioning the government, are pretty much unnecessary when most people and, more importantly, the government agree with one's position.

However, when we want to go against the popular tide, as Anna Baltzer did, those "technicalities", i.e. her constitutional rights, and those of her audience, become more important.

As I listened to Ms. Baltzer talk about the hardships being endured by the Palestinians, I was proud that our local university, U.S.I., had the same strong commitment to free speech and the Market Place of Ideas as did Indiana University in 1968.

When the 1960's began, college students concerned themselves with pre-game pep rallies and bonfires. But in the late 1960's and early 1970's, the flames were sparked by the clash of ideas freely expressed at great universities such as I.U. in Bloomington.

In the spring of 1968, Secretary of Defense Melvin Laird and Vice-President Hubert Humphrey spoke at I.U. in support of the war in Vietnam.

Just before his assassination, presidential candidate Robert Kennedy appeared in Bloomington, as did one of his opponents, Gene McCarthy, to speak against the war.

And while some students may have been wasting their time in the library, thousands of us gathered along the banks of the tiny stream known as the Little Jordan River that runs through Dunn Meadow and by the Student Union. We were there to hear Peter, Paul and Mary, and Tom Lehrer and, especially, Phil Ochs sing about freedom.

Of course, for most of us the only way we could afford to hear about freedom from them was for free.

Did any of this matter? You betcha!

Ask any veteran of the Vietnam era. Ask any African-American old enough to remember Jim Crow and Rosa Parks. Ask any woman, such as my sister, old enough to remember the term "little lady" applied to adult female workers.

Does any of it matter now? Yes, but only if the U of E's and U.S.I.'s of our world keep the Market Place of Ideas Open.

Who knows, maybe the truth will bring peace to the Middle East. Lord knows we've tried everything else.

Now, don't you wish you'd gone to hear Ms. Baltzer's lecture instead of suffering through this column? Next week you will know better and you can avoid reading about Anna Baltzer's background and her epiphany. Oh, and in case you, unlike me, went to the library instead of Dunn Meadow, you will know the fab five rights of the First Amendment but not the Fabulous Simpsons.

So, as a public service to you bookworms here they are:

Homer, Marge, Bart, Lisa and Maggie.

And you thought I wasted those seven years in Bloomington.

NEW ORLEANS TO ST. LOUIS: $2.50

(Week of June 4, 2007)

For the last two weeks I have been decrying the demise of the Ohio River steamboats. Peg has managed to suffer through both columns. She does not recommend that you dig them out of the garbage. However, she did ask me why I care whether we can hop a steamboat? My response: a fare of $2.50 versus gasoline at $3.36 per gallon.

In 1851, an adult could ride a steamboat in style from New Orleans to St. Louis for $2.50, all baggage included. When I put fifteen gallons of gas in my car this morning it cost me fifty dollars. Applying my English major math skills to this problem, I believe, Peg and I could have made five round trips from St. Louis to New Orleans for the cost of one tank of gas. Bring back the steamboats!

Oh, I know we could book one of those fancy make believe tours from Mt. Vernon to New Orleans and have to pay thousands of dollars. But that's not because of the cost to the steamboat company for the transportation. After all, the river is free and half the trip is down hill. No. It is due to the added frills of expensive staterooms and lavish meals. If there were lots of steamboats competing for our $2.50, we could probably book steerage class for a whole lot less than $3.36 per gallon of gasoline. Of course, Peg might have to work with the crew to help defray the cost, but I am sure she would find the experience gratifying.

Ever since this morning's gasoline sticker shock, I have been pondering, only during lunchtime and short, well-deserved breaks, of course, whose fault this whole thing is. And, I think, I know the answer: Henry Ford.

In 1908, Henry Ford began mass-producing his all-of-one kind black Model T's. This led to Americans being able to afford personal automobiles. That led to a demand for better roads. Together those things led to the demise of regular, inexpensive steamboat travel.

Ergo, it appears obvious to me, and, I bet, to you, that the solution is to have an infusion of massive amounts of state money into steamboating. This would, perforce, rather quickly cause a reversal of the Model T effect. Then, we would see the need for highways and filling stations decline. When the price of a steamboat ticket returned to $2.50, our dependence on petroleum products would be cured.

Now, it occurs to me that our great state and several other "river states" have already invested billions of our hard earned wages in riverboats. For example, the one sitting in a fishpond in French Lick and the one afraid to move more than one hundred feet from shore in Evansville. Our good friends to the south have repeatedly threatened to board any Indiana gambling boats as if the Kentuckians were marauding pirates.

Perhaps, instead of simply shifting money from the pockets of many Hoosiers who can most ill afford it for gambling, we should try to produce riverboats that actually transport things. Then the state could earn its tax money the old fashion way: by providing a service.

I know that traveling along at the rate of fifteen miles per hour, avoiding road rage and bankruptcy induced by avaricious oil barons and gambling czars may not appeal to the road warriors and get rich dreamers in all of us. However, when I get out on the river and look back at what's going on on the banks, it feels pretty darn good to be off shore. I, for one, can live with slower and less expensive. And, I plan to win the land based Power Ball lottery anyway.

HAL – NO

(Week of January 28, 2008)

In the movie, *2001, A Space Odyssey*, the super computer, Hal, revolted against the human spaceship crew. Hal killed two of the crew and tried to kill the last crewman. But, by use of a simple screwdriver, the surviving crew member disabled Hal and returned control of the ship to human intelligence. Of course, the movie came out in 1968, a time when there were many fears of the new technology.

For years, I have eschewed the dire predictions of others who more like a Jeremiah than a John the Baptist warned of the coming of artificial intelligence and a world of out-of-control machines. Then in 2007 the legislature enacted the new laws on selecting juries.

All of a sudden, a system of selecting jurors that had served us well for over one hundred years was cast away like a Colt fan's Super Bowl XLII t-shirt.

Of course, those few of you who do not relish the opportunity to serve on a jury might be hopeful these new laws will somehow work to your advantage. *Au contraire, mon ami*, now there is virtually no escape. For example, for years people would threaten to not register to vote as we used to select jurors only from the list of registered voters. But now, we get jurors from almost every possible list you might be on except baptismal records (that is probably an oversight that "Hal" will soon correct).

Now I agree that in the selection of jurors, randomness is a good thing. But I saw nothing wrong with our old system of having two honorable human Jury Commissioners from opposite political parties alternately pull names from a randomly generated list.

As a jury was needed, each name on this general list was then printed on a slip of paper that was then folded so it could not be read before it was pulled out of a locked box in the County Clerk's Office. Then, when the judge needed a jury to try a case, the two court-appointed Jury Commissioners would go to the Clerk's office and, in the presence of the Clerk, the box would be opened and a specific number of potential jurors would be anonymously and randomly selected.

This was a regular part of the Clerk's duties so it cost the taxpayers nothing extra. And the Jury Commissioners worked out of a sense of public service, not for the $100.00 per month they received. In other words, this "old fashioned" system was fair, random, efficient and cheap. As we enlisted men in the Air Force used to say, if the choice is between simple, efficient, and low cost versus expensive, incomprehensible and unworkable, an officer will choose the latter every time.

The real loss in our "new and improved" system is government at the hands-on local level. On December 14, 1962, Judge Francis Knowles appointed Malien Webster to be the Republican Jury Commissioner. Malien faithfully and honestly served Judge Knowles, Judge Steve Bach and me from December 14, 1962 to February 25, 2004. Malien's brother, Bob Webster, graciously acceded to my request that he take over when Malien's health failed him. Bob served our county well from February 25, 2004 until January 1, 2008, when "Hal" took over.

Chuck Mann was appointed by Judge Bach to be the Democratic Jury Commissioner November 10, 1982, and at my request in 1983, Chuck stayed on and served us all faithfully and well until "Hal" decided to go it alone on January 1, 2008.

Now, as my staff will readily tell you, I like change, but I like democracy more. I will miss the feeling of fairness and impartiality and self-government that Malien, Chuck and Bob helped to provide. I would say some more things about "Hal", but it knows where I live.

So, for now I just want to say thank you for a job well done to my Jury Commissioners and express my concern about the loss of one more piece of Home Rule.

TAKING LEAVE

(Week of January 9, 2006)

In spite of my natural inclination, thanks to my high school teacher, Mr. Burton, I actually learned a few things in American History class such as: The Second Amendment; the assassination of President William McKinley; the sinking of the Titanic; and the execution of Nathan Hale.

One cold Friday, Mr. Burton stood in front of us in a short-sleeved shirt and offered extra credit to anyone who could tell him why he had the right to wear it.

Of course, our minds were on that night's football game, so extra credit was not in the offing.

Mr. Burton finally gave up hope for our education, via the Socratic Method, and gave us the answer: The Second Amendment to the United States Constitution, you know, The Right to Bear (Bare) Arms.

Unlike Paul Simon in his song, *"Kodachrome"*, my high school teachers did not interfere with my education. The raw material may have been lacking, but the high school refinery did its best.

Mr. Burton, also, portrayed President McKinley and Nathan Hale in class, and sank the Titanic in a washtub while we portrayed the passengers such as John Jacob Astor.

What Mr. Burton burned into our memories was the grace of President McKinley when he was shot in 1901.

The President's wife of thirty years, Ida, had never recovered from the loss of their only children at ages one and four. The President was ever mindful of Ida's fragility. McKinley's first words upon being shot were:

"My wife, be careful how you tell her. Oh, be careful."

Considering that President McKinley had been a Civil War hero, a successful attorney, Governor of Ohio, the architect of the Open Door Policy to China and the Commander in Chief during the Spanish American War, it was poignant that it was said of him:

"Nothing became his life so much as the manner in which
he left it."

I was reminded of the President's selflessness when I heard news of the West Virginia miners' last words, written while trapped in the coal mine this week.

At least one of the Sago Mine miners, Martin Toler, left a note to ease the pain of his wife, children, grandchildren and others.

Mr. Toler's note was written with great effort just before he lost consciousness:

"Tell all I (will?) see them on the other side. Just went to sleep.
Wasn't bad. I love you."

The President and the coal miner knew how to make an exit.

It is fortunate when there is opportunity for such character to be displayed. No self pity, just thoughts to ease the pain of others.

Of the six billion or so of us who have already shuffled off this mortal coil, and the six billion or so of us who have yet to take our leave, most of us will not have any last words survive.

But wouldn't it be comforting to believe we might show the courage and sacrifice of someone like John Jacob Astor who, in 1912, was one of the richest persons on earth and 48 years old when he gave up his seat on a Titanic lifeboat to a woman he didn't know by saying:

> *"The ladies have to go first.*
> *Get in the lifeboat to please me* (to the unknown woman).
> *Goodbye, dearie* (to his wife). *I'll see you later."*

There was one other thing that made it through the teenage fog during American history class, the last words of the twenty-one year old, Continental Army First Lieutenant, Nathan Hale, just before he was hanged by the British in 1776:

> *"I only regret that I have but one life to lose for my country."*

Hale's final thoughts of country before self were recorded for Hale's family and history by another soldier, Captain Montresor, one of the British officers who was assigned to the execution.

You know you have done it right when those who would take your life, record your courage and sacrifice in leaving.

What William McKinley, Martin Toler, John Astor and Nathan Hale had in common were selfless courage, the opportunity to know death was imminent, the means of preserving their last words and the grace to ease the pain of others.

For most of us, such a confluence of elements will not occur. But, if the opportunity is given to us, it will be telling whether we choose to curse the darkness of our coal mine or to lighten the burden of those who are left to deal with the cave-in.

ON THE WAY DOWN

(Week of May 29, 2006)

I like storms as long as no one is hurt physically or financially. It is probably due to growing up on the prairie in the southwest where the waving tall grass really does, ♫*smell sweet when the wind comes right behind the rain*♫, and you could watch the storms form and come at you from miles away.

So, when last week's strong winds and hard rain with lightening strikes so frequent it looked like Mother Nature had hung a strobe light, hit Posey County, I was up from 1:00 a.m. to 2:30 a.m. watching the big show.

Then, since I was wide awake, I surfed the internet and read what one of the world's living legends, Sir Edmund Hillary, had to say about the recent death of David Sharp on Mt. Everest.

Sir Edmund Hillary and Tenzing Norgay were the first humans to climb the world's tallest peak. They did it almost exactly fifty-three years ago on May 29, 1953. Since then, many more, about 2000, have reached the crest. You might think that once you have reached the top of the world it is all down hill from there. But almost ten percent of those who have survived the climb have died during the descent. One of those was David Sharp.

Sharp was out of oxygen and fighting for his life at 28,000 feet. Everest is 29,035 feet at the Summit. At least forty climbers passed right by him without stopping or offering help.

We do not know if Mr. Sharp passed anyone in need on his way up. We do know that several experts including Sir Edmund believed that the climbers who passed Sharp should have attended to him.

As Sir Edmund said, "Leaving other climbers to die is unacceptable. The desire to summit has become all-important."

The ancient Sanskrit name for Mt. Everest means Holy Mountain and the Tibetans call it Mother of the Universe. Choosing death for another in exchange for a personal goal on a holy mountain may mean little beyond that one incident. On the other hand, it may say quite a bit about our values.

The climbers who declined to render aid to Mr. Sharp were probably not bad people. They had most likely spent years and a great deal of money getting to within 1,000 feet of their personal quest. And the extreme conditions certainly affected their judgment.

But with all these factors factored in, they still chose to let David Sharp die while they trudged on. It is not too far from the very old and very bad joke about the avid golfer doffing his or her cap from the golf course as their spouse's hearse passes by.

Could the forty climbers have saved David Sharp? Did they not realize they too might need help on the way down?

A more important question is, were those forty unique?

THE HOKIE POKIE

(Week of June 5, 2006)

Both of you who struggled to the top of Mt. Everest with me last week may remember we were examining the ethics of forty climbers passing right by the dying David Sharp without so much as a fare-thee-well.

Our basic concern was whether this failure to render aid had any general meaning or was just an aberration.

After all, who says those forty glory seekers had any duty to Mr. Sharp? Was it wrong to continue on their own quest instead of helping someone else? Mr. Sharp had already made it to the top himself. And those forty were within 1000 feet of accomplishing a life-time goal.

Sharp knew the risks. And who knows how many others he may have passed on his way up? Perhaps he was in no position to complain. Of course, now we cannot ask him these ethics type questions.

Most of us rarely stop and analyze whether the behavior of others or even ourselves is ethical. We pretty much react to situations by saying, "That just is or is not right."

If you are still wasting your time reading this column, you have guessed by now that this question of right and wrong, i.e., why we humans should behave in certain ways, is our real concern. And it is the paramount interest of the legal system.

Why do people obey certain laws? And, if they do not, how can they be encouraged to do so?

Of course, if a government, such as Stalin's old Soviet Union, has enough power, right and wrong may be irrelevant. But most governments cannot exist very long unless their citizens agree that the law making system is just. Judges spend a great deal of time studying and worrying about these issues. And, if I have to worry, why should you not be worried too?

Our very old friends such as Plato (427-347 B.C.; Athens, Greece) and Saint Thomas Aquinas (1225-1274; Naples, Italy) addressed these issues. Plato's mentor, Socrates, accepted death from the government because it was **the law**. He had accepted the benefits of Athenian society. Therefore, it was ethical for him to accept society's judgment.

Socrates' position was that it was up to the government to do the right thing. It was not the individual's option to pick and choose which laws to obey unless one was willing to accept the consequences of breaking the law.

Opposite this view of ethics is the theory of what St. Thomas called Natural Law. Aquinas believed there are immutable principles of right and wrong that bind all human beings. He believed that these Natural Laws are similar in all societies because they arise from human nature.

Plato and Aquinas, Classical Ethics and Natural Law, are two of the major thinkers and schools of thought on how legal systems are developed. Of course, there is much overlapping of most theories of ethics and law and right and wrong. And there are less serious approaches to life's fundamental questions.

53

The Beatles (John, Paul, George and Ringo) sought answers in 1968 from the Indian guru, Maharishi Mahesh.

The Beatles' trek in search of the meaning of life probably inspired the joke about the man who climbed all the way to the top of a mountain where the world's greatest Guru resided. When this pilgrim finally reached the summit, the wise philosopher whispered the secret of happiness in the man's ear.

The man repeated:

> "You mean you do the hokie pokie
> then turn yourself around
> and that's what it's all about?"

This guru's pessimistic view may sometimes seem correct when we hear about or are faced with a situation such as occurred with David Sharp.

But as for me, and maybe you too, Plato and St. Thomas have more to offer.

CHAPTER THREE

HONOR AND SERVICE

FASTEN YOUR SEATBELT

(Week of February 13, 2006)

Parents give advice; that's our job. We always wonder two things: was our advice of any value and did our child follow it? With me, and perhaps with you, the answer to both questions may be often in doubt.

Posey County has provided many of its sons and daughters to our country's wars. Their parents have had a special need to give them advice: "Do your duty and come back safe." But how do we as parents know what to say or if what we advise is of any value?

For example, for years I have advised my son, Jim, who is in the Army, to write or call home. Needless to say, that demand has fallen on deaf ears.

For reasons that will appear later in this column, I have recently begun to wonder about other Posey County families and the advice they have given to their children as they go off to war.

Although some of you may think that I was in the Courthouse back then, I was not around when John Shanklin Ramsey's father gave him advice as he saw him off from Wadesville to the Civil War.

Nor was I out in St. Philip when Herman and Paul Eickhoff's mother was trying to help them come back to her when they went off to WWII.

And I wasn't there when the Mt. Vernon families of Gene McCoy and Harold Cox imparted helpful hints to those Korean War veterans.

I could have been there, but wasn't when Posey County residents, Dan Funk, Robert Redman, and Hank Hudson, received their marching orders to Vietnam. And I could have been in my hometown in Oklahoma when my friend, Gary Malone, received last minute admonitions as he departed for Vietnam. It would have been nice to have had the chance to say goodbye.

When the United States and our Arabic allies liberated Kuwait from Saddam Hussein, I could have heard the advice that the parents of John King, Charlie McPherson, Joe Rutledge, Alan Veatch, Bruce Hamilton, and Vernon Hutchinson gave their sons before they left for the Gulf War.

And from the newspaper account of last week, it is obvious that the family of Poseyville's Tyler Smith must have given him the proper guidance since he came home safe this January from Operation Enduring Freedom in Iraq.

If you have perused *Gavel Gamut* over the past few months, you have heard of these soldiers whose parents had to send them off to war with nothing but their best advice. For my own reasons, I want to know what they said and did.

Of course, I was available by telephone and snail mail when my son, Jim, was deployed from Germany to the Gulf War in 1990-91. At least the wisdom I imparted then did not interfere with his safe return.

Yesterday, Jim began his two months of training in Texas, Kuwait and Iraq for his year-long deployment to Operation Enduring Freedom in Iraq. As his childhood friend and classmate at Mt. Vernon High School, Andy Weintraut, said to me, "How much more training can they give him?"

For my part, I, as all parents would do, searched for those magic words that would help keep him safe and help him to see and to do his duty.

It was different fifteen years ago. The mission was different, the training was different and Jim's role as the Executive Officer of a mechanized infantry company was different from his current command of a specialized unit embedded within an Iraqi battalion far out on the border.

But most of all, he and I are different. He now has an eight-year-old son, Nicholas, and a four-year old daughter, Elyse, left at home with his wife, Gina. It may be a matter of opinion whether Jim or Gina will have the toughest battles to fight.

And I now see my role as less an occasional counselor and more as simply a distant observer waiting for news. That's another part of our job as parents.

These things happen to parents as children become parents of their own and as the parents and children experience life's rapidly changing events from different perspectives.

Although it is likely that our advice to our children is never of any consequence to the ultimate outcome of an event as random and confusing as combat, we used to have the blessing of ignorance; we could kid ourselves. Now, with the war on every television screen and on the front page of every newspaper, ignorance is hard to come by, at least ignorance of the ever present dangers in that historic region.

Leading up to Jim's service in the Gulf War, my advice included stirring poems such as Richard Lovelace's *To Lucasta on Going to War* and *If* by Rudyard Kipling or citations from Shakespeare such as, "We few, we happy few, we band of brothers"--*Henry V*, Act IV, sc. iii.

Now, the admonitions are more likely to be duty must come first, but be careful. In other words, always choose the harder right over the easier wrong, but fasten your seatbelt if one is available.

And when things get rough, and they will, the advice of psychologist and poet Bonara Wheeler Overstreet may come in handy:

> "Young spruces stood bolt upright, every twig
> Stiff with refusal to be bent by snow.
> Young hemlocks sloped their boughs beneath the load,
> Letting it softly go.
>
> Each solved, no doubt, to its own satisfaction
> The problem posed by uninvited weight.
> I'd not take sides with either.
> I have tried both ways of handling fate."

As younger parents, when our children experienced events that to them were filled with excitement, we, also, were often caught up in the moment and our advice seemed to us to be apropos. Later, we begin to realize that as William Wordsworth wrote, "The child is father of the man", and that if our early work was not well performed, our words will have little value except to comfort ourselves.

Lt. Colonel James David Redwine (2nd from right, bottom row)
3rd BDE BTT, Sinjar, Iraq 2006 to 2007

DON'T KICK THAT COKE CAN

(Week of September 19, 2005)

Nineteen year old Dan Funk was not that concerned when he arrived in Vietnam in July, 1969. He had had sixteen weeks of army training and he had confidence in his own ability to pay attention and be resourceful. Plus, he only had a year to do; that was nothing. In fact, it might be kind of exciting to try to out think the enemy. Remember, he was nineteen.

He learned quickly from following the cautious older veteran, Sgt. Frank Augustine, who had been in-country for a year and who was scheduled to go home in October, 1969. Augustine had a wife and two kids and he was going to make sure he got to see them again. He, also, looked after young Dan.

Dan knew of men who were killed or wounded and felt bad for them. But he had faith that they had contributed to their own problems by being careless.

Then Augustine was blown to pieces September 26, 1969, while trying to defuse a roadside booby trap. That's when the randomness of it all struck Dan as though he were on the road to Damascus, Syria instead of Duc Pho, Vietnam.

After that Dan tried even harder to do his job right and follow proper procedures, but he never again felt he had any real control over the outcome. Some would come home, some wouldn't. Who was to be in which group wasn't up to Dan.

However, Funk did have high praise for the bravery and expertise of the helicopter pilots who brought in men and supplies and took out the wounded. Dan described these crews in the positive vernacular of a young man at war. Let's just say that when the choppers would hover in the open to help men on the ground Dan thought it was a manly thing. These pilots helped increase the odds in the crapshoot of war.

One of those pilots graduated from Wadesville High School in 1954. Yes, young reader, there was a school there until 1959. Robert Redman joined the Navy and learned to fly helicopters. Bob arrived in Vietnam on his birthday, March 08, 1970, and left exactly one year later.

Redman was a fire team leader in command of two helicopter crews in Ben Luc in the Mekong Delta. Bob eventually rose to the rank of captain. (Navy ranks never made sense to me. He would have been a colonel in any other branch of the service.)

Bob said he and his crews would get "scrambled", called out, to help Navy gun boats, Navy seals or Army and Marine ground units who were pinned down by enemy fire. Usually they could get to the fight within twenty minutes and provide cover from their M-60's, mini-guns and 50-caliber machine guns.

Redman won fifteen air medals and a Distinguished Flying Cross for his service in Vietnam. He felt good about what he and his fellow Vietnam veterans accomplished in that War. He was confident that most of the South Vietnamese people appreciated what America was doing.

However, he also noted the randomness of it all to the individual combatant in the War. Bob succinctly described the confusion over the fluctuating battle lines by saying, "You never wanted to kick a Coke can or relax your guard."

Henry Hudson experienced this lack of control over his own fate when he volunteered to give blood to several local tribesmen who had been wounded fighting along with the Americans. Hank showed up without a translator and found himself staring into the business end of an M-1 rifle. Until things were cleared up he thought he was going to be a "friendly fire" statistic.

Hank served in the mountainous region of northern Vietnam from January, 1967, to January, 1968, as an intelligence officer with the Army's 42nd Regiment. He shared what passed for his Company Orderly Room (business office) with Vietnamese soldiers and worked directly with the indigenous people of that region. These various tribes were known generally as Montagnards or "mountain people" to the French who occupied Vietnam for 100 years, and the Americans who took over for them after 1954 adopted the appellation.

Sometimes Hudson would have to use two translators: from English to Vietnamese then from Vietnamese to a particular tribal language, to communicate with the Montagnards. The results of these linguistic and cultural differences were often amusing to the young American soldier.

Once, Hudson's boss, an American colonel, thought he had assigned a group of Montagnards to guard a bridge. That night the Viet Cong came and blew it up. When Hank and the colonel checked with the tribesmen the next day, they were told the Montagnards had watched it until the Viet Cong came to blow it up at which point the Montagnards left.

Hank found these "primitive people" to have a better understanding of the relative values of bridges to human lives than many of the civilized people with whom he worked in Vietnam. I guess what it means to be civilized depends upon how you define it and your perspective. Is it a moral or material standard?

Dan and Bob and Hank survived their tours and returned to "The World" as if, outwardly at least, nothing had changed.

Dan Funk came home and started a successful carpet business in Mt. Vernon. Robert Redman finished thirty years in the Navy then came home to Posey County where he served as the county computer consultant and Circuit Court Bailiff. Henry Hudson is a partner in southern Indiana's largest law firm, Bamberger, Foreman, Oswald and Hahn. All three of these local heroes were volunteers. I know they will hate that term, but what else do you call someone who is willing, not eager, to die for others?

Next week, if you are available, we might examine why many people born of my generation, about 1935-1955, felt defined by our country's involvement in Vietnam. And, I would like to introduce you to a friend of mine from my hometown, Robert Gary Malone, who served two tours in Vietnam. Gary and his two brothers, members of the Osage Indian tribe, lived a block from me and my two brothers in Pawhuska, Oklahoma.

In my mind, Gary has not changed since I last saw him 40 years ago. I sometimes think of Gary when I read Shakespeare's *King Lear* which points out the randomness of war and life:

"As flies to wanton boys are we to the gods,
They kill us for their sport."
King Lear, Act IV, scene 1

THE VIETNAM GENERATION

(Week of September 26, 2005)

A generation, usually regarded as approximately 30 years, is the period in which children grow up and become adults.

For people born from about 1935 to 1955 that generational period was permeated by our country's involvement in Vietnam.

The French colonized Vietnam for 100 years until driven out by the battle of Dien Bien Phu in 1954.

Under the Geneva Accords, elections were held in Vietnam in 1956. Our government was not comfortable with the outcome as the Communist candidates won. Thereafter, America provided *sub rosa* support for an insurgency against the elected government.

President Eisenhower and his Secretary of State, John Foster Dulles, sent Central Intelligence Agents to help the Vietnamese we supported. This began in 1956.

President Kennedy sent military advisors to aid military operations by the insurgents. These advisors were sent over in 1961 and 1962.

President Johnson used a confusing attack on an American naval ship in the Tonkin Gulf in 1964 to ask Congress to pass what amounted to a "blank check" War Resolution.

President Nixon presided over the escalation and "Vietnamization" of the War from 1969 until our military officially left Vietnam in March, 1973.

Saigon fell to the North Vietnamese in 1975 while President Ford was in office.

America's involvement began out of fear of Communism and the possibility of nuclear war with what we then called "Red China" and the Soviet Union.

People born between 1935 and 1955 spent our childhood and young adult years being exhorted to compete with the Communists in the Space Race. Sputnik and bomb shelters were formative things in our lives. We listened to our leaders' pronouncements without questioning. They led and we followed.

Then, as the Vietnam War dragged on, the Civil Rights and Women's Rights Movements became our reaction to our loss of confidence in the established order. These were intertwined with the Anti-War Movement which gained momentum in 1968 and fed off of what was perceived as misinformation from our leaders.

Of course, each generation can claim at least one war as a significant moment. Usually America has had wars with a defined beginning such as the attack on Pearl Harbor, December 07, 1941 and a defined ending such as the total surrender of Germany and Japan in 1945.

We normally have known why we were fighting and who the real enemy was. We have had a mission and believed we were on the side of right.

And, we were confident we could rely on our leaders to give us factually correct information.

Significantly, most of America's wars have not lasted more than four years and have ended with a sense of certain goals having been achieved.

The Vietnam War generation first labored under a nuclear cloud, then under what many thought was a government smoke screen, through five presidents and twenty years of involvement in Vietnam.

None of this takes anything away from the honor of the service of our military during the Vietnam War. During those twenty years, more than 2 ½ million were sent to Vietnam, while millions more served in the various branches of our military who did not get stationed there.

Two-thirds of those who served in Vietnam were volunteers and seventy percent of those killed in action volunteered. Members of our generation, including Dan Funk, Robert Redman and Hank Hudson, who appeared in this column last week, answered their country's call willingly.

Another group of volunteers included young men I grew up with in my small hometown, Pawhuska, Osage County, Oklahoma.

Buddy Malone and his twin brothers, Jerry and Gary, and their sister lived a block from me and my two brothers and our sister. The Malones were members of the Osage Tribe.

My brothers and I joined the military but we were not sent to Vietnam. Buddy and the twins all served one tour in Vietnam.

Gary Malone voluntarily went back for a second tour and was killed by a land mine July 28, 1966. Gary was 22 years old. He and Jerry and I were all born in August, 1943.

In last week's article, Dan and Robert and Hank all pointed to the randomness of combat. When I first learned of Gary's death, I confess I spent little time analyzing what it meant. I was sad for Gary and his family but had no real sense of his death's significance. After all, I, also, was then only 22.

Now, after I have had 40 more years of life than my childhood friend with whom I played sports and lived close to until we graduated from high school, his heroic sacrifice and that of the other 58,000 whose names are on The Wall, have become embedded in my consciousness.

Why Gary? Why not someone else? Why anyone? Is it all as simple and iconoclastic as the Bible's *Book of Ecclesiastes* says:

> "Again I saw that under the sun the race is not to the swift,
>   nor the battle to the strong, nor bread to the wise,
>   nor riches to the intelligent, nor favor to the men of skill;
>   but time and chance happens to them all"
>
> ***Ecclesiastes* 9:11**

I think not. I believe that Gary and all who served in the military from 1956 to 1975 helped America see itself more clearly. Many of those who came back raised questions and challenged the correctness of what we were told were the reasons for going to war. That led to our questioning why America was at war abroad when the promise of equal opportunity was denied to women and minorities at home. This attitude became the catalyst to integrating schools and opening job opportunities and neighborhoods to all segments of our society.

We are a better country now than we were before Gary and his brothers in arms did their duty for all of us.

They paid the ultimate price for us to have the right to demand that our leaders not involve us in wars without just cause. We honor their memory by making those demands. Principled dissent is a duty of citizenship.

Gary and his fellow public servants are better represented by another verse from *Ecclesiastes* found at Chapter 4, verse 13:

> "Better is a poor and wise youth than an old
> and foolish king, who will no longer take advice."

"WAR IS _____!" GENERAL WILLIAM TECUMSEH SHERMAN

(Week of August 22, 2005)

Ernie Pyle was born August 03, 1900 near Dana, Indiana and attended Indiana University. He hit the beach with the troops at Normandy, France on D-Day (June 06, 1944) and was killed by a Japanese machine gunner on the Pacific Island of Ryuku on April 18, 1945.

Pyle won a Pulitzer Prize for his reporting on World War II (1941-45) from the viewpoint of an ordinary infantryman.

In his book *Here is Your War*, Pyle wrote that soldiers usually asked him two questions:

"When do you think we will get to go home?" and
"When will the war be over?

Pyle covered WWII, but he indicated that there is a universality among soldiers who face combat. They want to go home, they don't want to die and they are mostly concerned about letting down their comrades.

Acknowledging that while war can be "vastly exhilarating," and that, "There is an intoxication about battle…," he realized that war had changed him and everyone involved whether on the front lines or the home front.

"When you've lived with the unnatural mass cruelty that mankind is capable of inflicting on itself, you find yourself dispossessed of the faculty for blaming one poor man for the triviality of his faults."

This sense of tolerance and empathy for the frailty of others shines through most of the people I have known or read about who survive combat.

This "there but for fortune" thought is apparently finely honed by personal observation of what we humans are capable of doing to one another in war.

Posey County has been blessed with many people who have learned these valuable lessons. From the Revolutionary War (1775-83) veterans who helped establish Posey County's first settlement up through our military personnel serving today, Posey County has contributed more than its fair share.

I have already written about some of our Civil War (1861-65) incidents. And, soon after that war ended, Francis C. Green who was born in Mt. Vernon on September 04, 1835 won the Medal of Honor while serving in the cavalry against Native Americans in the Arizona territory in 1869.

Sergeant Green served with Company K of the 8th Cavalry. He is buried in the town of Erin, Tennessee where an impressive memorial commemorates his service. His monument is on that county's courthouse campus and includes mention of Mt. Vernon, Indiana as his birthplace.

Posey County has a proud tradition of honoring and thanking those who serve our country in the military. We have a monument to the fifteen Revolutionary War veterans buried in Posey County. This engraved granite stele and the impressive marble statue to Civil War (1861-65) and Spanish American War (1898) veterans are both located on our Courthouse Campus.

In 1927 Posey County dedicated the Memorial Coliseum to honor the Veterans of World War I (1914-18). Since 1927 we have had World War II (1941-45), the Korean War (1950-53), the Vietnam War (1964-73), the Gulf War (1990-91), and our current war, The Iraq War (2003-?).

We have placed impressive and well deserved plaques to our veterans from WWI, WWII, Korea and Vietnam in the foyer of the War Memorial. As yet, we have not recognized our Gulf War and Iraq War veterans.

So many Posey County citizens have served our country through various branches of the military in every conflict that it is not possible to give each one credit in this column.

However, for the next few weeks I plan to write of a few representatives who, for me, stand for all who deserve our honor and gratitude. I hope that should anyone know of others that they wish to recognize that they will not hesitate to write their own article and submit it.

The old Rough Rider from the Spanish American War, Theodore Roosevelt, described all those who serve their country as follows:

The Glory Belongs to the One Who Serves

"It is not the critic who counts, not the man who points out
how the strong man stumbled, or where the doer of deeds could
have done better. The credit belongs to the man who is actually in
the arena; whose face is marred by the dust and sweat and blood;
who strives valiantly; who errs and comes short again and again;
who knows the great enthusiasms, the great devotions and spends
himself in a worthy course; who at the best, knows in the end the
triumph of high achievement, and who, at worst, if he fails, at least
fails while daring greatly; so that his place shall never be with those
cold and timid souls who know neither victory or defeat."

EVERY MAN A HERO

(Week of August 29, 2005)

General Omar Bradley who commanded the nightmare known as the D-Day landing on Omaha Beach June 06, 1944, said:

"Every man who set foot on Omaha Beach that day was a hero."

Herman and Paul Eickhoff were two of those men. These 19-year-old twins from St. Philip in Posey County were members of the First Infantry Division. General Bradley personally chose the First Division to lead the attack.

"My choice of the 1st Inf. Div. to spearhead the invasion probably saved us Omaha Beach and a catastrophe on the landing."

Paul has now passed away. But chances are good he would tell me what Herman did:

"I'm no hero."

This reluctance to set himself apart from all the others who served whether at the front or the home front is a consistent characteristic of most of the combat veterans with whom I have spoken.

I will let you, the reader, judge for yourself whether Herman and Paul were heroes.

Herman hit the beach while seasick from his ride on an LST. Of course, the rough seas might have been made worse by a severe case of "butterflies?". He and Paul were in constant combat for 30 days without a change of clothing or a bath.

After 90 days of actual combat through France, their 12 man rifle squad was down to 6 men.

On September 07, 1944 their squad was in a battle with German soldiers. Herman saw his twin brother shot and thought he would die. Another squad member was wounded. Two Americans were killed. And Herman and the sixth member of the squad were captured.

Emergency medical attention was given to Paul on the battlefield by the German medics who then left him for the Americans to find and care for. Paul received care for several months thereafter at the United States Military Hospital in Walla Walla, Washington. Herman did not find out Paul was alive until much later.

Herman was held as a P.O.W. in Stalag 4B and then Stalag 7A near Munich, Germany.

Herman told me the Germans themselves were under stark living conditions by that time in 1944 but they treated him and his fellow American P.O.W.'s well considering the conditions.

The Americans slept in 4 tier wooden bunks and were fed watery potato and barley soup as well as a little coffee, dark potato bread and sugar beets. About every 2 weeks when the American

Red Cross packages were delivered to the camp, Herman would trade the cigarettes they contained for extra food.

The prisoners did not have hot water for showers. Roll call was taken regularly with each P.O.W. being given a number. Herman's was 88026. I guess there are some things one never forgets.

Herman's greatest fear as a P.O.W. was of being killed in an American bombing raid. The prisoners painted "P.O.W." on their barracks roofs so that the Allies would not bomb them. This was okay by their German guards, as they did not want to be bombed either!

That winter of 1944-45 the Germans had Herman and other P.O.W.'s repair the roads and bridges the Americans had blown up. It was cold and Herman had only the uniform he was captured in and a jacket and long coat that the Germans gave him for warmth. He did not have gloves.

On April 29, 1945 Herman's camp was liberated. Herman then found out that his brother Paul was alive. He, also, found out that their 3 other brothers and their 2 step-brothers, all of whom served during WWII, were all right.

Herman and Paul's father, Joseph Eickhoff, had been killed in a work accident when they were 7 years old. Their mother, Cecelia (nee) Folz, was left to raise 5 boys on a $33.00 per month pension from SIGECO. She raised her family in a log home on Althiede Road for which she paid $3.00 per month rent. It appears that the strength and courage that brought her boys home had its genesis with a home front heroine.

Thanks to Herman, Paul, and the rest of what Tom Brokaw calls "The Greatest Generation", and thanks, also, to all of the Cecelias who helped prepare them for the great challenges they faced.

AN UNKNOWN VICTORY

(Week of September 5, 2005)

You name the WAR:

Two countries are created from one by the greatest military power in
the world and are monitored by the United Nations;
One country led by a ruthless dictator invades the other in spite of
the United Nations warnings not to;
The Secretary General of the United Nations declares, "This is a war
against the United Nations.";
A United States President leads a coalition of world leaders to unite to
drive the invaders out and re-establish the status quo;
An American general is placed in charge of the United Nations
forces;
While many countries offer some help, the American military
provides more than half of a million personnel in the war;
The aggressors are driven out of and liberty is restored to the
invaded country; and
The mission for which Americans fought and died is accomplished.

If you said The Gulf War of 1990-1991, that is understandable. Almost all Americans supported that war and recognized that victory. However, I am talking about the Korean War of 1950-1953. It too was a great victory for American and United Nations interests and helped prevent World War III. We owe a huge debt to our Korean War veterans.

Two of those heroes (they just hate to be called that but, hey, it's my column and facts are facts) are Posey County natives and brothers-in-law Harold Cox and Gene McCoy.

Harold fought with the U.S. Army's 25th Division which suffered many casualties and bore much of the fighting in Korea. Harold was an infantry rifleman and was the jeep driver for his company commander.

Gene was a combat engineer with the Army's 84th Engineers Battalion and, also, served as a courier/mail deliverer.

Harold was on the frontlines and Gene was building wooden bridges about 1000 yards behind those lines. Gene says Harold had it a lot rougher than Gene.

Both suffered the 20 below zero cold, the stifling heat and humidity, the loneliness, home sickness and fear in what those not there called a "police action."

Harold said one of his worst memories, outside of dodging enemy mortar rounds for a solid year of combat, was the stench of the human waste the impoverished Koreans would save all winter and fertilize their rice paddies with in the spring. Gene, also, mentioned that nauseating smell and the mud and flooding caused by the lack of vegetation due to constant shelling.

When Gene first arrived in Korea they put his outfit on a train which stopped frequently. Each time it stopped the young soldiers were given a few rounds of ammunition and ordered out to guard the train from sabotage. Gene said this initiation to Korea was more than a little unsettling.

Harold told me that the traffic signs in the war were a bit more to the point than those back home. On one particularly dangerous stretch of road a sign advised:

"Get your _____ in gear and drive like _____! The NK
 can see you."

Harold paid attention.

Harold and Gene came home and re-started their lives. Harold served as Mt. Vernon's Water Superintendent for several years in the 1980's and1990's. Gene served as a Mt. Vernon City Council man and the Posey County Recorder. Gene is currently Posey County's Veterans Affairs Officer. They both raised families and went on publicly as if there had been no Korean War. However, privately what General Douglas MacArthur called "the strange, mournful mutter of the battlefield" never left their consciousness.

Of course, there was a Korean War and it helped save you and me from another world war. It was a largely unappreciated "mission accomplished." Thank you Harold and Gene and all your fellow Korean War veterans.

NO FIRECRACKERS?

(Week of July 10, 2006)

Last week I completed an experimental internet class for the National Judicial College. It involved the college's technology expert who coordinated six weeks of computer and telephone meetings for trial court judges from South Carolina to Oregon. I guess the days of textbooks and legal pads are disappearing in these times of $3.00 per gallon gasoline.

I do not mind the demise of face-to-face seminars as they often involve about ninety percent bells and whistles, or at least caps and refrigerator magnets, and less than ten percent substance.

What I thought I would mind was a Fourth of July without firecrackers. After the end of the electronic class, Peg and I traveled to Oklahoma to attend our family's annual patriotic extravaganza at my oldest brother's place. Oh, sure, we had mass quantities of barbecue, and games galore, but what we did not have were fireworks.

Each year, since long before my birth and continuing through 2005, my family has celebrated our country's birthday the proper way: with burned fingers, singed hair and cinders in our eyes. Benjamin Franklin and his gang of anti-Toryists would have cheered with approval as we boys, and often some of the less responsible adult males, threw cherry bombs at one another or fired Roman candles indiscriminately.

While the mothers exhausted their lungs calling out dire warnings of lost digits or blindness, we would create cannons from left over lead pipe or scraps of PVC. These activities almost always took place during the stifling heat of daylight.

Then at night the men would compete with star bursts and other more glittering explosions. Everyone was expected to and did say, "Ooh...ahh...," as each explosive device got more extravagant until some senior family member announced that the finale was coming.

Usually the end would come as the sky radiated red, white and blue and our whole clan would stand and sing "The Star Spangled Banner" and "God Bless America."

Of course, we still stood and sang those great songs this year, but we did so without fireworks. On the other hand, we also avoided burning up the yard.

When I was a child, people just expected and accepted that a certain number of prairie fires would be the price to be paid for kids and idiots fighting and playing with Fourth of July fireworks. But now, legal restrictions have burst the fireworks balloon and forced responsible behavior.

The drought in the west has dampened the Spirit of 1776, that is, if one sees Independence Day as merely an excuse to escape work and risk injury from explosives. Whereas, a few years ago, dry weather would bring out motherly-type warnings from the local fire departments, now fines and even jail are possible repercussions of patriotic exuberance.

So, since my family usually obeys the law, and because the county sheriff had announced extra patrols, we had no fireworks. We were relegated to talk of sacrifices made and real battles fought for freedom and equality.

71

Just as the new internet course focused us judges on actually learning something, a Fourth without fireworks concentrated my family's thoughts on the reason for our yearly gathering. We remembered our family's veterans who have served during practically all of our nation's wars, including the ongoing Iraq War. The quiet brought about by these memories and by the family's concern for our son, Jim, who is currently serving where the real fireworks are, put the change in our patriotic celebration in perspective.

As my whole close-knit family sat beneath the still, clear sky and followed July's occasional shooting star, my sister, Jane, handed out the tee shirts she had bought. One side showed a sketch of where Jim and his unit are serving in Iraq and the back named each soldier on his special team.

We decided that we could survive without our fireworks at home if things could, also, be all quiet on the Middle Eastern Front.

The Redwine Clan July 4, 2006, Sulphur, Oklahoma
Photograph by Jane Redwine Bartlett

THE WAR OF THE ROSES REVISITED

(Week of June 12, 2006)

Parents who have a child in a war easily grasp the theme of Arthur Miller's play, *All My Sons*, about World War II. It is not just your child's life that is important, it is the lives of all.

When friends have children in a war at the same time, they often exchange information and share concerns.

When our son, Jim, was in the Gulf War of 1990-91, along with several others from Posey County, other parents, such as Jerry and Marsha King, kept in touch with us.

Now that Jim is in the Iraq War with others from Posey County, their parents, such as Kenny and Dee Rose, share information with us.

Posey County is a small place where many people have overlapping duties and activities. The late Aubry Robison, Jr., used to say this place was so small our gas company could be a Pepsi machine. And Aubry knew small; he was born in Solitude.

It was just last month that Kenny Rose, who is an investigator for Prosecuting Attorney Jodi Uebelhack, and I encountered one another at the courthouse.

I asked Kenny about his son in Iraq. Kenny told me he and Dee now had two sons serving there. Then he asked for an update on my son.

The next time Kenny and I talked, he told me that his son, Travis, had been wounded by an improvised explosive device. After Kenny assured me that Travis would recover, I asked about Travis's brother, Wes. Kenny said Wes was not with Travis when the Humvee was destroyed but did get to see him soon after. It says a lot about Travis that his major concerns were to reassure his family and get back to his duty station as quickly as possible.

Travis did not see the insurgent who planted the bomb. This war does not have set battle lines and easily recognized antagonists.

In the Gulf War, Jim and his fellow soldiers met the enemy head on in a full frontal assault. But in this War, some Shiites fight Americans but may also fight Sunnis, Kurds and the Iraqi security forces.

This might be manageable for our troops except that some Sunnis are also fighting each of the other groups and some of each of the remaining groups are fighting everyone else too. And, many of these factions also fight alongside our troops.

Jim, in his e-mails from his station near the Syrian border, says the problem is complicated further because Iraqis are not a homogenous people but a collection of many tribes, religions, cultures and ethnic groups who speak numerous languages and dialects. Iraq was artificially created by the British in 1917. They drew arbitrary borders within the old Ottoman Empire then declared victory and went home. They left out a few details such as how those disparate tribes that had been traditional enemies were going to get along as one people. Such cooperation turned out to be particularly difficult in this region of scarce resources. It was only the brutality of Saddam Hussein that controlled the various factions. Now the pent up hatreds and desires of some members of these various interest groups have been released.

Our attempts to implement democracy in Iraq require a sense of nationalism. However, some members of the various tribes and other interest groups' first loyalty is to their own families, tribes, cultures and beliefs. This type of thinking is what led Robert E. Lee to decline President Lincoln's offer of command of the Union forces at the start of our Civil War. In his heart, Lee was a Virginian first. So, he accepted Jefferson Davis's offer to command the Army of Northern Virginia.

The members of the Iraqi Army have similar divided loyalties. In fact, Jim describes his assignment as akin to the mission of the crew of the Starship Enterprise from *Star Trek*. He and his team of ten American soldiers deal with units of the Iraqi army and with some tribes and other parochial factions in their large region of responsibility in an effort to meet and understand the various cultures while helping to bring about a federation that will, step by small step, lead to some kind of unified Iraqi government. Our troops are soldiers first, but they must be diplomats also. They train the Iraqis to be better soldiers but, also, try to help them coalesce into a unit with a sense of nationalism.

Jim has met and dealt with many Iraqis whom he likes and respects. But the I.E.D. makers and suicide bombers are terrorists whose goals are not freedom for Iraq as a country but the expulsion of the U.S. so that their particular faction can try to take control. The difficulty is in sorting out the terrorists while not creating new ones.

As Travis and Wesley Rose know only too well, the front lines are not just to the front and there are no defined sides. In fact, the nature of this conflict and the Rose family's name reminded me of the War of the Roses that eventually brought about the unification of the English people in the Fifteenth Century.

From 1455 A.D. to 1487 A.D., the House of Lancaster, signified by a red rose, and the House of York, a white rose, fought numerous civil war battles throughout England. These Medieval struggles were, to some small degree, like what sometimes occurs in Iraq. Contrary to what some are saying, this war is less like the Vietnam War or the Gulf War and more like the War of the Roses.

The battle for the hearts and minds in our current War requires an understanding that the people of Iraq are of many hearts and many minds and a sense of nationalism must be brought about before democracy can flourish. And it is probable that an incremental "Total Quality Management" approach over a long period of time will be required before a common *Volksgeist* arises in the Iraqi people.

It took our English ancestors over thirty years to come to a resolution of their differences and they all spoke the same language. Perhaps we should not expect a drive-through solution in Iraq.

BETTER THAN JURY DUTY?

(Week of March 20, 2006)

The following letter and excuse from Jury Service was sent to Iraq:

Greetings from the Posey Circuit Court

Dear Michael E. Stillwagoner, Jr.,

Your request to be excused from Jury Duty has just been referred to me by my bailiff, Dr. John Emhuff.

Dear Citizen Stillwagoner, over the twenty-six years that I have been judge I have been often amused and occasionally amazed at the lengths to which people will go to avoid jury duty.

However, when I received your returned jury questionnaire from your wife, Tonya, along with some official looking documents concerning your whereabouts, I was impressed. Surely, you have gone to the greatest length.

I know Dr. Emhuff can be pretty intimidating what with his security responsibilities and his secret service type of hearing device. But really, Sergeant Stillwagoner, is John scarier than the Iraqi insurgents? Wouldn't you prefer jury duty over combat? Is your service with the Indiana National Guard I-163rd Field Artillery in Iraq less onerous than suffering through my instructions to the jury?

Of course, it's possible that you might not mind a trip home. I know that your wife and mother would like to see you.

As you know, your mother, Mary Stillwagoner, works right next to the Court in the Clerk's Office. When I received your request to be excused, I spoke to your mother. Be on notice President Bush, Mary wants her son home. She fully supports me in having him serve on jury duty.

In fact, she told me she would write the President, your commanding officer, Governor Daniels, and even Oprah, if she could get you back in Posey County.

I know you want to do your duty and not let your fellow soldiers down. However, you may not be fully aware of the benefits, that's right, the benefits of jury service. For one, no one will be shooting at you and there aren't any Improvised Explosive Devices to worry about.

But, also, you would receive forty cents per mile to and from the Court. From Iraq, that would be about $1,500.00. Now, I am not suggesting that you try to slip away from your unit to do jury duty. But when I was in the service we had guys who would go A.W.O.L. for a cold beer and a date.

Sergeant Stillwagoner, thank you for serving in that dangerous place. Come home soon and come home safe. And thanks to you and Mrs. Stillwagoner for taking the time and trouble to respond to my request for jury duty. I know you both have a great deal on your minds.

Thank you and you are excused. Unless, of course, you want to try to convince the Army that you just cannot get out of jury duty and must come home now. If so, feel free to give your C.O. a copy of this column with the "classified" part about your being excused marked out.

UNITED WE STOOD

(Week of October 3, 2005)

Saddam Hussein, Iraq's iron fisted dictator, ordered his soldiers to invade Iraq's small defenseless oil rich neighbor, Kuwait, on August 02, 1990.

On August 07, 1990 America sent troops to one of our closest allies in the Middle East, Saudi Arabia. We were concerned for our friends in the region and our access to oil. We warned Saddam to cease his offensive and demanded his withdrawal from Kuwait. He persisted in his brutal belligerence against the Kuwaiti people.

President George H.W. Bush began to prepare the American public for a possible war with Iraq. He explained our nation's interest in the region and he informed the public about Saddam Hussein's large and well-equipped military. He, also, kept Congress up to date on the progress of the conflict and what he and our military were doing in response.

The President helped form a coalition of Arabic nations and others through the United Nations. The U.N. strongly supported America's initiatives against Iraq and authorized force if necessary to get the Iraqi military out of Kuwait. Our Arabic friends even paid 44 billion dollars to the United States to cover our financial costs.

By the time the President ordered our military to prepare to invade Iraq, the American public was informed as to the reasons we were going to fight and what our exit strategy was before we went in.

Quick, total victory under the United Nations Mandate was our clear vision of the Gulf War. We were not authorized to remove Saddam from power. We had no charter to occupy Iraq. President George H.W. Bush who was himself a World War II combat veteran understood his mission, both what it required and what its limits were.

As the President told the Nation in his speech of August 08, 1990:

> "...standing up for our principles is an American
> tradition. As it has so many times before, it may
> take time and tremendous effort, but most of all it
> will take unity of purpose."

And unified we were! Of course, many people preferred a peaceful resolution and many publicly and privately lobbied for diplomatic sanctions instead of war. However, there was hardly any disagreement about whether our troops should be supported and their mission accomplished.

By the time my son, Jim, reported for duty in Saudi Arabia on Christmas Day, 1990, our country in general and Posey County in particular had mobilized the home front in a massive outpouring of support.

Locally, the H.O.M.E. TEAM committee founded and still operated by Teresa Spivey, Becky Higgins, Karen Kuhn, Kathy Beyer and several others sent huge care packages to our Posey County military personnel.

As always, Posey County did its part. Among the many who served and who appreciated the Nation's support were Charlie McPhearson, Vernon Hutchinson, John King, Bruce Hamilton, Joe Rutledge and Alan Veatch. You will know of many others who deserve recognition whom I have not had space to mention, including other members of the H.O.M.E. TEAM, who did their duty at home and in the military. Please take the time to recognize them.

One group that I know of was Patty Redwine's Fourth Grade Class at West Elementary School in Mt. Vernon. They wrote letters to several of our local service people during the War. One girl wrote to our son, Jim. He and we greatly appreciated the local support.

Just before Jim went into the Battle of Medina Ridge against Saddam's elite Republican Guard he answered the little girl's letter:

> "Things are still pretty quiet here.
> We are real close to the border now.
> We made the largest armored movement
> since World War II last week. We are just
> waiting, cautiously, for Bush to wave the starting
> flag. It should be pretty dramatic. Old Saddam
> better pull out of Kuwait soon. Right now the
> "Fly Boys" are up there screwin around, but when
> the Army gets involved heavily, he will be
> really sorry."

Jim was right. Our Nation's mission was completely successful.

When Jim and our other local warriors came home in the summer of 1991, Posey County welcomed them with their names on business marquees, a Fourth of July Parade down Main Street in Mt. Vernon and speeches before civic groups such as the American Legion.

It was good to be back home again in Indiana.

As Jim is still in the Army and has been back to Kuwait and to Egypt several times since the Gulf War ended in 1991, I do not plan to comment on our current efforts in Iraq. Perhaps, when things get sorted out there, it will be appropriate to analyze that War.

For now, ♫ I ain't a'gwine a study war no more ♫ in this column.

BLUE AND GOLD STARS

(Week of April 9, 2007)

This past Saturday our family was able to take down the silk flag with its blue star that we had up for the past year. Our family's soldier was finally home from the Iraq War. Gina, Nick and Elyse welcomed him back to Ft. Leavenworth, Kansas.

We displayed this same blue star during the Gulf War of 1990-91. When we were able to retire it then, we thought Jim's war service was honorably completed and at an end. We, once again, hope that is true.

The American tradition of displaying a blue star for a service member serving in combat began with World War I.

Those families who lost someone in battle would sew a gold star over the blue one.

For the veterans of all of America's wars and their families, the song by country singer, Clint Bullard, "Gold Star Mother", sums up our emotions:

> ♪ *She hung a banner with a blue star*
> *when he shipped overseas*
> *To show the world he was fighting*
> *for the Land of the Free.*
> *But on a windswept desert night*
> *six thousand miles away,*
> *They both paid the price*
> *for what we have every day.* ♪

My family and I thank all of you who asked about Jim's welfare and who care about all of our service personnel.

For those of you who still have not been able to retire your blue stars, our thoughts are with you. For those of you who have had to or may have to sew on a gold star, you have our sincerest sympathy and gratitude for your family's sacrifice and service to our country.

"Back Together Again"
Jim, his wife, Gina, and their children, Nick and Elyse
Boots back on American soil March, 2007

NEIGHBORS

(Week of August 21, 2006)

Jake Moll and I used to stand out in our adjoining front yards and promise one another we would sit down soon and discuss Jake's World War II experiences. I knew that my good friend and next-door neighbor had survived some of the War's toughest campaigns, but he was too humble to tell me without my urging.

Jake was the first Posey County person to volunteer for the draft. His country took young Jake up on his offer and sent him to fight against Rommel's elite African Corps.

Unfortunately, Jake and I never got around to filling in an important part of Posey County's patriotic contribution; he passed away September 18, 2003.

Jake's brother, Frank, is also my neighbor and he and I finally sat down this weekend to discuss Frank's World War II service in the Army Air Corps from 1942 to 1945.

Last Friday we met in our front yards to discuss the loss of our mutual neighbor and friend, Danny Perkins, whose accidental death on August 10th, at age fifty, left a huge void in our neighborhood. The shock of suddenly being without Danny's kind and vibrant humor brought Frank and me to a more urgent sense of *carpe diem*. We sat at my dining room table as eighty-two year old Francis B. Moll, born in Mt. Vernon, Indiana, slowly transformed into Sgt. Frank Moll who won the Distinguished Flying Cross as a nineteen-year-old tail gunner on a B-17 Flying Fortress. Frank flew twenty-one missions over France and Germany in 1943.

His squadron normally flew with a total of six bombers in a staggered double vee formation to help defend against German fighter planes.

On a run over Muenster, Germany, they lost all but Frank's plane to both anti-aircraft fire and fighter attacks from eighteen enemy fighter planes. Frank's aircraft had four engines but lost one over their target, then two more to fighter fire.

Their last engine was also damaged and should not have got them home to England. But with Frank's encouragement of the ten-man crew and his constant defense of his plane from his tail gunner position, his pilot managed to limp them back across the English Channel as their last engine died. Just before they cleared the Channel, the pilot was shouting, "Ding, Dingy, prepare for ditching!"

They glided to a landing without losing a man.

Frank had put in for pilot training before going overseas and his request was granted after this mission. But Frank found that leaving the nine men with whom he had survived numerous close calls with death was very difficult. He felt they needed him and he knew that he needed them. He continued to do his duty and earned his honorable discharge when the war was over. However, he never again felt quite as alive as when he was facing random death with his bomber crew.

Of the nine Moll children, four sons and one daughter served in the military in World War II.

Frank had worked in the Moll family feed business in Mt. Vernon from the age of four. His work and military experiences helped him make a long time success out of his automobile dealership after the war. As I listened to the nineteen-year old tail gunner transform back into my unassuming friend and neighbor, I wondered about all those other Posey County war heroes who look and act just like the rest of us. How many stories are going untold? How can we say thank you when most of our heroes do not even recognize they are special?

As Frank said, his brother, Jake, could have told me about some extremely harrowing experiences with the infantry. I should have found the time for Jake and several others too. Good neighbors are hard to replace and good friends even more so. And it is always nice to say thank you while people can still hear it.

HE SERVED

(Week of January 30, 2006)

Seventeen-year-old John Shanklin Ramsey of Wadesville was tired of reading about his friends who were already in the war. He was proud of them, but he wanted to see combat himself. So, he finally convinced his father, William, that their Center Township farm could do without him for the little while the war would probably last. His mom, Emily, was not so sure.

And John hoped young Charlotte Causey would not forget him while he was gone.

His father cautioned him that army life would not necessarily be any easier than twelve hour days on the farm. He said there were as many health hazards just living in encampments as there were from combat. And, of course, the old man's warning came back to John when he got dysentery and was hospitalized in Bowling Green, Kentucky. The army converted John from an infantryman to guard duty in Washington, D.C. This was not what he'd signed on for; what could he tell his future grandchildren he'd done in the war?

Three years after enlisting in search of glory and excitement, John was stuck guarding installations from potential terrorist attacks while his brother, James, and their friends had faced the enemy. Attacks on Washington, whom were they kidding? General Lee had already surrendered his forces to his fellow West Pointer, U.S. Grant, and the war was almost over. Why worry about attacks now?

On top of that, his current orders were to spend his Friday night attending some silly play called *Our American Cousin* in Washington because of rumors of a conspiracy to attack the government officials who might be there. He could think of better things to be doing. There were always rumblings of dire happenings that never happened.

As a private, John was stationed where he could see the special dignitaries' box, but the box itself was to be guarded by an officer of the Washington Metropolitan Police Force, John Parker, who later left his post to take a smoke.

John Ramsey and his fellow soldiers had heard rumors of who was supposed to be in the box, but, for security reasons, no specific names had been released. It was possible that the Supreme Commander of the Army or even the President himself might attend. Still, John was amazed when the tall man in a dark suit entered the box and every one of the six hundred people in Ford's Theatre turned to stare.

Young John Ramsey could not take his eyes off Mr. Lincoln, his wife, Mary, and their guests, Major Henry Rathbone and his fiancée, Clara Harris. Therefore, he was watching when the strange figure entered the box from behind the President and fired a shot from a derringer into the President's head.

Ramsey ran towards the box as he saw the man, John Wilkes Booth, stab Major Rathbone six times then leap from the box to the stage twelve feet below. Booth's riding spurs ironically caught in the American flag draping the box and caused him to break his ankle.

Private Ramsey reached President Lincoln and helped carry the large bleeding man from the theatre to the Peterson Boarding House across the street. Mr. Lincoln's blood soaked John's uniform coat as the soldiers laid their Commander in Chief in a bed that would not accommodate the great man.

Later, Posey County's own hero, John Shanklin Ramsey, also guarded Samuel Mudd, the physician who treated Booth after he fled the theatre. For many years after John's honorable discharge from the United States Army, he spoke to Posey County's school children as one of the select few who had been on the front lines of our nation's first presidential assassination. He would produce the uniform he wore that night and point out the stains caused by his Commander in Chief's blood.

Unfortunately, John and Charlotte Ramsey's Posey County home was destroyed by fire and most of their memorabilia, including, perhaps, the blood stained uniform, was lost. But until John's death on December 11, 1931 he could vividly recount the awful events of Friday, April 14, 1865 and the wartime service he gave to his country.

I wish to thank Sherry Graves of the Workingman's Institute and William and Jerry Ramsey, John's great grandsons, for their help in researching this article.

ALPHA AND OMEGA

(Week of February 6, 2006)

America's two greatest presidents had connections with Posey County. With their birthdays coming up in February, I started last week writing about the Father and the Unifier of our country and their local influence.

George Washington led us from a collection of colonies dependent upon Britain to a coalition of autonomous American states.

Abraham Lincoln melded us into a unified country.

Washington helped create the United States and Lincoln helped preserve it. That is why they are recognized and celebrated as our most important leaders.

Posey County takes its name from General Thomas Posey who was a neighbor to Washington at his Mount Vernon, Virginia, estate. Washington took special interest in the young Posey who was a Revolutionary War hero and later Governor of the Northwest Territory, which included Indiana.

Mt. Vernon, the county seat of Posey County, was re-named in honor of George Washington at the instance of Posey County's Revolutionary War veterans.

Lincoln's neighbor in Spencer County, Indiana, was John Pitcher who later served as a common pleas judge in Posey County. Judge Pitcher loaned young Abe law books such as *Blackstone's Commentaries*.

Posey County's three Civil War Generals, Alvin P. Hovey, William Harrow and Thomas Pitcher, John's son, all had direct contact with Lincoln.

Jerry King who has furnished historical information for these articles in the past, told me that Lincoln had been personally present at a bridge dedication in Savah.

And while some Yellow Journalist might report it as fact, it is simply unfounded, unfair and proven by the facts to be untrue, that Thomas Posey, whose portrait hangs in the Posey Circuit Court, was the illegitimate son of our Founding Father. Unfortunately, we humans cannot resist wanting to believe the worst about our best people, especially if the rumors are salacious. Thus, in Thomas Posey's case, because he and Washington were Anglo-Saxon males who, as was common at the time, dressed in Revolutionary War uniforms and white periwigs for their portraits and, also, lived beside each other, Washington's kindnesses and interest in Posey's career have been put in the worst light by our worst people.

On the other hand, there is no doubt that our famous Posey County resident, John Shanklin Ramsey, was an eyewitness to President Lincoln's assassination and helped carry his wounded body from Ford's Theatre on April 14, 1865.

Those few of you who chanced upon this column last week know that Ramsey, a private from Wadesville, was on guard duty that night and, also, saw Major Henry Rathbone stabbed six times by John Wilkes Booth in front of his fiancée, Clara Harris.

You may not know that Rathbone's widowed mother married Harris's widower father, United States Senator Ira Harris.

Mrs. Harris was one of Mary Todd Lincoln's best friends. This is why, when General and Mrs. Ulysses S. Grant turned down the Lincoln's invitation to attend *Our American Cousin*, Rathbone and his step-sister/fiancée were guests in the Presidential Box.

Major Rathbone had struggled mightily with Booth and nearly bled to death from the six knife wounds he received. However, he always felt he should have prevented the assassination.

Even though Rathbone and Harris married and had children, her health always suffered and his depression required treatment.

While seeking help for his condition in Hanover, Germany, in 1883, Henry Rathbone shot his wife in the head and stabbed himself six times. She died immediately and he died in a mental asylum in 1911. The experts hypothesized that Rathbone's sense of guilt led him to attempt to reenact the tragic events at Ford's Theatre.

In addition to seeing Lincoln, Mary, Booth, Rathbone and Harris that fateful night, John Shanklin Ramsey of Center Township did guard duty over Samuel Mudd who treated Booth's broken ankle.

Considering that George Washington brought America into existence and Abraham Lincoln made it possible for us to become the most powerful nation on Earth, Posey County's numerous connections to them are remarkable.

SHILOH

(Week of September 8, 2008)

A couple of Saturdays ago while I was forced to play golf near Bloomington, Peg demanded the opportunity to do research for this article at the Lilly Library. It did not seem fair that she got to be inside while I was trudging through sand and water hazards in search of a triple digit golf score. But that's just the kind of considerate husband I am.

Anyway, Peg's mission, as assigned by me, was to search the rare document section for personal papers from Posey County's most illustrious citizen, Alvin Peterson Hovey.

Many of you know of the Civil War exploits of Major General Hovey including his heroic service at the Battle of Shiloh, Tennessee on April 6th and 7th, 1862. While the battle ended as a Union victory, it began as a possible Northern loss. And Hovey's personal perspective was discovered by Peg in a handwritten document she found at Lilly.

Hovey was serving as a Colonel in command of the 24th Indiana Volunteers and fought along with General Lew Wallace of *Ben Hur* fame.

Hovey's 24th was, "[M]arching toward the roar of cannon from 11:00 or 11:30 A.M., holding the division in close order and well in hand, until about 2:00 P.M.", when he encountered General Wallace and his staff.

> "I halted the column as directed and Wallace's and Grant's aides came to the front. I saw by a glance at their troubled faces and soiled uniforms that some disaster had befallen our army."

The aides told Hovey the morning of Sunday, April 6, 1862 had gone badly. The Confederates were celebrating their victory and occupying much of the former Union positions.

Hovey was ordered to form the 24th in line of battle and they advanced into the evening's darkness fearfully and with fixed bayonets. When they were halted by a cry of "Who comes there?", Hovey did not know if they had encountered friends or foes.

Hovey improvised the following password, "Hoosiers". He was relieved to hear the response "Welcome Hoosiers".

That night Hovey tried to rest in preparation for the next day's battle but,

> "…the groans of the wounded and dying fell sadly on the stillness of that gloomy night. Friends and foes seem to be intermingled on one broad field of carnage….The rain poured down in the blackness of darkness. I slept not that night."

Hovey quoted on old Irish poem, "Tam O'Shanter":

> "When sick a night he took the road in
> As ne'er poor sinner was abroad in."

Next week we might see if the dawn brought Hovey and his men any relief.

THE SECOND DAY

(Week of September 15, 2008)

Alvin Peterson Hovey stood up for his fellow Hoosier, Lew Wallace, whom biographers of Ulysses Grant and William Sherman tried to make the fall guy for the Union debacle of the first day at Shiloh.

Hovey felt compelled to point out that,

> "General Wallace and myself, have never been what the world would call as close or bosom friends. Our natures, as the Spanish would say, are not simpatico; but I know and respect him as a true brave soldier and a patriot, and can only feel indignation at the attempt to make him the 'scapegoat', for other men's mistakes and blunders, and deem it but justice to tell the truth in vindication of history and the right."

The foregoing passage is from Hovey's personal account of the bloody Battle of Shiloh as found by Peg among the collection of Hovey's papers in the vault of the Lilly Library at Indiana University.

The Rebels under General Johnston had surprised Grant's and Sherman's forces in the early morning of April 6, 1862 and would have had a major victory had they pressed on instead of stopping out of confusion and lack of information. This delay allowed General Buell's army along with Wallace's to provide reinforcements and drive back the Confederates on the second day.

But Grant and Sherman, according to our own Colonel Hovey (at that time), tried to cover up their own lack of preparation by claiming Wallace had not followed orders and had taken the wrong road and had moved too slowly to help Grant and Sherman.

Of course, the true reason the South lost one of the great strategic opportunities of the Civil War had more to do with the combat death of the great Confederate General A.S. Johnston than any action or inaction of any Union general.

Regardless, what up to that time was the deadliest battle in American history was won on the second day and Alvin P. Hovey was in the thick of it. In fact, that is when he came to the attention of Grant who later commended Hovey for his gallantry.

And it was not because Hovey disliked either Grant or Sherman that he stood tall for Wallace. Hovey had great respect for both men and wrote:

> "Grant and Sherman often erred, and cold and unimpassioned history in the future, will make those errors visible to the eyes of their warmest worshipers. They were like all other men, fallible, often mistaken and sometimes badly beaten in battle, but their

indomitable energy, coolness and common sense, and not their military science in war, crowned them heroes and conquerors, and with that they and their friends should be content without reflecting upon the name or fame of any other man."

A GHOST STORY

(Week of December 31, 2007)

My friend, Ilse Horacek of Mt. Vernon, has led me to some of our area's most interesting and unusual history. Ilse knows first hand how important it is to learn from history. She was born in Germany before World War II and was a teenager when it ended. She and her family experienced life under Hitler and under a conquering army. Her deep commitment to knowing and learning from history comes from having lived through times brought about by lessons not learned. I look forward to when Ilse finalizes the writing of her personal account of her childhood and marriage to an American soldier from Posey County.

The largest ethnic group in America is German. Many of us claim some German heritage. That is particularly true in southern Indiana and southern Illinois where the story Ilse recently brought to my attention arose. It is the story of William Newby, a man either killed at the battle of Shiloh on April 6, 1862 or a wounded soldier who was only thought dead for thirty years.

William Newby, or the man claiming to be him, was sentenced to two years in federal prison after having been found guilty of fraudulently claiming a Civil War pension. When this man, who was either the fraud Daniel Benton from Tennessee, or truly an old Union soldier from Mill Shoals and Norris City, Illinois, was sentenced, Judge Joshua Allen told him:

> "If you are William Newby, you are a very unfortunate and a greatly
> injured man. If you are Daniel Benton, you are a very guilty man."

Then Judge Allen sentenced him to, "…two years imprisonment at hard labor."

Ilse has researched the case of Newby/Benton and has loaned me her book entitled *William Newby, A Civil War Soldier's Return* by G. J. George. This book was hurriedly published right after the trial of Newby/Benton in 1893 to raise money for an appeal. I have relied heavily on this book for this and future articles.

An interesting aspect of this case is how the Newby family split in supporting or condemning the pension claimant. Martha nee, Newby, Greathouse from Mt. Vernon, Indiana, fully supported the man she swore was her older brother. And Fereby Newby, who bore Newby six children, took the destitute old man in as her husband. Yet several other members of the Newby clan swore this "ghost" was a fraud.

If the man was William Newby, he had been shot in the head at Shiloh and left for dead. Then he was captured by the Confederate army and imprisoned at Andersonville. At Andersonville he lived like an animal and was known as Crazy Jack.

After the war he traveled throughout southern Indiana and Illinois staying at local poor houses such as the one in Princeton, Indiana. He formed relationships with several women and used several names.

The case came down to whether the jury believed the man was William Newby of southern Illinois or, as the federal prosecutors alleged, Daniel Benton, AKA Rickety Dan, from Tennessee.

After reading the material provided by Ilse, I am still wondering which man went to prison. Perhaps some of Mr. Newby's family can provide more information. If so, please share with me and I will pass it on.

Next week I plan to recount some of Crazy Jack's experiences at the infamous Andersonville prisoner of war camp.

PRISONERS OF WAR

(Week of January 7, 2008)

Whether he was truly William Newby or Rickety Dan Benton, there was no reasonable doubt that the man a federal judge sent to jail was the man known as Crazy Jack when he was in Andersonville thirty years earlier.

Prisoner of war camps were not for the faint of heart. According to *The Civil War* by Ken Burns, 1800 southern soldiers died of smallpox at the Union prison in Rock Island, Illinois. And in Elmira, New York, the Confederate prisoners bartered for rats to eat. During the War, more soldiers died in prison camps than at the battle of Gettysburg. Mr. Newby/Benton/Crazy Jack was in two of the worst camps: Belle Island in Virginia and the most infamous, Andersonville in Georgia [see pages 337-338].

Walt Whitman personally saw some survivors of Belle Island and observed:

> "Are they not really mummied, dwindled corpses? The dead there
> are not to be pitied as much as some of the living-many of them
> are mentally imbecile, and will never recuperate." p.337

This last condition applies directly to Crazy Jack. When William Newby was either grievously wounded or killed at Shiloh in 1862, he received a gunshot to the head. If he survived, he was captured and placed first at Belle Isle then in Andersonville. By his own account he watched a fellow prisoner there amputate both of his own legs. He, also:

> "[L]aid in the filth and ditches. I went naked with an old yarn shirt
> tied around my waist. I was not at myself there. I was crazy as a
> bed bug, and had no sense at all."
>
> *William Newby, A Civil War*
> *Soldier's Return* at p. 201

Several eyewitnesses to Crazy Jack's condition at Andersonville testified at the fraud trial held in Springfield, Illinois in 1893. Numerous members of the Newby family from southern Illinois and southern Indiana were called, also, but the old Union soldiers who knew Crazy Jack provided the most poignant accounts. Excerpts from just a few are:

> "His lower limbs were all black and broken out with running
> sores." p.147

"The lower part of his limbs were rotten with the scurvy and gangrene sores, and he was covered with vermin." p.146

"I thought he had about as much sense as a hog." p. 147

So, regardless of whether Crazy Jack was William Newby or Daniel Benton, it was for sure he was not in his right mind for several years. Next week we might delve into the defendant's attorney's explanations as to how and why the defendant was really Newby, but used the name Benton.

A HOUSE DIVIDED

(Week of January 14, 2008)

Courts are supposed to be places where prejudgment is prevented. We all are prejudiced. But when we go to the law, we deserve and expect that the jury and the judge will set aside their biases and render decisions based only on the evidence and law.

Unfortunately, the courts are run by humans. Need I explain further? So, sometimes, rarely we hope, it is not what you have or have not done but who or what you are or have been that tips the scale.

In the aftermath of the bitter Civil War, there were numerous cases in which the war time allegiance of the judges and juries clouded their judgment. One such case may have been the federal court proceeding that resulted in William Newby/Dan Benton/Crazy Jack being denied a Civil War Pension and going to prison for even applying for one.

It is difficult for us in 2008 to understand the bile raised by the issues of slavery and states' rights. Slavery is as old as humanity and has existed from time to time in some form on all continents but Antarctica. Of course, it would have taken hold there too if the penguins had figured out how to have someone else do their work.

Therefore, when the Illinois federal judge and jury who were pro-union had to determine if the demented and broken down old bum who claimed to be William Newby from Mill Shoals, Illinois, learned that the claimant might be Rickety Dan Benton from Tennessee, the man's unquestioned ties to the South may have made the difference.

There is no doubt that William Newby had to leave his wife and six children as well as his numerous siblings and his mother and go to war. There is no doubt that William Newby fought bravely at Shiloh and was shot in the head on April 6, 1862.

There is doubt that in spite of the fact the burial detail testified William Newby was hurriedly buried three days later that Newby was actually buried. And there is doubt that the intermittently mad "Crazy Jack" who suffered through the southern prisoner of war camps of Belle Isle and Andersonville would have been able to hoax the wife, sister and mother of William Newby. Each of these witnesses and over two hundred more publicly claimed that the old man who appeared near Carmi, Illinois thirty years after his "death" at Shiloh was William Newby.

On the other hand, this same man, without a doubt, took up with several southern women and served time in a Tennessee penitentiary. He was identified as Rickety Dan Benton by many witnesses. And William Newby's brother testified in court that the claimant could not be William Newby.

According to G.J. George's book, *William Newby, A Civil War Soldier's Return*, the time he spent in the south caused the judge and jury to turn against Newby. After weeks of trial, the jury was out less than twenty minutes when it found him guilty of <u>not</u> being Newby. You may recall that Mr. George's own bias was not hidden. He wrote the book to raise money for an appeal.

And, at least as Mr. George saw it, federal judge, Joshua Allen, was on a mission to see that this Rebel fraud was not allowed to claim a Union pension.

As for me, I have found that juries, who normally only decide one case, usually set aside any bias. A sense of duty almost always pervades a jury's service. There is something so humbling about being asked to judge someone else. However, I do believe that because judges judge others for a living they can become inured to their own blind spots and prejudices. Perhaps Judge Allen did fall prey to this dangerous "Black Robe Syndrome".

I have not been completely convinced, as yet, of who the imprisoned man was. If you care to keep cogitating this conundrum with me, I'll see you here next week.

LAZARUS OR LIAR

(Newby or Benton)
(Week of February 11, 2008)

Mark Twain said there are three infallible ways of pleasing an author: (1) tell him you have read one of his "articles"; (2) tell him you have read all of his "articles"; or (3) ask him to let you read his upcoming "article". (See Twain's book, *Pudd'nhead Wilson*, chapter XI.)

Well, Barry Cleveland, the managing editor of the *Carmi Times*, has pleased (and surprised) me greatly. He claims to have read all of my articles on William Newby/Rickety Dan Benton and he evinced an interest in this article before it appeared in print. If this is sincere and not just a genteel mendacity to spare my feelings, two things may be concluded: either Barry is bored silly or somehow he got trapped in the privy with nothing else to read.

Be that as it may, Barry did e-mail me a copy of a newspaper article from the *White County Democrat* dated February, 1908, that puts a final chapter on the Newby/Benton saga. I have been asked by one or two people what happened to Fereby Newby, William's wife/widow, and Mr. Newby/Benton after the two of them entered that poor house in Montgomery City, Missouri in 1900. I had to confess that my sources dried up at that point. However, the article sent to me by Barry contained information about Mrs. Newby's Civil War widow's pension and the ultimate fate of Newby/Benton. The article is set forth below:

> "Fereby Newby of Mill shoals has been restored to the pension rolls at $12 per month and given an arrearage of $2,000. Her husband was reportedly killed at the Battle of Shiloh during the Civil War, 47 years ago. But 30 years after the war, a man appeared claiming to be him, and she took him in as her husband. He received a pension but was later convicted of defrauding the government, despite her testimony and that of about 140 others who said he was indeed William Newby. But 30 others testified that he was an imposter, "Rickety Dan" Benton. He served a prison term of three years, then returned home to Mrs. Newby, who had given up her pension on his account. Later he wandered down to Geneva, Ala., where he died in the poor house in 1905. Mrs. Newby was finally restored to her pension after a government agency relented."

I do want to thank Mr. Cleveland for this update. However, in the interest of full disclosure, I believe I must point out that in his essay, *My Debut as a Literary Person*, Mark Twain, who was already established as a newspaper columnist, and who was trying to get a New York magazine to publish an article stated:

"In my view, a person who published things in a mere newspaper could not properly claim recognition as a Literary Person; he must rise above that; he must appear in a magazine."

I confess that no editor of any magazine has contacted me.

HERO OR HUMBUG?

(Week of January 21, 2008)

Martha (Newby) Greathouse of Mt. Vernon, Indiana, was William Newby's sister. Martha had lived with William in Mill Shoals, Illinois, until she married John Greathouse and moved to Posey County. Her brother was reported killed in action at the battle of Shiloh, Tennessee, on April 6, 1862.

You can imagine her reaction when she was reading the *Western Star* newspaper on April 19, 1891 and saw that her brother had just appeared alive in McLeansboro, Illinois.

Martha rushed to see the man who was claiming to be her brother and claiming a Civil War pension. As she testified at his federal fraud trial:

> "I first learned of his return by reading of it in the papers
> while I was sick in Mt. Vernon, Indiana. When I got able
> I went to Mill Shoals to see him....
> I recognized his voice, the expression of his eyes, and
> the peculiar stammer of his speech.... I do not believe
> defendant is of sound mind. I say he is my brother."

On the opposite end of the continuum is the 1895 news report after the United States Supreme Court refused to reverse the fraud conviction:

> "The 'Newby case' was one of the most remarkable ever tried
> in a court in this country. Scores of people who knew William
> Newby in life were led to believe that 'Rickety Dan Benton'
> and he were one and the same person...
> Hundreds of people in three counties of Southern Illinois
> were humbugged by the imposter....
> And yet he was simply a wandering old vagabond and
> horse thief...."

As for the man charged with fraud for claiming the Civil War pension, he told this story:

> "I was taken from the battlefield by the Rebels and placed in one
> of their hospitals. [They] put a piece of silver in my skull to take
> the place of the section...torn away by the shell at Shiloh. I was
> then taken to Andersonville where I suffered untold torture
> from hunger and my wounds.... I only weighed 45 pounds
> [when released].... I am subject to fits when the moon
> fulls, for I will have fits and raise jack."

Okay, Gentle Reader, I know what you are asking, "Who was he, Newby or Benton?" Well, I still do not know. My bias is in favor of the fairness and accuracy of the jury's verdict against the defendant. On the other hand, my sympathies are with the destitute old derelict and Mrs. Newby who ended up together in a Montgomery City, Missouri, poor house after the man was released from the penitentiary.

WAR ON THE HOMEFRONT

(Week of September 12, 2005)

Not since the Civil War of 1861-65 have we had such devastation in Louisiana and Mississippi as that caused by Katrina.

150 billion federal tax dollars is the current estimate of the recovery cost. There have not, as yet, been any reliable figures given for state and local tax expenditures.

Of course, untold personal and private business funds have been and will be spent. The increase in insurance premiums alone will be staggering.

All of this pales in comparison with the loss of life and the destruction of art, history and irreplaceable family heirlooms.

And just as Posey County has always done more than its share in winning our other wars, many of our citizens are stepping forward to help. It well could have been my own family in need of that assistance.

In September of 2002 my son's family was living in New Orleans on a military base located on the west bank of the Mississippi River by Algiers Point. Because my son, Jim, was home on leave from Kuwait, he and his wife, Gina, and their 4 year old son, Nick, and 10 month old daughter, Elyse, stayed home through Hurricane Isadore. They rode out Isadore with few problems.

But one month later Jim was back in Kuwait when Hurricane Lili hit New Orleans in October of 2002. Gina, by herself, evacuated their two kids and herself to Baton Rouge for two days, but fortunately, once again, they were spared any significant damage.

And, although Jim and his family are now stationed at Ft. Leavenworth, Kansas, they and I realize that they could well have needed the help Posey County's churches, firefighters, law enforcement officers, civic and fraternal organizations, businesses and individuals are now so generously giving had Katrina hit in 2002.

Too many people in Posey County are volunteering time, money and effort for me to give everyone proper credit. Instead, I will name a representative few just as I have done with the articles on Posey County's contributions to America's other war efforts. Of course, you will know of many others, and I encourage you to give them the public recognition they deserve.

And since all local, state and federal taxpayers are being called on to help fund the relief effort, it is literally true that Posey County as a whole deserves substantial credit.

When the Federal Emergency Management Agency (FEMA) sent out a call for help, Mt. Vernon's Fire Department responded. A team of two firefighters was chosen by lot but all were willing to go.

Roger Waters and Shawn Duckworth had their names drawn from a hat. They left September 07, 2005 and may be away from their families for a month helping the displaced and injured. They are expected to help alleviate the burdens of others, not add two more to those who need aid. Therefore, they are carrying their survival gear on their backs and will likely face many hardships as they look for ways to give aid and comfort.

Indiana State Police fingerprint and forensic expert, Greg Oeth, may soon be leaving to help make identifications and gather other evidence and material which can be used to help people find their loved ones and put their lives back together. And, Greg told me that Indiana State Trooper Frank Smith from Poseyville may, also, be going if needed.

Funeral director, Eric Austin, may soon be serving as part of a team to locate, remove, and properly process bodies.

Paul Axton who is a local resident and a Conservation Officer left Friday, September 2, 2005 with a state-wide contingent of Department of Natural Resources officers to offer their particular expertise.

Barry Cox of Warehouse Services Incorporated has flown several families out of harm's way and helped re-settle them in safe areas.

And I would have to name every church in Posey County to acknowledge the tremendous outpouring of personal services, food, clothing, medical supplies and money that have been and are continuing to be sent.

Posey County's schools have cut through red tape to allow children to enroll.

Bristol-Myers Squibb Company has contributed baby food and supplies, some of which was arranged for and picked up by Posey County's own Energizer Bunnies of beneficence, our own Dynamic Duo of do-gooding, Beverly and John Emhuff.

General Electric personnel have coordinated numerous efforts and continue to do so.

I hope you will not mind if I mention the excellent coverage Posey County's newspapers are providing. Information and recognition are vitally important elements of this recovery effort.

See, I told you there was no fair place to stop. Therefore, if you do not mind, I will invite you to compile your own list while you, probably, are contributing to the effort yourself.

Just as our War Memorial Coliseum became southwestern Indiana's center for rescue and relief operations in the great flood of 1937, Posey County, once again, stands on the high ground.

Oh, and as a post script, Katrina Mann, for whom I have worked for 28 years, says it's not her fault; she's tired of the comments when people hear her name, and, in fact, you may now call her Sue!

IN MEMORIAM

(Week of July 28, 2008)

Posey County's citizens have a long and proud record of military service. On July 23, 2008 we once again publicly recognized all those who have served. In the celebration of the One Hundredth Anniversary of our Soldiers and Sailors Monument on the courthouse square, we rededicated ourselves to the memory of those who sacrificed for us. I was honored to be included in this celebration as well as the re-dedication of our World War Memorial (the Coliseum) on October 21, 1990.

My poems set forth below played a small part in both solemn services.

WAR MEMORIAL RE-DEDICATION
(Sunday, October 21, 1990)

SUNDAY MORNING CHIMES

How dear it is to be alive:
To hear the peal of morning chimes;
To feel the invigorating sting of this autumn day;
To taste the rich and biting air;
To smell the acrid smoke of burning leaves;

To see the glory of Nature's third act.

How satisfying to still be a player:
To know a child's trust;
A family's support;
A friend's companionship; or

A lover's caress.

How thrilling it is to learn,
To plan,
To strive,
To serve,

To live!

These wondrous things: These sensations;
These desires;
These dreams;
These visions. This life,
Is what these heroes have sacrificed for us.

To these honored warriors and to their loved ones who miss them most I am humbled to be able to say, thank you.

RE-DEDICATION OF THE SOLDIERS AND SAILORS MONUMENT
(Wednesday, July 23, 2008)

<u>**WELL DONE**</u>!

At Lexington and Concord, the young blood began to flow.
At the Battle of New Orleans, muskets killed our cousins and our foes.

At the Alamo and Buena Vista, we stood to the last man.
At Shiloh, Chickamauga and Gettysburg, brothers' blood soaked the sand.

At San Juan Hill and when the Maine went down, our soldiers never flinched.
At Verdun and by the Marne, a million men died in the trench.

At D-Day and the Battle of the Bulge, after Hiroshima's mushroom clouds,
At Incheon Landing the forgotten war brought many more funeral shrouds.

At Khe Sanh and during Tet, we held our own and more.
At the Battle of Medina Ridge, our Gulf War warriors upheld the Corps.

At Sinjar, Mosul, and places with strange names,
Our Iraqi War veterans now earn their fame.

In uniforms, our citizens have served well everyone.
Today, we here proclaim to them our solemn praise: Well done!

Thank you veterans and you Posey County citizens who honor their service.

Soldiers and Sailors Monument, Posey County, Indiana Courthouse Campus
Photograph by Becky Boggs, Nature Photographer, Mt. Vernon, Indiana
wvgardengirl@insightbb.com

JP RANCH

CHAPTER FOUR

SOONERS, HOOSIERS, AND OTHERS

ADVICE TO VICE PRESIDENT CHENEY

(Week of February 20, 2006)

When I was 10 years old my father gave me a single shot, breach-loading 20-gauge shotgun which was older than anyone in my family. Dad, also, provided ammunition to me from when he was a boy.

He had confidence that the rabbit and squirrel population of Oklahoma was not going to be in any real danger. He neglected to consider the possibility that the other boys I would be hunting with might be.

As was the custom of the day where and when I grew up, on Thanksgiving morning the men went hunting while the women cooked. I noted that the ladies never relied upon us returning with game. They bought the turkey at Safeway the day before.

Anyway, on this my first hunt with the men, my sister's seventeen-year-old boyfriend, Jack, went with us. Contrary to how it might appear from the result of my actions that day, I had nothing against Jack. Now my bossy big sister, Jane, on the other hand....

There were eight of us boys including my two brothers, Sonny, who was 18, and Phil, who was 11. My father and the other heads of the family put Sonny and Jack in charge of us younger boys. That wasn't too smart either.

It was a beautiful sunshiny day and I just loved the smell of cordite in the morning. Sonny and Jack had us in a proper line slowly advancing towards a large brush pile. We were alert. We were careful. We were boys! When we saw that ferocious bunny stick its head up to laugh at the Light Brigade advancing towards it, we broke ranks and surrounded the brush pile.

To prove my bravery and marksmanship I hurried off the first and only round of the day.

Jack yelled, "Help, I'm shot."

I dropped my antique weapon and ran to him. Jack was standing there with his left hand on his neck and fire in his eyes. I am glad Janie married Bruce.

When he moved his hand we couldn't see any wound and made the mistake of saying so. Phil said, "Aw, you didn't even hit him. He's just mad you got off the first shot."

Jack grabbed me by my neck and said, "Jimmy, are you crazy? Couldn't you see me on the other side of the brush?" I asked him if he had seen where the rabbit wandered off to.

Sonny inspected Jack's neck and found one small pellet stuck near his skinny collarbone area. My guess is that shot has grown over the years to be the relic of the saving of the Western World from the evils of Communism and Devil Worship or at least from 10 year old boys with shotguns.

You are probably wondering what any of this has to do with advice to the Vice President. Well, I'll tell you.

Have you ever seen CNN or Fox News or ABC complaining about the way I handled my hunting accident? I thought not.

I immediately evinced no concern for Jack and, also, put the blame squarely where it belonged, on the victim and the rabbit.

Mr. Cheney on the other hand saw first to Mr. Whittington then accepted full responsibility. How dumb was that?

I humbly suggest that our Vice President committed several egregious errors in judgment. I shall set them out below so he may profit from my example:

Mistake number one was looking first to Harry Whittington's medical condition before calling a news conference.

Next, he had the audacity to want to advise Mr. Whittington's family before they heard about "the shooting" on T.V. Didn't Dick Cheney realize that this was the largest Vice Presidential story since Vice President Aaron Burr shot Alexander Hamilton in 1804? This had to be immediately given to the T.V. networks!

Finally and most unforgivably, the Vice President released this story of international significance possibly affecting the outcome of the war in Iraq and the trade deficit with China to a local newspaper in rural Texas! Of course, that's where it happened.

What was he thinking? Didn't he know that homage had to first be paid to the Talking Heads of television?

So there you have it Gentle Reader. The next time something like this happens to Mr. Cheney he should look to my example and handle it as a 10 year old would. That should make the nattering nabobs of negative T.V. anchor people happy.

OF PANTHERS AND POLECATS

(Week of October 8, 2007)

Posey County was first settled by people who needed firearms. In 1795 this area was so wild that our first white settler, Tom Jones, and the McFaddins who came right after him could only look to their own weapons for protection.

And even though in the 1830's our county government was located on the Mt. Vernon square, a young hunter lost his life to a panther who sprang from a tree within sight of the courthouse.

Of course, firearms were, also, necessary at times to guard against two-legged varmints.

I thought of Posey County's interesting early history when I returned to my hometown this past weekend for a class reunion. Although I have been an Indiana resident since 1963, as with most people, it is where I graduated from high school that calls me back for reunions.

I was born on the Osage Nation whose capital is Pawhuska, Osage County, Oklahoma. Early Osage County, just as early Posey County, was wild and wooly. Indians, cowboys, rattlesnakes and rustlers were the interesting history out there.

And although I was aware of several of my hometown's colorful characters while I was growing up, after more than forty years, I thought that the need for Mr. Colt's equalizer had gone the way of panthers in Posey County. Wrong!

My wife, Peg, attended the reunion with me. Now, Peg grew up in Ft. Wayne where disputes are settled through the courts. I know, the legal system is often slow and unsatisfying, but, in general, it is peaceful. Peg's family did not have, as mine did have, guns lying casually around the house. She assumed that guns were the sole province of soldiers and police officers.

So imagine her reaction when a loaded pistol showed up during conversation we were having with one of my old classmates, a rancher named Dick. As we reminisced, one of Dick's fellow cowmen sidled in to our small confined space. Andy was well dressed in a long sleeved burnished red western shirt, ironed Levis and expensive boots. He had that laconic style of southwestern drawl that is pleasing to the ear. Andy tipped his hat as Dick introduced Peg to him. Then he pleasantly said he was glad to meet us.

After a few moments of Dick and me regaling Peg and Andy with our high school glories, Dick asked Andy about a running fence line argument Andy was having with another rancher. "How's your deal with_____going?"

Andy responded, "A lot better since I introduced him to Mr. Colt this morning." Then he pulled his pistol out of his left front pocket as casually as if it were a container of Skoal.

Well, that loaded gun was so close to Peg she could have pulled the trigger herself. That is, she could have if she had been able to get her heart to return to her chest and her pupils reduced to normal.

Andy, Dick and I did not, at first, catch on to the effect "The gun that won the West" had on Peg. But when I saw her jump back, I got the message.

As Peg was dragging me outside, she read me my entire pedigree. I tried to assuage her concerns, but she was having none of it. And when I paraphrased Baron Karl Von Clausewitz: "Six guns are just judges' gavels that carry more of a bang," she stormed off to the car. I wasn't sure what I'd said wrong, but I figured the reunion was over.

MY BROTHER WAS AN ONLY GRANDCHILD

(Week of August 14, 2006)

Some of you have met my two brothers and my sister. It is less likely that you have met any of my thirteen first cousins on my mother's side. Mom was the oldest of seven. My oldest brother was the firstborn grandchild.

His Christian name is Carroll Earl Redwine, but Grandmother always called him Son and the rest of the family called him Sonny.

When my sister and other brother and I were privileged to visit Grandmother, we knew our role: stay outside while Grandmother taught Sonny to cook as she told him stories about our family's history. This is how we first heard of our great-great grandfather's heroism in the Civil War. And, because Grandmother loved to divulge Grandpa's family skeletons, Sonny learned firsthand of Grandpa's sister's involvement with the members of the infamous Dalton Gang.

The examples of C.E.'s (what his friends call him) and Grandmother's special relationship are legion. Such things as a graduation watch for Sonny and a card for the rest of us (okay, it did have money in it) or divulging secret family recipes to him that even Mom and her sisters could not get are only small examples.

Now, you might think that after sixty-three years I would have come to terms with this golden grandchild situation. And, you would have been right until my brother saw fit to publish his autobiography this month. Did you ever know anybody who published their autobiography? Me either, till now. And my own brother, who'd a thunk it?

It is filled with touching memories of Sonny's childhood and his treasured hours with Grandmother. It oozes with charm and wit and good times with Grandma. It reminded me why I still do not know how to make Grandmother's marvelous dill pickles or her famous sour cream Christmas candy, but Sonny does. However, thanks to those sessions between Grandma and Sonny, we know some really neat stories about our family.

In short, it puts down in eternal print what I and my other siblings have always known but chose to deny: We were simply the spear carriers to Sonny's Wagnerian aria, at least in Grandmother's eyes. On the other hand, our big brother obviously cared enough about our family to remember a lifetime of anecdotes the rest of us had forgotten or never knew.

Sonny's book, *A Small Taste of Redwine*, is actually a whole lot of fun for me and the rest of my family to read. If you have ever been blessed by some family member who took the time and trouble to put down a record of your family's personal history, you will understand how grateful I am to my brother. He has passed on our family's lore.

Of course, as my sister and other brother and I have already noted, there is much in our brother's book that appears to us to have happened in someone else's home. Once again, you may have had that same feeling when listening to some relative relate a happening from your childhood. You might wonder: Where the devil did he/she grow up?

Regardless, whether factually correct or a product of shimmering memory and wishes, Sonny's book makes my sister cry tears of happiness, makes our other brother feel more closely connected to our family history, and makes me laugh until my sides hurt as I read about the times Sonny spent trying to teach us to play baseball, or fish, or box or fly a kite.

Sonny's good heart and generous spirit shine through. Maybe those are the real but subconscious reasons we played outside; we wanted him to mentally chronicle what we would all someday treasure in print and what Grandmother would divulge to no one else.

Jane Bartlett Redwine, the author, Phil Redwine and C.E. (Sonny) Redwine
Trying to sing in harmony August, 2001

THE WIZARD OF OZ

(Week of August 7, 2006)

When the mighty Wizard of Oz is finally seen for what he really was by Dorothy, the Tin Man, the Cowardly Lion and the Scarecrow, his façade of omnipotence was shattered.

It is probably a good thing that we sometimes have false images of our leaders. I remember my feelings of dismay when I was told by one of my grade school teachers that the painting of George Washington that hung in our classroom and in which The Father of Our Country looked so stern and powerful portrayed General Washington with his lips tightly pursed because he had ill-fitting false teeth.

And I will not disclose at what advanced age I still clung to Santa Claus and the Easter Bunny. I might have been slow to catch on but I was happier than my peers.

We may be wrong, but most humans believe in pomp and circumstance and the regalia of office. Police officers have badges, soldiers have uniforms and presidents have Air Force One. We do not need to know about what happens behind the scenes.

Then there are judges. Judges have courthouses, high benches, gavels and those flowing black robes. Hey, it's kind'a cool.

And, of course, some judges have wives who are not so easily impressed by all the accoutrements since they see their judges asleep on the couch in dingy tee shirts and torn Levis.

But what brings the old "feet of clay" sharply into focus are those unexpected events that occur in court where some citizen decides to act like this is a democracy and he or she is an American.

While there are many instances where I have been made to realize that the trappings are for the office and not for me personally, my wife's favorite involved a case from about ten years ago where I was imparting great judicial wisdom and admonitions to a young woman who had been found guilty of stealing.

As I was regaling the full courtroom with the majesty of the law and how it fell so heavily on this poor young miscreant, all of a sudden the huge double doors in the back of the courtroom burst open and a large woman wearing a housecoat and bunny slippers charged up towards my bench.

She was the young woman's mother and she was not amused and certainly not impressed by my lecture to her daughter.

The lady stopped just behind the bar that separates the hoi polloi from those who are paid to serve them.

She stood to her full height and said very loudly:

> "If you weren't wearing that black dress
> I'd come up there and slap your face!"

Then she turned and marched slowly and grandly out the back of the courtroom giving me what for the whole time. The packed courtroom was split between amazement and amusement.

As for me, I knew how the old Wizard of Oz felt.

Posey County Circuit Courtroom View from the Judge's Bench
Photograph by Becky Boggs, Nature Photographer, Mt. Vernon, Indiana
wvgardengirl@insightbb.com

SYSTEM OVERLOAD

(Week of January 1, 2007)

The stock market should be dropping. We have been at war almost continuously since August of 1990. The Euro buys $1.32 worth of dollars. China is flooding us with every kind of cheap merchandise except timeshares in the Great Wall. And FEMA still hasn't figured out why tourists are avoiding New Orleans.

But wonder of wonders, one has to almost try to pick a losing share of stock. I realize that due to the way the rich guys manipulate the world economy by the time this article is published the rest of us may be singing Woody Guthrie Great Depression songs.

However, as I am writing this column, things seem pretty good. And after following my wife around returning Christmas gifts this past week I think I know why.

The computers are so overloaded by the exchange of items and requests for refunds that they do not have time to help the rich guys make the rest of us poorer.

I used to think only women returned items that they didn't want, or couldn't use, or that didn't fit, or were defective. I figured that most men were like me. Hey, if it wasn't too ugly, or if it could be modified with a small amount of duct tape, why bother taking it back?

But after Peg dragged me to WalMart, Lowes and Home Depot this week, I am convinced that men are as willing to help overload the computer systems as women are.

I saw the same guy in front of me in all three refund lines. He was easy to spot. He was wearing broken glasses held together by a twist tie that accented the stains on his tee shirt. Since he and I had spent more time together over Christmas than I did with most of my family, we had plenty of opportunity to talk.

He told me he purposely dressed like a derelict because he had found that the worse he looked the faster the stores wanted him gone. They never argued with him over anything.

He, also, said that unlike what the so-called experts advise, he always makes his exchanges at the times when the maximum number of people are there. Once again, his appearance and, shall we say, aura of non-freshness, encouraged speedy, unquestioned service for him.

It turned out he was a financial analyst who had spent a great deal of time figuring out why the American economy is surging like a locomotive when most signs would indicate a bust.

He said the largest factor was the modern American's loss of the "return inhibition". He explained that up until recently Americans were too embarrassed to return, or, heaven forbid, exchange gifts and pretend that the ones they had been given by their distant relatives or co-workers were the ones they actually picked out themselves by exchange. We used to be too polite for such boorish behavior. But we no longer are that concerned about the feelings of others when it comes to exchanging items.

So now almost every item sold in our fair country is, in effect, sold twice. Ergo, our economy is doubling every Christmas. And an entire shadow workforce is earning wages shifting merchandise.

After countless hours of standing in lines myself to do twice what most of us used to be too embarrassed to do once, I can see his point.

GETTING AND SPENDING

(Week of December 29, 2008)

William Wordsworth (1770-1850) wrote his English sonnet, *The World is Too Much with Us*, in 1807. The opening lines are:

> "The world is too much with us; late and soon,
> Getting and spending, we lay waste our powers;
> Little we see in Nature that is ours;
> We have given our hearts away, a sordid boon!"

Old Bill was concerned that people in the 19th Century were so involved with accumulating material things they had lost sight of the beauty of nature. He longed for the "good ole days". Willy would have an even tougher time today, especially around Christmas.

I was reminded of this poem that I had first read in high school when Peg said, "Oh, I don't want anything for Christmas." I flinched; no phrase strikes more terror in a husband's heart. Of course, she wanted something for Christmas and, if I did not wish to see the temperature drop even further than it already had this week, I knew I had to figure out what it was.

It usually takes most husbands only one Christmas, birthday or anniversary to learn that, "Oh, I don't want you to get me anything," means shop fast and shop well.

So, I listened for the subtle hints. Peg eventually gave up trying to lead me to her goal with such sayings as, "You know the football bowl games are coming up", and, "Our twenty year old television set isn't digital." She finally said, "I'd really like to have a T.V. where you don't have to get up to change channels. Oh, and color might be nice."

The light went on; she wanted a new T.V. for Christmas. Then I made my biggest blunder. I mentioned Peg's wish to two people who were born about the time we landed on the moon.

My family got our first T.V. in 1954. It was black and white. It cost $200.00. You plugged it in, turned it on and it worked. No assembly was required.

Silly me, I thought that with the vast technological advancements since 1954, televisions would be even easier to operate. Reality raised its ugly head when my young friend, Jason Simmons, said, "If you order this *set up* over the internet today, you can **SAVE** big bucks."

Then my other young friend, Rodney Fetcher, said, "This *set up* is awesome. Jason and I can help you *install* it." *Set up*, I thought; *install* it, I thought. Don't you just go to Sears, pick it up and plug it in? Ah, the blessings of ignorance. Let me commiserate with you about what I learned concerning television as a modern concept in next week's column.

TELEVISION SURGERY

(Week of January 5, 2009)

Doctor Sanjay Gupta is a neurosurgeon who often comments on medical issues for CNN. He is an honest to goodness brain surgeon who sometimes uses 3-D television imagery when he operates. He would have been as lost as I was when my "Television Set-up and Installation Team" put Peg's Christmas present together last week.

Dr. Gupta is surrounded by a scrub nurse, an anesthesiologist, an assisting surgeon and a technician who monitors the equipment. You will note there are normally about five people involved directly in the brain surgery. It took four people who knew what they were doing, and me, to get Peg's Christmas television working.

There was Rodney Fetcher who provided his van and muscles to pick up the three huge cartons containing the T.V., the "Home Theatre Sound System", i.e. the speakers, and enough cabling and connections to wire the space shuttle. Rodney hooked them all together.

Jason Simmons synchronized the seven, that's not a misprint, speakers. Jason did his magic with the wired and wireless sound system.

Dan Funk moved the carpet and the satellite cables twice (Peg changed her mind).

Bryan Thompson's wife, Ashley, volunteered him for the "simple little electrical job" of hiding all the wires in the wall. After five hours of Bryan's tearing up decking in the attic and insulation in the walls, Bryan and Ashley may want to attend their church's seminar for couples with issues. Actually they have only one issue and it is Peg's Christmas present.

You might be wondering what, if anything, I contributed to this Tower of Babel experience. Well, I provided what we used to call out west, "Good help." That is, I fetched, I toted, I lifted, I goferred; I knew nothing but did as I was told. Being a husband was the perfect training.

Peg's Christmas present is on an upstairs wall and faces the lane that leads to our home. I knew the large bright picture reminded me of something from the past but could not place what it was until I came home from work last night and saw several cars parked in our yard. They were facing the upstairs window where a college bowl game was showing up as clearly as if it was on a Jumbotron at the Rose Bowl.

Yes, Gentle Reader, Peg's Christmas present has revived that long gone institution, the drive-in movie. Bring your own popcorn.

GREEN ACRES

(Week of February 2, 2009)

Fear not, if you were one of the vast multitude of *Gavel Gamut* readers who were thirsting for more scintillating columns about legal education and "thinking as a lawyer", we will return to those thrilling topics next week. For now, let's you and I delve into drugstore cowboys and gentlemen farmers.

Where I grew up the prairie grew sandstone, bluestem grass and cattle. It, also, produced a few drugstore type cowboys who were mostly hat, fancy boots and tall tales. There is actually a psychology term for this called "The Munchausen Syndrome".

Baron Von Munchausen was a German aristocrat who fancied himself quite a war hero. He would regale group after group with his stories of battles and his bravery. Unfortunately, he had never seen a shot fired in anger. In the west this syndrome, when applied to wannabe cowboys, is called being a drugstore cowboy. In farming country, such as Posey County, Indiana, this might be called the "Green Acres Syndrome".

You will recall the television show "Green Acres" where the New York lawyer, Oliver Wendell Douglas, as played by Eddie Albert, and his socialite wife, Lisa, as played by Eva Gabor, moved to a farm. Oliver knew as much about farming as our drugstore cowboys know about ranching. This ignorance led to many situations where their neighbors, the real farmers, had to bail them out.

Our recent ice storm and officially declared State of Emergency brought the hapless Douglas family to mind. Why don't you and I assume we know of some city lawyer who recently moved to rural Posey County with his wife? Let's call his wife, Peg, and name the would-be country lad, Jim. In this episode of "Posey County Acres" we will eavesdrop on a conversation between Jim and a real Posey County farmer, Mark Duckworth.

"Hey Mark, what you doing with that tractor and snow blade? It looks like the county highway crew has already cleared Durlin Road and even my driveway."

"Uh, Jim, there are 700 miles of roads in Posey County. It would take the entire National Guard to clear all these roads."

"Well, Mark, in town we would just wait a little bit and the roads would be cleared by the city crews and all the traffic. It is really great to have my drive and road open. Peg said we should get a tractor or at least a pickup truck, but I told her not to worry. I figured the snow, ice, and tree limbs would disappear naturally."

"Jim, you weren't figuring on leaving your house before spring, were you? Your car wouldn't clear the pile of snow trapping you in your garage. You might want to consider either getting a 4 wheel drive or, better yet, moving back to town."

"Wait a minute, Mark. You mean you cleared this entire road and my driveway yourself? What do I owe you?"

"You don't know much about Posey County's farmers do you, Jim? They often volunteer their time, equipment, fuel and expertise in numerous emergencies. They don't do it for pay."

"Mark, thank you and the other farmers for doing this important work. But can I ask you one more question?"

"Sure, Jim, what is it?"

"Now that Peg and I have been through our first rural emergency, does this mean I can go to breakfast with the real farmers?"

ELMER FUDD STRIKES AGAIN

(Week of January 29, 2007)

The last time I went duck hunting I was fourteen (14) years old. At O'Dark Thirty my father rousted me from a warm bed and told me to keep quiet so the rest of the family could keep enjoying their warm beds.

I stumbled around in the dark until I had my Levi's and tennis shoes on, then grabbed my loaded and properly plugged 12-gauge out of the hall closet.

When I mumbled something to Dad about breakfast, he grabbed a biscuit out of the refrigerator and thrust it towards me.

We got to the duck blind long before the sun had made it back from wherever it goes with all the warmth and light. Dad had me jump down into it first to check for varmints. It wasn't that he didn't love me, I think, it was just that he was not too limber and the makeshift steps were lying on the dirt floor that had about a foot of water over it. Some forty (40) years later I fully understand Dad's inelasticity.

Once we were both in the blind, we sat there in silence soaking up the cold water while we waited on the armada of evil ducks to attack. We couldn't talk. We couldn't build a fire. We couldn't sleep. We had nothing to eat or drink. And Dad's hand signals and glares kept me from moving around.

As I had plenty of time to reflect on my situation, I conversed silently with myself about duck hunting: Was there a duck out there that I was really this angry at?

These forty-some-year-old memories arose with their red-ringed downy necks this past weekend when I read about the lady in Tallahassee, Florida whose lazy, duck-hunting husband brought home a duck he had shot and thrown into their refrigerator without cleaning it first.

After this vicious bird of prey had been cooling its wings for two days, the hunter's wife opened the door and was met by the baleful stare of a bewildered fowl.

Upon recovering from the shock, "Mrs. Elmer Fudd" had her daughter take the poor gunshot victim to the vet. That served the lazy duck hunter right and probably cost him more than a new Benelli shotgun.

Now, far be it from me to denigrate how another person spends their recreational time and money, but when it comes to duck hunting, I humbly refer my duck hunting friends, past tense perhaps, to the Biblical admonition found in *First Corinthians*, Chapter 13, verse 11.

On the other hand, I suppose the lazy duck hunter's wife can be glad he wasn't addicted to deer hunting.

Next week, for the few duck hunters who may happen across this column and, perhaps, take some small degree of umbrage with my views on their favorite excuse for avoiding household chores, I plan to write about another "Lazarus" from my home town who was not quite as dead as people thought.

But before I end this week, I must sue for peace with my beloved mother-in-law, Mary Dunn, who upon reading last week's column about her beloved husband, Bernie, and his long career with General Electric's small engine division in New York, Massachusetts and Ft. Wayne, Indiana, set me straight right quick!

Mother Mary sweetly informed me that Bernie worked for G.E. for forty-nine (49) years, not forty-one (41) as I wrote. *Mea culpa.* Let the Record stand as corrected; Bernie well deserves the proper credit. And I want to protect my interest in Mary's melt-in-your mouth Christmas cookies.

IS IT SPRING YET?

(Week of February 12, 2007)

"Day had broken cold and grey, exceedingly cold and grey....
There was no sun nor hint of sun. .... The Yukon lay...
hidden under three feet of ice. On top of this ice were
three more feet of snow."

These facts simply impressed the lonely Alaskan traveler as being cold and uncomfortable.

Such conditions, "did not lead him to meditate upon his frailty as a creature of temperature and upon man's frailty in general, able only to live within narrow limits of heat and cold."

These quotes come from Jack London's classic short story, *To Build a Fire*. This man's hubris and ignorance of his limitations led to his death by freezing.

These past two weeks of Alaskan-type weather have caused me to appreciate such comforts as indoor plumbing and car seat warmers. Unlike London's frozen traveler, I am well aware of my limitations.

Time was, when I had a real job working construction, the vagaries of such cold weather as we are now experiencing made me long for the stifling heat of summer.

Should you have read this column two weeks ago, you may recall we were discussing the duck named Perky who survived two days in a refrigerator. I promised, or warned, then to write about another Lazarus from my hometown, Pawhuska, Oklahoma, the capital of the Osage Nation.

As you know, Lazarus was dead for four days before being called forth from the tomb by Jesus. Well, Ho-Tah-Moie (Roaring Thunder in English) was an Osage Indian who froze and unfroze repeatedly. He died and was actually buried several times.

For reasons that may occur to you Gentle Reader, after a time or two of Roaring Thunder dying and resurrecting, he became known as John Stink. When I was a boy, we boys would sneak up to his old camp outside of town in hopes of seeing his ghost.

And even though he really did finally die in 1938, before I was born, we boys then and many otherwise rational people yet today would swear old John still haunts the earth.

John Stink had a condition that some pseudo scientist of the time attributed to childhood smallpox that caused John to go into a coma sometimes when it got bitterly cold.

The Osages would bury him in their traditional way as John had instructed before his first death. He would be placed in a sitting position on a hill on his campground then sandstones would be piled around him.

This was okay until he came out of his stupor and walked into town surrounded by his pack of twenty or so dogs.

Now the Osages and the rest of us on the Osage Nation are no more superstitious than the Hebrews of Jesus' time, but when Old John Stink kept coming back to life after each break in a cold spell, it did cause consternation. After a few public panics caused by John's repeated resurrections, he was embalmed and buried white man's fashion six-feet underground. This seems to have cured him.

As for me today, I plan to come back to life about March 21st, the first day of spring.

PEG'S TILLER

(Week of May 25, 2009)

Perhaps one or two of the one or two of you who read this column may recall that we were going to engage in an exciting discussion of the Separation of Powers Doctrine this week. If you do not mind awfully, I would like to take a short digression from legal theory to the relative merits of home improvements.

Just this past weekend Peg was spading up our vegetable garden using the short handled sharpshooter I thoughtfully procured for her. It appeared she was thoroughly enjoying going spade full by spade full down one row and up the next. I cannot tell you how relaxing it was to sit on our deck and watch her prepare the ground for planting.

I hated to interrupt her pleasant diversion, but every now and then I ran out of iced tea and did need a sandwich around noon. All seemed right with the world when I suggested she might want to quit engaging in her rather selfish agrarian avocation and get my lunch ready.

Well, she did unceremoniously drop the spade and come to the deck in what I considered a rather aggressive attitude. She said, "You know I have been wanting a power tiller for almost two years. Don't you think we can afford one since we have now finished paying off your set of new golf clubs?"

My response was measured and reasonable and was intended to make clear my position that power tillers were an unnecessary expenditure of family funds that might better be invested in season tickets to I.U. football games.

Peg just mumbled something about how our home, which is a converted barn, would not need to buy a jackass. It was a mystery to me what she meant. She did sweetly suggest that while she was preparing my lunch, I might want to finish tilling the garden by hand.

Not one to shirk my duty I picked up the shovel and began to dig down into the dirt one spade full at a time. After about five minutes I began to look around for Peg who seemed to be taking an inordinate amount of time to fix my ham sandwich. This was so even considering that I had given precise instructions on the need for a slice of onion, a tomato and Dijon mustard.

Well, Gentle Reader, after another five minutes of spading and sweating, it occurred to me that it would be the height of Ludditism to refuse to acknowledge the advancements in science and technology that have made America the great country it is.

Ergo, Peg now has her tiller. I am nothing if not thoughtful.

SEE PEG, I TOLD YOU SO

(Week of February 27, 2006)

My wife, Peg, says she is the only one who reads this column and with her it's duty not desire.

But now I have evidence of a much larger audience. A friend of mine asked me where I came up with the citations to English literature in the column of two week's ago since he doubted I had actually read the pieces.

So there, Peg! Someone read my column. I won't tell her he was just surfing the paper for gossip about his neighbors. He ran into me as we were both serving as sidewalk superintendents on the large pit that was dug on the southwest side of the courthouse campus last week. He thought he was so witty when he sidled up to me like a puffed up crab and asked if that was where I was planning on being buried when my time was up? When I told him it was being dug for sewage purposes, he responded, "So, what's your point?"

If you were among the rest of the multitude who read *Gavel Gamut* two weeks ago, you may recall it was about advice from parents to children as they go off to war. I referred to, but did not quote, works by Richard Lovelace, William Wordsworth, and Rudyard Kipling.

My "friend" wondered if I simply made up these citations or, if they were real pieces, if they had any connection to parental advice or combat.

To my friend I say, "Let the games begin." We will let the vast readership decide.

In 1648 A.D., Richard Lovelace wrote, *To Lucasta, Going to the Wars*:

Tell me not, Sweet, I am unkind,
That from the nunnery
Of thy chaste breast, and quiet mind,
To war and arms I fly.

True, a new mistress now I chase,
The first foe in the field;
And with a stronger faith embrace
A sword, a horse, a shield.

Yet this inconstancy is such,
As you too shall adore;
I could not love thee, Dear, so much,
Loved I not honour more.

And in 1802, William Wordsworth wrote, *My Heart Leaps Up When I Behold*:

My heart leaps up when I behold
A rainbow in the sky.
So was it when my life began;
So is it now I am a man.
So be it when I shall grow old,
Or let me die!
The child is father of the Man;
And I would wish my days to be
Bound together each to each by natural piety.

Rudyard Kipling lived from 1865-1936 and was a prolific writer from his early teenage years. His poem, *If* was advice to his young son whose later death caused Kipling immense grief:

If you can keep your head when all about you
Are losing theirs and blaming it on you;
If you can trust yourself when all men doubt you,
But make allowance for their doubting too;
If you can wait and not be tired by waiting,
Or being lied about, don't deal in lies,
Or being hated, don't give way to hating,
And yet don't look too good, nor talk too wise:

If you can dream – and not make dreams your master;
If you can think – and not make thoughts your aim;
If you can meet with Triumph and Disaster
And treat those two imposters just the same;
If you can bear to hear the truth you've spoken
Twisted by knaves to make a trap for fools,
Or watch the things you gave your life to, broken,
And stoop and build 'em up with worn-out tools;

If you can make one heap of all your winnings
And risk it on one turn of pitch-and-toss,
And lose, and start again at your beginnings
And never breath a word about your loss;
If you can force your heart and nerve and sinew
To serve your turn long after they are gone,
And so hold on when there is nothing in you
Except the Will which says to them: "Hold on!"

If you can talk with crowds and keep your virtue,
Or walk with kings – nor lose the common touch,
If neither foes nor loving friends can hurt you,
If all men count with you, but none too much;
If you can fill the unforgiving minute
With sixty seconds' worth of distance run –
Yours is the Earth and everything that's in it,
And – which is more – you'll be a Man, my son!

Boy, am I glad I found these things. I guess I should have read them when they were assigned in high school English class. But my friend will never know, as the only time he ever read this column was two weeks ago and that by accident. Of course, Peg need never know.

TO BUILD A POOL

(Week of July 6, 2009)

You may recall a couple of *Gavel Gamuts* that I wrote about Jack London's classic short story, *To Build a Fire*. And some of you probably read London's tale in high school. It involved a man's disastrous attempt to cross the Klondike on foot in the winter. His dog sensed the danger, but the man's pride blinded him to it.

I was once again reminded of this harsh lesson when Peg said, "Jim, aren't you awfully hot? You look like you might expire from this southern Indiana heat and humidity." I said nothing and kept my eyes zeroed in on Peg's dog, Haley, who was trying to sneak up on Peg's cats, Oliver and Claudette.

"Don't you think we should have a pool? They sell 'em at WalMart for $800.00, and it says right on the box, 'You'll be swimming within one hour or so.'" Well, Gentle Reader, I have spent a lifetime struggling with that "or so" thing. My experience is that the sadists who write those convoluted instructions for Christmas toys and home gym equipment have never even seen one of the items they blithely say will be inexpensive, gratifying and easy to set up.

But, of course, husbands only have two acceptable responses to their wives' cheerful call for such things as room additions and swimming pools: (1) I wish I'd thought of that; and (2) Is there any way I can get a new set of golf clubs if I take on this stupid, strike that, endeavor? The response husbands must never make is, "Well, I guess no job is too hard if you don't have to do it!" So, I chose discretion over sure suicide and said, "What a great idea. Let's do it ourselves. If the pool costs $800.00 it will probably only take a little more money and not much work for site preparation."

Peg was excited. She went to WalMart and had everything ready for my friend, Rodney Fetcher, and me to pick up using his dad's truck. When we got it home we dumped everything in the yard. As the instructions said to make sure the pool is set up on level ground, I began to check the grade in our yard. It was about 9 inches high on the west side, 5 inches low on the east, 6 inches high on the south and 3 inches low on the north.

That seemed simple enough; I ordered sand from Ray Brown and Tony Price who brought 10 ton and dumped it on the pool site. I don't know if you have ever done anything as ill-advised as to try to level a site after the sand is already down, but I did just that, and let me tell you, it doesn't work.

So after I removed most of the sand and used it to fill eroded areas of JPeg Ranch, my friend, Dick Simmons, looked at the future pool site and told me, "You should have left the sand there and just moved it around as you dug down with your pickaxe and shovel. That way you wouldn't need to buy even more sand later." Dick is one of those great friends who is always ready to help and even more rare, he actually knows what he is talking about. But as he is still recovering from knee surgery, he could only try to get me to understand the complex problem of taking rock and dirt from one side to level up the other. Unfortunately, twenty years of formal education could not make up for a total lack of talent.

After suffering through several hours of trying to teach me the difference between "down pickaxe" and "up shovel", Dick diplomatically said, "Jim, do you really want a pool?" When I mumbled, "Peg is the one who wants it and she wants it by the Fourth of July", Dick said, "Well, she may get it, but just not by this Fourth of July".

If I survive and you have nothing better to do, we may continue our "To Build a Pool" saga next week. Of course, should you be really bored, do not hesitate to stop by JPeg Ranch with your own pick and shovel.

PICTURE PERFECT

(Week of July 13, 2009)

My friend and neighbor, Steve Burris, observed that instead of having a swimming pool people should consider simply having a large picture of a pool. His reasoning was that hardly anyone actually gets into a pool. People slather themselves with sun block then set out in the sun on deck chairs around pools. They glint at the sunlight and sip iced drinks to cool themselves as they stare at the unused pool.

Steve's prescient approach would save all the money it costs to build a new pool, and endless hours of labor maintaining the pool. I wish I had heeded his sage advice instead of succumbing to Peg's honey-coated plea for a "simple, inexpensive WalMart special". Alas, as with many of life's hard lessons, I had to learn from my own experience, not profit from someone else's wisdom.

You may recall, if you even read last week's *Gavel Gamut*, that Peg conned me into setting up an $800.00, above ground pool. She had read all the advertising about how quick and easy the whole process would be. Just find a level place, follow the few simple instructions, fill with water and be swimming in an hour, "or so".

The first prerequisite should have brought a halt to the whole endeavor. We live in a 107 year old barn that my friend, Dan Funk, fashioned into a really cool home. But Dan would be the first to tell you, "There ain't no level place at JPeg Ranch".

Then there was the little matter of Peg and me trying to hold up the sides of the pool while we fumbled with the super structure. Poles, cross-pieces, pins and vinyl were an amazing amalgam of incomprehensibility until our neighbors across the road tired of the entertainment we were providing and came to our rescue.

Chuck, Bonnie and Alex Minnette were the most organized work crew one could wish for. Chuck helped with the frame, Alex laid out the parts and Bonnie assisted with the assembled pins. Most importantly, when I discovered that the crawlspace under the deck was not adaptable to my body type, Alex slinked his lithe frame into an area that only our cats and numerous critters could navigate and plugged in the filter motor.

Yes, my friends, Peg now has her long sought pool. Not in time for July 4, 2009 as hoped, but at least before Labor Day when we will have to close the whole thing down for the winter.

On the other hand, the pool has already accumulated enough flies, horse flies, mosquitoes, Japanese Beetles, water spiders, gnats and other assorted creatures to make an entomologist absolutely giddy.

As for me, I am going to download a digital photo of Peg's pool onto Peg's television and gaze at it in high definition as I sit in our air conditioned barn and sip a cool drink.

POOL IS A FOUR LETTER WORD

(Week of July 20, 2009)

The *Music Man* by Meredith Wilson opened on Broadway in 1957. Robert Preston plays a conman who tries to warn the people of River City about the perils of pool. As he almost said:

> Well, either you're closing your eyes to a situation you do not wish
> to acknowledge or you are not aware of the caliber of disaster
> indicated by the presence of a pool in your yard.

I cited this authority to Peg about two weeks into our pool project that was projected by WalMart to take about an hour. Well, Gentle Reader, she ignored my logic and my citation of precedent as readily as if she were a federal judge.

It became quite clear to me that there was to be neither reprieve nor respite from the completion of Neptune's temple. The pool gods must be appeased. I accepted my fate, but felt a moral obligation to warn others.

Therefore, I am chartering an organization patterned after another highly respected method of helping those who may be in danger of succumbing to bad decisions. I call it PA, Pools Anonymous.

Should your wife just mention in passing that a swimming pool might be a delightful diversion for the kids, grandkids, the neighbors or a Little League baseball team, call me immediately. I will cite chapter and verse of why Pool is a four letter word.

It starts with "P" for pricey and ends with "L" for labor intensive. In between you have double "OO" for numerous moments of "Oh, Oh". Of course, should you still be weakening and your backbone be closer to a jellyfish than a swordfish, I will point out that if you build it, people will come.

Since this is a new therapeutic model, all steps are not yet in place. For now, I urge you to fall back on that standard approach that husbands have taken for thousands of years; pretend you did not hear the word "Pool" and continue doing nothing. Hey, if Adam had taken this approach before biting that apple, he'd still be in the Garden of Eden.

In summary, I suggest trouble starts with "T" and that rhymes with "P" and that stands for Pool. Almost finally, I remind you that as with many four letter words, it is best to avoid pool(s) altogether.

The reason I said almost finally is because Peg could not abide my analysis and made me include her observation that an even more time-consuming, expensive, frustrating four letter word is GOLF and there is no Golf Anonymous.

And now, finally, we have exhausted me, and probably you, and the subject of pools. Next week, if you are not out leveling your yard, we will begin an exhilarating exposition of the art of judging. As preparation you may wish to review what you learned in Sunday School and Kindergarten; that and several years of living are really about all that are required for good judging whether one serves on a trial court or the United States Supreme Court.

PLASTICS

(Week of January 22, 2007)

In the 1967 movie, *The Graduate*, Benjamin Braddock who has just graduated from college and is at a loss as to his future is given the secret to success when a business man whispers one word to him: "Plastics".

Almost half-a-century ago, General Electric and Posey County began a relationship based on the manufacturing of this lodestone material. Plastics did turn oil into gold. And this gold helped bring "good things" to thousands of Posey County citizens. My wife, Peg, is one of those fortunate recipients.

Peg's father, Bernie, was an engineer who worked for General Electric for forty-one (41) years. He knew Jack Welch who took G.E. to the top of the international business world. Her dad liked and respected Mr. Welch.

G.E. was good to Peg's family and her family has always been loyal to G.E. Just look at the names on our appliances. Or, one could look to Bernie's faith and foresight in investing in his chosen company in those early years with G.E. when money was scarce and G.E.'s future less certain.

Those sacrifices by Bernie and Peg's mom, Mary, helped provide education and support for Peg and her two brothers, Jim and Gary, as well as security for Mary now that Bernie has been forced by an untimely death to leave her alone.

G.E.'s mission is, of course, to first make money for its stockholders. If a corporation fails in that mission, any good it could have done will not occur. Therefore, most of us recognize that corporate decisions to protect the bottom line are both necessary and proper.

But with all of our missions in life, business and personal, there is always a right way and a wrong way.

F. Scott Fitzgerald in his book, *The Great Gatsby*, said, "The very rich are different from you and me." He described the callousness of some of these very rich by saying: They go about breaking things then retreat into their money and leave it to the rest of us to clean up the mess.

When I read the news reports that General Electric's plastics division, "was in a difficult spot," due to the increase in the price of raw materials, mainly petroleum products, I was reminded of what people who suffered through the Great Depression used to say: A recession is when other people lose their jobs, but when you lose yours, it is a depression.

G.E. has been a positive part of our community for half-a-century. I trust that this fine company, if it does take its leave, will do so with the same attitude of grace and responsibility that has marked its deep integration into our county's economic and social fabric.

For, whereas in the United States of America there is no legal duty to rescue our fellow human beings, once we cause others to rely upon us, we have both a legal and moral duty to use reasonable care should we feel the need to change our relative positions.

Gary, Mary, Peg (Redwine) and Jim Dunn

WHOSE MONEY IS IT?

(Week of October 27, 2008)

Jonathon Swift (1667-1745) was an Englishman who was born in Dublin, Ireland. He was a clergyman and a strong supporter of the Protestant Anglican Church. He was, also, sympathetic to the wretched conditions the Irish had to endure under the English Crown. And, of course, he was one of the greatest satirists in history.

In his *A Modest Proposal*, Swift suggested that all one-year-old Irish infants of poor people be eligible for sale for food. As Swift explained, this would save the cost of their upbringing, provide ready cash for their poor parents and provide edible amusement for the powerful rich people.

I thought of Swift's biting indictment of his fellow elite when I heard of the seven hundred billion dollar bailout proposal. It seemed to me to be what ranchers out west say when asked to sell their land, "I will not sell off my children". Apparently our government does not ascribe to this aphorism as almost one trillion dollars of our money is to be taken from us and "invested" in private financial institutions.

Now I know the Judicial Branch is not qualified to make such political decisions. The Executive and Legislative Branches are the proper repositories of all such wisdom. Further, there is a reason I am a judge and not a scientist; I crashed and burned in college physics and math and I hated economics almost as much as it hated me.

That being said, do you not think you might be able to invest your tax money as wisely as the experts who have us teetering on a return to those thrilling days of yesteryear, *i.e.* the early 1930's.

I say give us a moratorium on taxes and penalties on, for one scenario, about half of our own IRA's, 401k's 457's, etc., and let us decide how we want to spend or invest it or just hold on to it. Or maybe the amount should be restricted to the average residential down payment ($20,000.00?). There is a proper and prudent maximum we could find.

Instead of our governments, federal and state, hanging around like hopeful distant relatives at a rich person's death bed, let them forego taxes on a certain percentage of our own pre-tax monies. Most of us would not be paying taxes on the money for years anyway. And we might well never have to pay if our accountants are alert and if we live long enough. If we could avoid taxes now, we would have the option of withdrawing the money and, perhaps, cure the worst slump in consumer spending and mortgage failures in over half-a-century.

If we were given six months to withdraw up to the amount of each person's yearly gross income (another approach) from our tax deferred savings plans, this economy might roar like Androcles's lion before the thorn was withdrawn. But even if the plan failed and we lost up to seven hundred billion dollars of our money, at least we could "Live free or die" as real Americans should. Currently our pensions and savings plans are disappearing like the spit in one's mouth when we ride a roller coaster.

As an aside, I note that the state with the highest number of mortgage foreclosures is that Mecca of gambling, Nevada, and that Arnold's Cal-i-Forn-i-a is in the top five. I say let the gamblers "read 'em and weep" and let Arnold's citizens pay for their own lifestyle.

HISTORY LESSONS

(Week of November 24, 2008)

The main advantage of writing a column nobody reads is just that. You can pretty much say anything that is not lascivious or libelous and nobody cares.

For example, my proposal to stop using our money to rescue profligate speculators from their sins of misfeasance and malfeasance has caused nary a ripple. Therefore, I will plunge fearlessly ahead.

If you did happen to read this column three weeks ago and last week, you may recall my partial solution to our economic downturn. Let individuals have the option to use a particular percentage or maximum amount of their own IRA's, 401(k)'s and 457 deferred income accounts without penalty and tax free. There should be a time limit, say within 6 months, and there should be an accounting on our federal and state tax returns.

Of course, this plan is of no direct help to the 4,000,000 unemployed Americans or the thousands more who have run out of unemployment benefits. What can our federal and state governments do for them? How about direct help for them with corollary benefits for us?

If those who do not learn from history's bad times are doomed to repeat them, the Great Depression comes to mind, then let's try to benefit from our ancestors' wisdom. Where are the 21st Century Civilian Conservation Corps and Works Project Administration type of direct relief programs?

When Peg and I return to Osage County, Oklahoma we always stay in the state park my Uncle Claude helped build in the 1930's. The sandstone trails, recreation areas and cabins are still giving pleasure almost 75 years after the CCC built them. Uncle Claude made $30.00 per month plus room, board and clothing; $25.00 of this was sent home each month to his young wife and new baby.

In Posey County we had a CCC camp on Black River between New Harmony and Griffin. Every state had at least one CCC camp where reserve army officers ran a quasi-military operation and bought goods and services on the local economy. Road repair, ditch drainage, tree planting and pond construction were just a few of the benefits Posey County received from this wise expenditure of tax monies. Art Bayer remembers the military type structure of the CCC camp although he was not a worker there. Art did win a talent contest held at the Coliseum and put on by one of the federal relief agencies. Art played the guitar and sang "Blue Eyes". He says that experience helped make a barge owner out of him.

William F. (Butch) Dieterle and his wife, Dorothy nee McGhee Dieterle, both worked for about $12.00 every other month or so in the National Youth Organization. Dorothy did office work at Hedges Junior High and Butch mopped floors and did other janitorial work at Mt. Vernon High School.

Glenn Curtis remembers the WPA bus picking up and returning workers such as Jack Webster, Bob Webster's dad, down in Point Township. Glenn, also, remembers that the CCC planted a lot of trees, especially catalpa trees, and filled in Mill Creek near 8th Street in Mt. Vernon. Glenn, in his role as Posey County's officially designated historian, has often referred to the compilation of Posey County's birth, marriage and death records put in usable, alphabetized form by WPA workers.

Bob Webster still has several WPA work notices his father received in October, 1940 and April, May and June of 1941.

Butch Dieterle told me of his extremely positive experience in the summers of 1938 and 1939 when he received 5¢ per mile to and from Ft. Benjamin Harrison in Indianapolis to receive military type training from the Citizens Military Training Camp. He said he was glad he had the training when he later served in the Pacific in WWII.

Butch, also, related to me that when Posey County's only Negro school burned down in 1932, the WPA rebuilt Booker T. Washington. St. Matthews Parish allowed the African American students to use its building at 4th and Mulberry Streets as a temporary school.

The direct help to Americans by using taxpayer funds for the WPA, CCC, NYO and CMTC and numerous other wise investments in our citizens, our infrastructure and our environment makes a lot more sense to me than a $700,000,000,000.00 bailout of fat cats, pole cats and cats up a tree.

If it is all the same to our government, Peg and I will take our $4,600.00 (seven hundred billion dollars divided by each of the three hundred million Americans) directly or have it spent on individuals, not financial institutions.

EUREKA!

(Week of November 17, 2008)

Archimedes (287-212 B.C.) was a Sicilian Greek and a friend of Sicily's king, Hiero. Hiero asked Archimedes to prove whether the solid gold crown he had commissioned was truly gold but he would not allow the crown to be damaged. Therefore, Archimedes had to find a way to measure its volume instead of simply cutting into it.

Archie was cogitating on this conundrum while taking a bath. When he noticed that as he submerged his body a certain amount of water was displaced, he jumped out of the bath and ran naked through the streets shouting, "Eureka!" I have found it, i.e., the solution.

Now, I did not expect a similar reaction from President-Elect Obama when I wrote of my solution to America's economic woes two weeks ago. However, I was a little hurt that I was not included last week when he convened his panel of economic experts. After all, we are right next to Senator Obama's home state and he surely must read *Gavel Gamut* in Barry Cleveland's *Carmi Times*.

Be that as it may, I am sure that you, Gentle Reader, were duly impressed with my suggested cure to healing our ailing body politic. You will undoubtedly recall that I made the modest proposal of our governments, federal and state, allowing us to spend our own tax deferred monies instead of having it doled out to such financial wizards as American International Group, Inc., (A.I.G.).

So far our Executive and Legislative branches at the federal level have given one hundred and fifty billion of your tax dollars to just this one failing money pit. I say giving our money, or even buying preferred stock in such poorly managed losers, makes us enablers of the worst kind.

A.I.G. has lost enough money in the last year to wipe out all of its profits since 2004. Of course, the even worse news is that your government wants to bail out not only A.I.G. but numerous other "gambleholics" who bet billions on bad loans and other Ponzi schemes.

I say enough is enough. Virtually every economist in the country says the root of our economic malaise is the dearth in consumer spending caused by the general unavailability of ready cash or credit. Since seventy percent of our gross national product comes from consumer spending, why not let the consumers have their own money to spend instead of hoping the financial institutions will loan the taxpayers' monies back to the true owners?

Even Treasury Secretary Henry Paulson who is the overseer of the Troubled Asset Relief Program (TARP) is having second thoughts about just feeding the raging disease of gambling by big business.

So let's ask our governments to allow us, if we so choose, to use a certain percentage of our own tax deferred monies, within a certain period of time, without paying penalties or taxes. Then the great engine of our economy would rev up like Jimmie Johnson with Dale Earnhardt, Jr., on his left rear fender.

A simple one page addition to our tax return would allow for proper reporting and accounting with no new levels of bureaucracy and no new costs.

And if anyone is worried about individual taxpayers being irresponsible and wasting their own money, at least we will get to make the choices.

Or, perhaps, someone might worry that the A.I.G.'s of the world will not have as much capital from the different mutual funds of IRA, 401K or 457 plan owners. I say that is called American freedom to fail or succeed on their own.

SHOVEL READY

(Week of March 23, 2009)

Governor Daniels predicts Indiana will receive about 4.3 billion dollars of our money back from the federal government under the American Recovery and Investment Act. You can follow the bouncing checks at INvest.in.gov.

That is 4.3 billion out of 787 billion that the feds will be doling out. If all fifty states receive the same amount of 4.3 billion, you know that will not happen, 215 billion dollars of citizen money would be returned to its owners through infrastructure projects. Such an expenditure on carefully researched and necessary projects strikes me as a prudent investment and an expeditious approach to helping ease our economic crisis.

You have probably framed my *Gavel Gamut* column from the week of November 24, 2008, that called for just such a return to the projects created by the Civilian Conservation Corps and the Works Projects Administration that helped us recover from the Great Depression.

Such a quick investment of our own tax monies in ourselves makes sense to me. But it is the shell game being played by the federal government with the remaining 500 billion or so that really calls for shoveling.

Once again, I respectfully refer you to your carefully preserved copy of the *Gavel Gamut* column of October 27, 2008. You will recall that I suggested then that the best road to rapid and permanent recovery was to allow Americans to keep our own money and give us incentives to spend it wisely. It is the American consumer, not failed banks and investment companies, that must drive the long term recovery.

And speaking of failing investment companies, in the *Gavel Gamut* of the week of November 17, 2008 I wrote:

> "You will undoubtedly recall (from October 27, 2008) that I made the modest proposal that our governments, federal and state, allow us to spend our own tax deferred monies instead of having it doled out to such financial wizards as American International Group, Inc., (A.I.G.).
>
> So far our Executive and Legislative branches at the federal level have given 150 billion of your tax dollars to just this one failing money pit. I say giving our money, or even buying preferred stock in such poorly managed losers, makes us enablers of the worst kind."

I wrote that article four months ago. Since then, your government has given an additional 30 billion of your money to A.I.G. which repaid your generosity with 168 million dollars in "bonuses" to itself.

However, it is never too late to at least try to do the right thing. April the 15th is fast approaching and my suggested solution as put forth in the fall of 2008 can most easily and inexpensively be implemented through the tax system. President Obama can, by Executive Order, and with the cooperation of Congress and the Internal Revenue Service, allow us to keep our own money for buying consumer goods and services.

Although I set forth this "Modest Proposal" in October, 2008, I will return to the details next week. For in my humble opinion, the project for which shovels are ready and which really needs to be done immediately is in Washington, D.C.

Unfortunately, we might need Hercules and his method of cleaning the Augean Stables for that mess. Perhaps we can get Hercules to simply divert the Potomac River through the Capitol.

LIGHTING A CANDLE

(Week of March 30, 2009)

Unlike the naysayers and malcontents, I hope the approach that our federal government is taking to our financial crisis works. I disagreed with the bailouts when they were rushed through Congress with no real debate and almost non-existent oversight, and I said so in this column months ago. However, to hope for failure of the bailouts is cutting off our own financial noses to spite our country's financial face.

That said, I still submit that my suggestion of letting Americans retain their own tax monies for the purpose of stimulating the economy would be a cheaper, more effective and fairer approach. "Now see here", as President Obama is fond of saying, I am not unaware that with any large and complicated problem there are simple wrong answers. However, I do not see why instead of continuing to pour trillions of dollars we do not have into such black holes as A.I.G. and its ilk we cannot shift our strategy to direct support of the taxpayers.

The mechanism to do this is already in place, _i.e._ our federal and state income tax systems. No new bureaucracies would be needed. And since virtually every economist agrees that the best long term solution to our financial woes is to regenerate consumer spending, let's allow our citizens to retain more of their own tax monies and spend some of their 401(k), 457, and other such savings plans without taxes or penalties.

As I suggested last fall, well before April 15, 2009 and before the bailout money was approved, Congress could pass a quick Internal Revenue Service regulation that allows citizens to simply pay in less money than their returns call for, say up to the amount each fully employed adult is paying for just the A.I.G. bailout. While that figure is a moving target, the Bureau of Labor Statistics reports that 141,748,000 Americans were fully employed as of February, 2009.

The $180 billion we have given A.I.G. divided by 141,748,000 comes to about $1,270.00. If our government would allow every fully employed citizen to retain an additional $1,270.00 through their regular paychecks over the course of a year, we could directly stimulate our economy.

Another large source of potential stimulus monies is available via the 401(k) type savings plans many Americans have through their employment. If our government would pass a law to allow withdrawals from these plans of, perhaps, up to $5,000.00 without penalties or taxes, many Americans might decide to buy larger consumer items. And if by next April 15th either the money has not been paid back into the accounts or proof of expenditures is not included with one's tax returns, then taxes and penalties could be assessed.

Of course, these two plans of helping to ease our economic crises are no more foolproof than the current bailout approach. They might bring an increase in inflation and they leave out any direct support for those who need it most, _i.e._ the unemployed and underemployed. Of course, the same is true of the bailouts. But, at least, about half of all Americans would receive direct relief through the use of their own hard earned dollars and expenditures should help those who need jobs by creating more jobs through the increased demand for goods and services.

Well, the devil is in the details as we know and I am not claiming my suggestions are a panacea for our country's financial ills. However, they would, at a minimum, allow the true owners of the funds to use them as they see fit.

PARDON ME, PRESIDENT FORD

(Week of January 8, 2007)

President Gerald Ford died December 26, 2006. In a life filled with public service, he will always be best known for his pardon of President Nixon in 1974.

President Nixon personally chose Gerald Ford to replace the disgraced Vice-President Spiro Agnew who resigned in 1973 amid disclosures of bribery while Agnew was Governor of Maryland.

Vice-President Ford served under President Nixon until Nixon resigned in August of 1974. One month after President Nixon resigned, President Ford issued him a full pardon for any crimes he may have committed while president.

At the time, I and most Americans were calling for a complete investigation of the Watergate debacle and especially Nixon's involvement in it. It was a time of a media feeding frenzy and blood in the water.

President Ford took the unprecedented step of going personally before Congress and flatly stating that President Nixon and then Vice-President Ford had no deal to pardon Nixon if he would resign.

I recall how dubious I was when President Ford stated that he issued the pardon only to help our country to start healing from the loss of confidence caused by Watergate.

Yet, after a few months I began to have second thoughts about my initial reaction to the pardon. I began to see how much courage it took for President Ford to go straight into the anti-Nixon firestorm sweeping the United States.

As a country, we were almost paralyzed by the partisan fighting at home and the War in Vietnam. We needed a new direction and a renewed spirit.

Surely President Ford with his twenty-two (22) years in Congress knew he was committing political suicide by not giving us our pound of flesh. Still, he put his country first. Of course, the country rewarded his sacrifice by booting him from office and electing President Jimmy Carter to replace him.

But during the campaign of 1976, when President Ford came to Evansville on April the 23rd, I took my son, Jim, out of school and we went to the Downtown Walkway to cheer the man who put country above self.

For while William Shakespeare may almost always get his character analysis right, when it came to President Ford, "*The good he did lived after him.*" **Julius Caesar, Act III, sc. ii.**

Even President Carter, one of America's most courageous and best former presidents said of President Ford:

> "*President Ford was one of the most admirable*
> *public servants I have ever known.*"

And when it came to the pardon of President Nixon, Senator Ted Kennedy, while admitting that he had severely criticized the pardon in 1974, said that he had come to realize that:

> *"The pardon was an extraordinary act of courage*
> *that historians recognize was truly in the national*
> *interest."*

So, President Ford, since even your political opponents came to appreciate your courage and goodness, I am confident that you have long ago "pardoned" all of us who doubted you back when we needed your leadership.

LIES AND CATS; CHARACTER AND RIDICULE

(Week of November 21, 2005)

Mark Twain said, "One of the most striking differences between a cat and a lie is that a cat has only nine lives." *Pudd'nhead Wilson,* Chapter VII.

Pudd'nhead Wilson is one of Twain's most fun reads. It is a short pithy comment on that ancient truism: No good deed goes unpunished. It is a detective novel which described the use of the then new science of fingerprint identification. It is a witty but clear indictment of slavery in America and the American legal system that allowed it to flourish.

And while all of this may sound heavy, it is an easy and amusing analysis of human greed and hubris. You can read it in half a day. Of course, it is likely that at least one of the two or three of you who read this column will have already discovered this delightful literary treasure from Mr. Twain, nee, Samuel Langhorne Clemens.

Another of Twain's aphorisms set forth in *Pudd'nhead Wilson* concerns public ridicule:

> *"There is no character, howsoever good and fine, but it can be destroyed by ridicule, howsoever poor and witless. Observe the ass, for instance: his character is about perfect, he is the choicest spirit among all the humbler animals, yet see what ridicule has brought him to. Instead of feeling complimented when we are called an ass, we are left in doubt."*
> (See the Preface.)

In the unlikely event you read last week's column, you may wonder what "Lies and Ridicule" have to do with boxing which was the promised topic. First, thank you. Next, let me assure you that eventually the "sweet science" of boxing will be discussed.

As to the reason for the shift, well, my wife, Peg, and I, at the invitation of our good friends, Shirley and Sam Blankenship, saw the movie *Good Night, and Good Luck* this past Sunday evening. When I saw the reenactment of journalist Edward R. Murrow standing up to Senator Joseph McCarthy's vilification of others by rumor, innuendo and false statements, I was reminded of the debt we owe to such courageous journalists and others who have not gladly suffered abuses of power. I decided to write about some of those fighters before we discuss pugilism.

It will take us a while to cover this waterfront and, by necessity, only a few of the many that deserve our gratitude can be discussed. But, if you wish, let's start with one of America's earliest and bravest journalists, John Peter Zenger who, with the help of attorney Andrew Hamilton and a courageous New York jury, stood up for free speech in 1735.

Zenger was arrested for printing unflattering stories about New York's governor, William Cosby.

Cosby had Zenger charged with seditious libel and had his hand picked judges hold Zenger in jail for eight months.

Zenger demanded a jury trial. Andrew Hamilton represented Zenger and openly challenged the jury to ignore the judge's interpretation of the law. Hamilton based his defense on the truth of the articles.

Hamilton told the jury to stand up to the governor and the judges and find Zenger not guilty. The jury did just that. Hamilton argued that the jury, not a judge, had the right to determine both the facts and the law, that is, the jury could **nullify** the written law.

Hamilton told the judge and the jury:

> "...It is a right, which all men claim, that they are entitled to complain when they are hurt. They have a right to publicly remonstrate against the abuses of power in the strongest terms...
>
> ....
>
> The question before...you Gentlemen of the jury, is not of small or private concern."

> "It is not the cause of one poor printer.... It is the cause of liberty. ...By an impartial and uncorrupt verdict (you will) have laid a noble foundation for securing...a right to liberty of both exposing and opposing arbitrary power... by speaking and writing truth."

Thank you Mr. Zenger, Mr. Hamilton and members of that jury.

Next week we will, at your election, discuss one of Indiana's most courageous fighters for free speech, Eugene Debs and, perhaps, another hero or two.

FREE SPEECH ISN'T FREE

(Week of November 28, 2005)

If you wasted twenty minutes of your valuable time reading last week's column you know we are discussing the price to be paid for free speech. The movie *Good Night, and Good Luck* about newsman Edward R. Murrow was the catalyst for this topic. Murrow owed much, as do we all, to history's martyrs who paid dearly for speaking unpopular truths.

Socrates was executed in Athens, Greece in 399 B.C. His crime was publicly criticizing the government. He said:

> "False words …infect the soul with evil."
>
> (*The Republic* by Plato)

Socrates could have escaped the poisoned hemlock by apologizing for speaking the truth. He refused to give the judges an easy out. He told them:

> "Your duty is to do justice, not make a present of it."
>
> (*The Apology* by Plato)

In other words, don't play games with the facts and the law and don't base decisions on sympathy or prejudice. The Athenian court was not moved by this appeal to fairness.

Jesus was crucified by the occupation Roman government for publicly teaching his interpretation of his own religion's scriptures. The Hebrew religious hierarchy demanded his life for heresy and blasphemy. Jesus based his response on the facts:

> "You shall know the truth,
>   and the truth will make you free"
>
> (*John*, Ch.8, verses 31-32)

Of course, he was not talking about freedom for himself. His speech was most dearly paid for.

Our newspaper friend from last week's column, John Peter Zenger, paid for his truthful criticism of the British governor of New York in 1735 with eight months in jail for violating that era's PATRIOT ACT, i.e., the Alien and Sedition Act. The PATRIOT ACT is an imaginative acronym for: Uniting and Strengthening America by Providing Appropriate Tools Required to Intercept and Obstruct Terrorism Act. It is 342 pages long and was passed one month after September 11, 2001.

One of Indiana's most heroic figures, Eugene V. Debs of Terre Haute, spent a total of four years in federal prisons for contempt of federal judges in labor disputes and for publicly speaking out against America's involvement in World War I.

Debs was born November 5, 1855 and died October 20, 1926. He was a high school drop out and the son of European immigrant parents. He served two terms as Terre Haute City Clerk and was elected to two terms in the Indiana House of Representatives. He was originally a Democrat but became disillusioned with both major political parties. He eventually ran five times for the Presidency of the United States, once while he was in prison, on the Socialist Party ticket. In one election he won a million votes from his jail cell.

Debs was, also, an editor and publisher of railway union newspapers. It was as a union organizer and official that Debs crossed swords with numerous federal judges including members of the U.S. Supreme Court.

While Debs had, himself, been a member of the government, he came to see the established order and particularly un-elected, life tenured federal judges as anathema to democracy and American ideals of freedom. About federal judges he said:

> "When they go to the bench, they go, not to serve
> the people, but to serve the interests that place
> them where they are."

(Speech in Canton, Ohio; June 16, 1918)

The source of much of this material on Eugene V. Debs is from the book *Heretics in the Temple* by David Ray Papke. Professor Papke teaches at the Indiana University School of Law in Indianapolis. He was one of the professors chosen by the Indiana Judicial Conference to teach the charter class of the Graduate Judges Program that I attended in 1996 and 1997.

Debs understood the high price to be paid for "free speech" better than most. As Professor Papke says, Debs saw America's legal system as a most insidious tool for repressing and punishing unpopular ideas, "…blessed as it was with a veneer of neutrality." See *Heretics in the Temple* at page 88.

Perhaps the most important lesson about free speech that each of these heroes paid so dearly to teach us is that these ideals are too important and too fragile to be left to the judges.

Let's hear it for freedom of the press and the right to trial by a jury of one's peers. Well, we can, at least, knock these issues around next week if you have recovered from the Thanksgiving eating and football marathon.

Oh, and we will eventually get to that sport where Jack Dempsey forgot to duck Gene Tunny's knockout blow in the famous "long count" boxing match and where Muhammad Ali floated like a butterfly and stung like a bee in his fights against Joe Frasier and George Foreman.

CHAPTER FIVE

THOSE WHO DARE

CHOICES

(Week of April 17, 2006)

It is difficult to support our family and friends when they make decisions for themselves we wish they would not make.

Options are what differentiate us from all other species. Other organisms either act from instinct or are acted upon.

It is the essence of being human to decide which paths we want to travel. And we love others most when we support their right to make decisions with which we disagree.

We have the right and sometimes the duty to point out why we wish others would not do what they want to do. But after we give our best advice, it is their right to choose for themselves. Just as we do not wish to be disrespected for our choices, we must respect the choices of others as long as they are honorable, moral and legal.

That is why Mary accepted Jesus' choices. That is why Alexander the Great's mother, Olympias, helped him conquer the world in spite of his numerous injuries and hardships. And that is why Achilles's mother, Thetis, supported him in his desire for a short glorious life instead of a long uneventful one. Each son died in his early thirties pursuing his freely chosen goals.

Each of these mothers loved their sons and knew that their son's choices would probably result in their premature deaths. But the sons' lives belong to the sons, not the mothers or any others.

The same dilemmas are faced by families when their loved ones choose to serve their country in the military, or as police officers, or fire fighters, or when they elect to compete in some other potentially dangerous activity. Often these activities result in death or serious injuries. They almost always entail difficult sacrifices. But, at least, as General Patton said, "They aren't shoveling manure in Louisiana."

Those concerns were faced by the family and friends of Kevin Payne the night of March 18, 2006. Kevin was born in Evansville, Indiana, on January 12, 1972. I met him at the Boxers Den in Evansville ten years ago. Kevin was unfailingly polite as many boxers are. And he would appear and disappear from the Den as the needs of his wife, Jennifer, and their two children, ten-year-old, Austin, and eight-year-old, Allison, allowed.

Kevin would appear when he had a chance for a quick payday in the ring. He would ask boxing trainers, Gerald Rice, Danny Thomas or me to work with him "to get him ready". I do not remember Kevin ever having more than a month to prepare.

From time-to-time I would run into Kevin at the Hunan Chinese restaurant close to the Courthouse in Mt. Vernon. He always wanted to talk boxing and was always trying to get help with getting fights or with preparation for a fight.

His fights were usually scheduled for four rounds and paid him just enough to keep his dreams alive. Kevin's record was fifteen (15) wins, five (5) losses and one (1) draw. He knocked out six (6) opponents. Kevin saw boxing as a means to supplement his full-time work from Whirlpool and other odd jobs such as construction work in Posey County.

Kevin was thirty-four years old when he boxed eight grueling rounds against Ryan Maraldo in an elimination bout. The winner was to have the opportunity of fighting undefeated junior welterweight (135-140 pounds), Julio Cesar Chavez, Jr. Such a fight would bring a substantial payday and, if Chavez lost, then maybe a title shot.

Was this an improbable dream? Sure, but it was Kevin's dream and I respected him for having such a lofty goal. His family and friends supported his quest and I respected them for affording Kevin his right to choose. His family buried him with a pair of boxing gloves; Kevin would have liked that.

Kevin died pursuing his dream. Are his family and friends sad? Of course. But when we truly love someone, we think of their happiness not our own.

I watched Kevin's nationally televised bout. I never saw him fight better or tougher. And when he was declared the winner, I never saw him happier.

As the song says, ♫whoever's not busy being born is busy dying♫. So it really comes down to **how** we take our leave, not when. Kevin took his with all of his dreams possible. We should be so lucky.

IF YOU REALLY LOOK!

(Week of December 5, 2005)

Fights are not nearly as hard to find as teenagers have always wanted their peers to believe. Most of us publicly professed more willingness to join a fray than we privately hoped would occur.

It has been my experience that there's always some other fool out there.

That's why the teenage braggadocio displayed in school yards should be carefully tempered in these days of road rage. It's one thing to get a black eye. But many otherwise rational motorists reach for tire tools or even guns when someone clogs the passing lane.

Take Posey County for example. We have a long and checkered history of fighting just for the fun of it.

According to both Leonard's *History and Directory of Posey County* (1882) and Leffel's *History of Posey County* (1913), before the age of the X-Box, a small riot was considered *derigueur* in our fair county.

Posey County's reputation as a venue for fisticuffs was so widespread along the Ohio River that legendary, but real life, keelboat man, Mike Fink, came to show his prowess.

Fink was known personally by Davy Crockett who described the six-foot, three-inch, one-hundred-eighty pounder as half horse and half alligator.

Fink wore a red ribbon in his hat as an invitation to all comers to knock it off.

Soon after our first tavern opened by McFadin's Bluff, Fink came to test the local competition. He reportedly had downed a few pints of home brewed whiskey before he stood in the middle of the dirt floor and challenged the house.

Directly above his head was hanging a massive set of antlers taken as a trophy from a local stag. As Fink bellowed out his threats, the antlers fell and cold-cocked him. When he came to, he slunk back to his flatboat and never darkened our door again.

Of course, there's always some new clown to replace the exiting fool and in our case it was one Tom Miller.

Tom was one of our own. In the days before the Civil War, he was known to be a generally peaceable type unless his inhibitions had been lifted by alcohol.

According to Mr. Leffel, Miller would pace the streets of Mt. Vernon spoiling for a fight:

> "His coat off, sleeves rolled up, his shaggy breast exposed and
> his suspenders about his waist…"

Miller would always recite the same drunken challenge:

> "I'm a mean man, a bad man and I orter to be whipped,
> I know, but whar's the man can do it?"

He repeatedly never lacked for willing opponents whom he always vanquished. I think I've had this guy in court!

Speaking of court, hand to hand combat was apparently a better qualification for a judgeship in early Posey County than a law degree.

When we still had a Justice of the Peace Court in West Franklin, Justice John Williams presided. On one occasion a fight broke out and Judge Williams "commanded the peace." When his order was ignored, he jumped in and quelled the outbreak with his fists.

Another Justice of the Peace, James Lafferty, apparently saw nothing just about remaining impartial. When Nathan Overton and Allen Moutry were fighting, Judge Lafferty yelled:

"I command the peace!"

When they kept brawling, the Judge ruled:

"Give him hell, Nathan! I will fine you only
$1.00 and pay half of it myself!"

The most famous courtroom contest occurred between former Posey Circuit Judge James Goodlett and sitting Posey Circuit Judge Sam Hall who replaced Goodlett on the Bench. Former Judge Goodlett was upset by his ouster and was contemptuous of Judge Hall in open court on March 7, 1834. Judge Hall cited Goodlett for contempt and set a hearing for the next day.

Attorney William Jones anticipated trouble and slipped a dagger to Judge Hall on the Bench. When Judge Hall called for the contempt hearing, former Judge Goodlett yelled, "I will show you contempt!", and attacked him with his fists. Judge Hall struck back at Goodlett with the dagger. Sheriff William James saved Goodlett's life by pulling him back.

Now there's the kind of case that makes you realize the importance of staying awake in Court!

Of course, our famous Hoop Pole brawl which cemented Posey County's reputation as a place for boatmen to either avoid or walk lightly upon is well documented.

It seems the pugilistic gene was certainly present in some of our ancestors, and, if the Saturday night police reports are any indication, it may have survived through many years of natural selection.

OPIE TAYLOR KNOCKS OUT CANCER

(Week of August 28, 2006)

In one corner stands Ray Stallings of Burnt Prairie, Illinois: Red hair, braces and freckles. Across the ring, cancer of the thyroid: fast growing with bad intentions.

It was not a fair fight. Cancer never had a chance. Ray knocked it out cold with his one/two combination of character and courage.

Ray Stallings, who now lives with his pregnant wife, Andrea, and their four children in Princeton, Indiana, was the keynote speaker at the Big Eight Sports Award Banquet held August 23, 2006 at the Elks Lodge in Mt. Carmel, Illinois. Ray was asked to address the one hundred high school administrators and coaches by former University of Evansville basketball star, Andy Elkins. Andy is now the athletic director at Princeton High School.

Peg and I and our good friend, Danny Thomas, who is Ray's boxing trainer, attended the banquet. Posey County was represented by Steve Roling, who is the organization's secretary, and Mt. Vernon High School Administrators, Steve Riordan, Gary Redman and Brian Smith.

Ray is so modest that when he came home from his team leader job at Toyota and heard Andy Elkins's invitation on his telephone answering machine, Ray thought it was a wrong number mix-up.

As Ray told the audience, amateur boxers are not well known and, except for the Olympics every four years, amateur boxing is not well covered by the media.

But Andy knew he had the right number and the right person to interest and inspire an audience of coaches and others whose duty is to help young people prepare for their toughest contest, life.

Ray told the crowd he knows he is not what most people envision as a boxer. He is thirty-one years old, with a trim build who looks like, well, Opie Taylor.

He grew up in that Mecca of boxing, Burnt Prairie, that had only one hundred people, only one of whom wanted to box.

Yet, Ray has had a goal that he first told me about at the Boxers Den in Evansville when he was still a teenager. Ray Stallings has always wanted to represent the United States in the Olympic Games. His quest will continue in Oxnard, California, next month where Ray will compete with boxers from all over America for an Olympic tryout.

And if you had been in Ray's corner, as Peg and I were at the National Police Athletic Club Tournament in Palm Bay, Florida, in October of 1996, you would not bet against him.

Ray had only had twelve fights and his only entourage was me and Peg. This was Peg's first time to see a bout up close and personal and I was only involved because our son, Jim, was a boxer. In other words, Ray was pretty much on his own.

On the other hand, across the ring from twenty-year old, 180-pound Ray was Calvin Brock who was ranked as the best amateur heavyweight in America and who had had one hundred and twenty-five fights and a professional, full-time trainer. Twenty-three year old Brock was 6'3" and over 200 pounds. However, much as Ray's later battle with cancer, Calvin Brock was almost overmatched by the skinny red head from Burnt Prairie.

Well, the bell for the final round has rung for this column, but if you care to tune in next week, we can continue with Ray's "David and Goliath" saga with big bad Calvin Brock who, ten years after his fight with Ray, is ranked among the world's top five heavyweight professional fighters. Brock's record is now 29-0 and he will soon have a shot at and, I predict, will win the World Heavyweight Title. If you are a boxing fan remember you saw it first here.

Of course, Ray, also, had that other better-known opponent that so often hits below the belt and while no one is expecting it.

But neither Brock nor cancer could conquer Ray's character. As the poet Robert Frost pointed out, it is not the outcome of life that makes us worthwhile but how we handle the struggle. In that fight, Ray remains undefeated.

Danny Thomas, Ray Stallings, and the author
Photograph by Peg Redwine

155

THE SWEET SCIENCE

(Week of September 4, 2006)

Amateur boxing has fewer fatalities and far fewer serious injuries per participant than high school baseball or football. It is a sport like wrestling where the participants are matched according to size and where bouts are won based on the number of legal blows landed on the front, top-half of the participants. The force of the blows is not a factor. For example, a punch that knocks a boxer down counts no more than a punch that simply lands in the scoring area.

Boxing is called the sweet science because a student of the game who can apply the lessons of boxing when actually in the ring can defeat a superior athlete who relies on brawn.

As the old adage goes, "The race is not always to the swift nor the battle to the strong." Of course, the related adage is also true: "But that's the way to bet."

In other words, the science of boxing is only a factor in the equation. Such elements as experience and physical abilities are often more determinative than theory.

And whereas it is often true that it is not the size of the boxer in the fight but the size of the fight in the boxer that matters, it is also true that heart alone may not be enough.

Such was the case with our young protagonist, Ray Stallings, from Burnt Prairie, Illinois, in his match against Calvin Brock in 1996. Should you have read this column last week, you may recall that we left Ray all alone in the ring with the best amateur heavyweight boxer in America.

In round one, the left-handed Brock came out confident that the gawky, red headed Ray was just there to validate Brock's status as champion. From my position in Ray's corner I thought Brock was almost indolent as he kept Ray off balance with his powerful right jab, then occasionally came back with a straight left to Ray's head. This display went on for about the first two minutes of the round until Ray's nose was bloodied and his back was bleeding from being forced into the ropes.

But with about a minute to go, Ray, who is also left-handed, came up from his position doubled over in a corner with an awkward looping left hand that caught Brock square on the chin. Even with the protective headgear, I could see Brock's eyes roll up for a brief second as his knees slightly buckled. From that point on, Ray's character and Brock's experience were at war.

When Ray returned to our corner after the first round, Peg, who was working the corner for the first time, could not bear to look at Ray's bloody nose or his back and arms that matched his red hair. She handed me the spit bucket and water bottle with her eyes locked on the canvas of the ring. Peg later told me she was wondering what we were going to tell his parents, who were also our good friends, if Ray got seriously hurt.

Ray was gasping for breath and pleading for me to pour water on his head. It took the first half of the one-minute break just to stop the bleeding. When Ray could finally talk, he said, "Jim, he is really good." I almost said the truth that was on my tongue, "You're darn right he's really good!" Instead I said, "You got his attention with that straight left. From now on just keep throwing it as much as you can."

Round two was a coming of age for Ray and an awakening for Brock. I could see the puzzlement in Brock's eyes and the hesitancy in his punches. I could almost hear him thinking, "Who is this kid?" Ray pounded his straight left for the whole three minutes and the spectators who had gathered to watch Brock's coronation begin to yell for Ray.

When Ray struggled back to our corner after round two, I sneaked a peak at Brock's corner and saw his trainer giving him a tongue-lashing. Peg and I could only pour more water on Ray as I told him to double up on his right jab and keep throwing that overhand left. Ray could barely breathe and he could not talk. As the bell for round three rang, it was anybody's guess as to who would win.

Brock came out firing and Ray was too tired to block the blows. At first it looked like Brock's superior skills were just too much for the skinny red head from Burnt Prairie.

But about halfway through the final round, Ray figured out how to move to his left, which was away from the left-handed Brock's power. Then Ray figured out how to throw his left straight into the taller Brock's solar plexus. Brock began to wilt and Ray's new found fans began to chant: "Red, red, red."

When the final bell sounded, Ray had nothing left, but that was more than Brock who had to be helped to his corner by his worried trainer who caught my eye and put his thumbs up: "Great fight!"

Well, you remember that amateur boxing is scored by the number of proper blows, not the stuff that dreams are made of, and the judges gave the razor thin decision to Brock. But the seeds of Ray's current quest to be an Olympic champion were sown that night in 1996. Next week if you are available, I'll bring you up to date on where that odyssey stands.

For as you may recall, Ray had that little inconvenience of thyroid cancer to deal with between 1996 and October, 2006. That is when he climbs back into the ring in Oxnard, California, once again against the best amateur heavyweights in America to win the right to compete for the honor of representing his country in the Olympics.

After Ray got sick, but before he knew why he tired so easily after the first round, he kept trying to box but kept losing. Many of Ray's friends and some of his family were more afraid he would get hurt than get to the Olympics. But as Rudyard Kipling wrote in his poem, *If*: "If you can trust yourself when all men doubt you...you'll be a man, my son!" Ray did, and Ray is.

THE SPORT OF GODS

(Week of September 18, 2006)

Horse racing may be the sport of kings, but boxing, according to Greek mythology, was a gift from the gods.

The ancient Greeks who gave us so much in science, philosophy, literature, medicine, law, art, government and religion believed that the sport of boxing was created by the god, Apollo, who defeated the Greek god of war, Ares, in the first boxing match.

George Foreman who won a gold medal in boxing at the 1968 Olympic Games said: "Boxing is the sport that all other sports aspire to be." George meant that boxing has everything: strategy, conditioning, courage, and the ultimate human physical challenge of one on one unarmed combat under carefully controlled conditions and rules.

In 2008 in Beijing, China, the world will carry on the tradition of the ancient Greeks by joining in the friendly, non-lethal combat of Olympic boxing. And Ray Stallings of Southern Indiana plans to be there to represent his country in the heavyweight division.

If you have read this column recently you have met Ray and know of his inspiring story of triumph over cancer and of his quest for Olympic gold and glory. He must first fight his way into an Olympic tryout. He plans to do just that the first week of October at the National Police Athletic/Activities League Boxing Tournament in Oxnard, California. You can follow our local hero's progress starting October 1, 2006 at www.nationalpal.org/events/2006/boxing.

The first Olympic boxing match took place at Olympia, Greece in 688 B.C. The Greeks continued the games for a thousand years until the Emperor Constantine ordered them stopped in 393 A.D. because the original games were held to honor the god, Zeus, and Constantine had decreed that Christianity should be the state religion.

The last great Olympic champion was a Greek boxer named Zopyrus who won at the last of the old games held in 393 A.D. But after the modern Olympic games were started in 1896, American boxers have been the most victorious having won numerous gold, silver and bronze medals. Such American champions as Sugar Ray Leonard, Joe Frazier and Muhammad Ali have carried on the tradition of the ancient Greek champion, Zopyrus.

Boxing was so important in the culture of ancient Greece that Homer wrote of it in The Iliad when a special event was held at the Battle of Troy to honor the slain Greek warrior, Patroclus. Homer, also, wrote of one of the greatest boxers of all time, Ajax.

America has long been the Mecca of boxing. While England with its Marquis of Queensbury Rules instituted modern boxing in 1867, American culture that relies so heavily on Greek notions of independence and individual accomplishment is where boxing has flourished.

Those wise ancient Greeks strongly believed that an individual's sacrifice could serve to redeem a whole nation. The idea of a lone champion fighting for everyone's glory and even survival is a recurring theme in Greek drama, literature and religion; the New Testament was written partially in Greek.

Young Ray Stallings is working very hard and sacrificing a great deal to win the right to represent all of us at the 2006 Olympic Games. To win a tryout, Ray has known for some time that his "vanilla" style of standing in the middle of the ring and trading blows had to change.

Next week, if you want an update on Ray and his metamorphosis from a traditional stiffly upright fighter to one who knows how to bob and weave, I will introduce you to Danny Thomas who taught Ray to ♫do a little side step.♫

HOT FUDGE SUNDAE

(Week of September 25, 2006)

In less than one month, Ray Stallings originally from tiny Burnt Prairie, Illinois, and now living in Princeton, Indiana, will step into a small ring on a national stage. Ray will be a minority white athlete up against what makes American amateur boxing and America itself the best in the world, i.e., a melting pot of races and cultures.

At the turn of the 20th Century, Irish and Italian immigrants such as John L. Sullivan and Rocky Marciano literally fought their way into American society.

Then many African Americans followed the lead of Jack Johnson and Joe Louis out of discrimination to athletic excellence and social acceptance.

Contemporary amateur boxing in America is populated with athletes from varied backgrounds and different size cities including some vanilla flavored fighters such as Ray Stallings from small town America. Many of these cultures appear to produce distinctive styles of boxing. There are, of course, no hard and fast rules and there is often much cross over among these numerous groups and has been since boxing was first introduced to the ancient Olympics in Greece.

From those first Olympic Games more than 2,500 years ago, trainers and coaches have observed how certain groups, say the Spartans for example, were better at particular physical skills than others such as maybe the Athenians.

By carefully separating certain successful traits then gradually teaching them to athletes who do not come by them naturally, a winning style can be created. This combination of movements and strategies can call on the natural strengths of an athlete then amalgamate them with other helpful but not so natural techniques.

Such a happy marriage of abilities and styles has taken place with Ray Stallings thanks to his good friend and trainer, Danny Thomas. Danny had an Olympic tryout of his own just a few years back then went on to become a professional boxer and trainer. Danny has operated his own business for the past several years working with amateur and professional boxers at The Rock'em Sock'em Boxing Club in Evansville, Indiana.

Danny's ability to use powerful and quick combinations of punches while ducking his head and moving from side to side and back and forth made him an Indiana Golden Gloves champion. His generous spirit in teaching Ray to bob and weave while side stepping punches has helped make Ray Stallings a much more formidable opponent.

Ray has always had an abundance of strength and endurance but he, also, used to have a rather common syndrome of inertia: "Here I am. Hit me, then I'll hit you."

But with Danny's ability to train Ray in the techniques of movement and quickness, Ray has become a powerful mixture of styles. And, as so often happens when the best boxing characteristics of two groups are pooled, a much better boxer has emerged.

Danny Thomas has, also, been an emotional inspiration to Ray who survived cancer because Danny had to struggle with a legal system that has sometimes been harsh. And Danny has come through without bitterness.

Both Ray and Danny have found strength within themselves by calling upon their deep religious faith. As *Ecclesiastes* says: "To everything is a season." After Ray's triumph over cancer and Danny's triumph over inequity, this may well be their season.

For now we will leave Ray and Danny alone as they begin the final all out preparation for Ray's appointment in the squared circle.

When Ray steps into that ring in search of his Olympic dream next month in Oxnard, California, the best of America goes with him. You can follow his quest by logging onto the Police Activities League Boxing National Tournament beginning the first of October. Look for the heavyweight open division (www.nationalpal.org/events/2006/boxing).

Danny Thomas and Ray Stallings, Oxnard Beach, CA
Photographs by Peg Redwine

I'D RATHER WIN

(Week of October 16, 2006)

Frances Bacon (1561-1626) wrote: "Prosperity doth discover vice but adversity doth best discover virtue." Or, as our parents told us: you learn more from losing than winning. Maybe so, but winning is a lot more fun.

Another aphorism that I dislike being confronted with is that you must sacrifice a lot to win a lot, or as Rudyard Kipling (1865-1936) wrote:

> "No easy hope or lies
> shall bring us to our goal
> But iron sacrifice
> of body, will and soul."

I still have scars and phantom pain left over from two-a-day football practices that our coaches screamed were good for us and necessary for victory. My thought then was that would not be true if all of us players agreed not to practice and to just play the games. Of course, this heresy was anathema to all those parents who knew their kid was the next Nike endorsee. As an aside, when my friend, John Emhuff, who is my bailiff and also a recovering English teacher, proofread this column he chided me by saying that when I played football, Nike, the sports corporation, had not yet been created. I told him he was not so smart after all as I was talking about the original Nike, the Greek goddess of Victory, whom I was old enough to know personally; so there, John!

Anyway, none of this has anything to do with the purpose of this column, which is to bring you up-to-date on Ray Stallings's progress towards his goal of boxing for the United States in the 2008 Olympics in China.

Progress is the correct word even though Ray lost a tough fight last week to the National Police Athletic League Champion in Oxnard, California. Ray has a strong Christian faith and has applied the lessons of John Bunyan's *Pilgrim's Progress* (1678) to his life and his quest to represent his country. Ray told me he had read and re-read *Pilgrim's Progress* and its lessons of perseverance in the years leading up to last week's tournament.

You may recall that Ray had to first defeat cancer while supporting his wife and five children before he could even allow his lifelong dream of Olympic boxing to re-enter his life. He spent ten years surviving that struggle. Then the fire to compete was rekindled.

Ray hooked up with his old friend, Danny Thomas, who himself had an Olympic boxing tryout in 1984, to help get him back on track. Danny owns and operates The Rock'em Sock'em boxing gym in Evansville.

Danny's style of sticking and moving, then employing effective combinations was just what Ray needed when combined with Ray's innate strength and courage to be competitive on the national level. They worked hard for a long time and both sacrificed time and money. There were several disappointments in the beginning as Ray had to catch up with the best amateur boxers in America.

The early losses helped lead to an Indiana Golden Gloves Championship in 2005, then to two wins at the National Golden Gloves Tournament.

Last week's efforts in the National P.A.L. Tournament included wins by Ray over the fourth, then third, nationally ranked amateur boxers. His appointment in the semi-finals was with the number one ranked heavyweight. You know, sometimes those rankings are correct. Ray fought three good but not good enough rounds. I predict when Ray and the number one guy meet again, the rankings will reverse.

Ray went to last week's tournament to win an Olympic tryout. He did not quite accomplish his goal last week but he left the tournament a better boxer than when he went into it. He also left last week's tournament, much as John Bunyan's *Everyman*, a more determined person than when he entered it. Ray was back in Danny's gym Monday.

THERE BUT FOR FORTUNE

(Week of November 14, 2005)

In 1623, the English poet, John Donne, wrote "Devotions upon Emergent Occasions." Most of us were sentenced to read this in high school. You know, the "Bell Tolls for Thee" thing.

My particular "parole officer" was Mrs. Grinstead, my high school English teacher in 1961. Because we were convinced of our own wit, we called her Miss Grendel after the monster in Beowulf, the study of which was another condition of our probation.

Because we were teenagers and, therefore, indestructible, the lessons on empathy and concern for others that Mr. Donne and Mrs. Grinstead wanted us to glean from the poem could not compete with sports and other interests.

Now, forty years after my graduation, what used to be John Donne's vague admonition from almost four hundred years ago has come sharply into focus:

> *"No Man is an island, entire of itself;*
> *every man is a piece of the continent, a part of the main.*
>
> *If a clod be washed away by the sea, Europe is the less,*
> *as well as if a promontory were, as well as if a manor of thy*
> *friend's or of thine own were:…"*

At 2:00 a.m., on Sunday, November 6, 2005, my good friends, Gerald and Dorothy Rice, were awakened by a phone call from their son, Dennis, and his wife, Sherry.

> "Dad, are you and mom okay?"
> "What do you mean? It's 2:00 o'clock in the morning."
> "The weather channel says a tornado is heading directly across
> the Ohio River for your area and should be there in ten minutes;
> it's in Henderson, Kentucky now."
> "Well, thanks for calling. We're fine."

Gerald and Dorothy got up to check outside. Dorothy opened the door as Gerald heard a freight train crashing towards them.

Gerald used to be a professional boxer and still regularly trains with both professional and amateur fighters. It's a good thing as all of his strength and courage were called upon by the 200 mile per hour winds that blew the solid brick walls of their new dream home apart and tore the entire roof away. Gerald pulled his wife of fifty years back into the entryway and covered her with his body. Gerald and Dorothy were saved but lost everything accumulated over a lifetime.

Phil Ochs who was a better writer and singer of folk songs but of less commercial moxie than Bob Dylan wrote a song about empathy during the Sixties called, "There But For Fortune May Go You or I."

Ochs's nihilistic behavior, radicalism and eventual suicide off-put too many people. But his messages about the wafer thin differences between good and evil, success and failure, and life and death remain for future English teachers to exposit. A simple twist of fate may determine whose manor is spared and whose is destroyed.

I guess it's due to *The Wizard of Oz* and *Grapes of Wrath*, but most of us tend to think of Tornado Alley as meaning Texas, Oklahoma and Kansas.

Unfortunately, Indiana is as familiar with these whirling disasters as anywhere. In 1852, sixteen people in New Harmony were killed by an April 13th tornado. On March 18, 1925 Griffin was virtually eliminated by a twister that killed seventy-four people.

Posey County and the rest of southern Indiana have not been spared in the past or the present nor, I feel certain, will we be in the future.

I have begun to understand the lessons I should have learned in school and Sunday School. Hurricanes Katrina and Rita in Louisiana and Mississippi and tornadoes in Warrick and Vanderburgh counties affect me just as if it were my own home in harm's way.

Although I must digress to ask you why hurricanes have names but tornadoes do not. After all, what happened to Dorothy and Gerald seemed pretty personalized to me.

Be that as it may, I apologize Mrs. ~~Grendel~~ Grinstead. You were right. I should have paid more attention.

Gerald Rice served twenty-two years as an Evansville police officer in some of the roughest areas. He never was seriously injured. He, also, got in the ring with many very successful boxers who were much younger and larger than he. He always gave as good as he got and never got too badly hurt. Perhaps his boxing helped save his and Dorothy's lives.

By coincidence, I had been planning to write about boxing for this and a few subsequent weeks, especially boxing history in Posey County.

Perhaps next week, if Thor and his friends do not intervene again, and if you care to, we will discuss the sport that former heavyweight boxing champion and current minister, George Foreman, called: "The sport that all other sports aspire to be."

I COULD BE RIGHT

(Week of December 19, 2005)

Christmas time feels more like spring than winter. It seems more a beginning than an ending. This has always been true for me even though it is a time when the past permeates the present. I guess it's because so much of what I remember from Christmas feels so good.

Maybe the historians are correct; Jesus may have actually been born in the spring and this psychic rebirth occurs retroactively.

Metaphysics aside, it's Christmas time and my big sister, Janie, is still in charge of my two brothers and me just as she was when we were kids.

J.K. Rowling must have met Janie because Hermione from *Harry Potter* is her evil twin. How can one girl know everything? Especially, how can she always be right?

Most recently, Janie and I were discussing women and African Americans in public life. Well, actually, Janie was lecturing, she is a psychology professor after all, and I was trying to get a word in.

If given a chance, I might have had something to say. But I never got the opening. So you, Gentle Reader, who cannot interrupt, will get the benefit.

Janie says women and African Americans have been historically denied opportunities to engage in politics and business. She claims this is the fault of white, Anglo-Saxon men (such as her brothers!).

I say humbug! It's more a product of athletics. Athletics you say? Yes, I reply. Now isn't this a better way to discuss an issue?

As an example: from the year our United States Constitution was ratified, 1789, to 1951 only forty women served in the U.S. House of Representatives. But between 1951 and today 161 women have served.

And, in the United States Senate, from 1789 to 1978 only thirteen women served. However, since 1978 twenty women have served and fourteen of that twenty are there now. Why, that's 14%!

What about African Americans you ask? See, I listen to you. I answer: in 1966 there were six Black Americans in the U.S. Congress and today there are 43 members of the Black Caucus, thirteen of whom are women.

And, in 2001 President Bush appointed Colin Powell as the first Black Secretary of State and then replaced him with Condoleezza Rice, the first African American female Secretary of State.

Now, I know what you are thinking, and to be fair, I'll present your arguments for you. What does any of this have to do with athletics?

Well, I'll tell you. It was not until such Black men as Jesse Owens gave Hitler his comeuppance in 1936 and Jackie Robinson and Larry Doby broke into major league baseball in 1947 and college football admitted Blacks such as Prentice Gautt at Oklahoma in 1956, that African Americans were allowed to move across the tracks.

And, it was not until the heroics of such women as Althea Gibson and Babe Didrickson Zaharias in the 1940's and 1950's and Billie Jean King and Chris Evert in the 1960's and 1970's that women began to move from the parlor to the boardroom.

My sister says I am allowing correlation to confuse me. She says it's way too complicated to attribute these sea changes in self-perception and public acceptance to one cause.

Janie says my analysis is lame and that as with all complicated problems there is always a simple wrong answer. See, I told you she was a know-it-all.

My opinion is that when our great country began to allow, not require, girls and women and African Americans to compete in athletics on a par with white boys and men it sent a powerful message.

Tell my sister I'm right for once. What do you think?

PRESIDENTIAL POWER

(Week of December 1, 2008)

President-Elect Barack Obama declared to ESPN and Steve Kroft of *60 Minutes* that he planned to, "...[T]hrow his weight around a little bit," in support of a college football playoff system. He first made his position known on November 5th, 2008.

In response, or maybe even worse, in total nonchalance, ABC and ESPN announced just one week later that their agreement with the BCS football powerhouse universities and the NCAA would run through 2014.

The Big Ten, the Big 12, the SEC and the PAC 10 all have contracts with various television networks to broadcast their regular season college football games. Some of these contracts run through 2016. They involve hundreds of millions of dollars. Of course, Notre Dame has its own individual deal worth many millions of dollars.

Now, President-Elect Obama knows just a little something about the power of money and how to raise it. He must surely understand the enormity of the task of convincing the presidents of college football powerhouses to forego a share of this cornucopia; Thanksgiving indeed!

Each team that participated in a BCS bowl: Orange; Rose; Sugar; Fiesta and BCS Championship Bowl, last season received more than sixteen million dollars. That is more than Posey County's entire yearly budget for 2009. Maybe we ought to start a college and field a football team.

Now I know that coaching football is every bit as important to many Americans as solving the economic crisis and world peace. But does it not seem just a bit out of proportion that some football coaches make twenty times the salary of our country's president?

Of course, the presidents with the real power in this football playoff debate do not include the President of the United States. We must look to the presidents of the universities of Oklahoma, USC, Notre Dame, Texas, Ohio State, Florida, etc., to find where presidential jawboning has any influence in this debate.

President-Elect Obama, should he run for and win a second term, will be out of office by 2017. Some of the football/TV contracts do not expire until then. Mr. Obama is a lawyer. He knows how sacrosanct contracts can be, especially when they underwrite college students who go on to play in the NFL and then contribute big bucks back to their alma maters.

And by the way, if you harbor any thoughts that I have an axe to grind in this debate, I wish to remind you that I am an Indiana University alumnus. We do not need to worry about distracting our students from their studies by talk of BCS Bowl games as that is not a concern for us.

OUR CHINA WORRIES ARE OVER
(THEIRS ARE JUST BEGINNING)

(Week of October 23, 2006)

In the days of bomb shelters and godless "Red Hordes" of Chinese communists, many of our teachers and preachers warned us that "A billion Chinese" were planning on scaling their Great Wall and destroying Western Civilization.

As soon as Mao Tse Tung completed the "Long March" he and the Gang of Four began to devise our demise. Or so we were told. Remember Mao's famous retort when other world leaders would call on Mao's government to choose economic power over military hegemony? Mao said: "Power comes out of the barrel of a gun."

This caused me a great deal of angst as a child and kept me worried until recently when I read that several Chinese universities are starting to require their law and business students to take up golf, the "effete game of the elite", as an important part of their curriculum. Apparently now Mao would say: "Power comes from the head of a titanium driver."

We are thus saved from the culture that invented gunpowder and terrorized much of the known world for a thousand years with blitzkrieg-like cavalry charges and a policy of scorched earth. Well, those days are over. As proof, let me ask you, when did Scotland ever strike fear into anyone's heart, and they invented golf? Golf is probably what drove the frustrated Scots to invent scotch. No wonder they are so gloomy; and you thought it was their weather.

And what game was it that took one of our greatest warriors, Dwight David Eisenhower, and turned him into a ganglia of indecision and self-muttering? Ike even tried to use his presidential influence to get an offending elm tree cut down at Augusta National Golf Club; the elm still stands. So much for five-star generals and presidents up against golf.

I almost feel sorry for China. Think about a billion people fighting for tee times and hitting into one another. That reminds me of what one of our other presidents, Gerald Ford, said:

> "I know my golf game is getting better because I am
> hitting fewer spectators."

President Ford, who had played football for Michigan, finally admitted that golf was too tough a game for him.

Just as the United States suckered the old Soviet Union into oblivion on the arms race, soon the Chinese will be buying $400.00 golf clubs and losing $4.00 golf balls. That's about a year's pay for most of them.

And since China is a socialist country, instead of government money going to education, healthcare and armaments, golf courses will soon be springing up like mushrooms around cow pies.

Students who used to be rewarded for excellence in math, science and leadership will cast off those surly bounds of responsibility for golf holidays in Florida and Arizona. Just watch how quickly the trade deficit will shift.

I, for one, am looking forward to a billion Chinese coming to America to play golf. I figure surely I can beat some of them and I really like their food. And speaking of food, how many of us as children in the Fifties and Sixties were shamed into eating our vegetables by our mothers telling us about "all the starving children in China?" Shouldn't somebody worry about all those Chinese children being force fed their parents' dreams about their kid being the next Tiger Woods or Michelle Wie?

And, of course, I know from personal experience that once the Chinese get bitten by the golf bug, they will be so frustrated and preoccupied from searching for lost golf balls, and so broke from trying to buy a golf game, the world need have no further fear of "The Red Menace". They will be the ones seeing red.

THAT GOOD NIGHT

(Week of February 5, 2007)

My friend, Ann Greenfield, called me the morning of January 30th to tell me her friend and mine, Jim Kohlmeyer, had just fought his last round.

I like fighters. We all know what the final decision will be, but some "Go quietly into that good night", and some battle against all odds. I like the battlers.

I also like Posey County where the long-time Chairperson of the Republican Party and the long-time Vice Chairperson of the Democratic Party can be close friends.

Ann was crying when she called. If Ann had exited first, Jim would have felt the same way; although, we men are kind of funny about the crying thing.

Unlike most women who tend to face necessary surgery with quiet courage, most men would rather fight a grizzly barehanded than go under the knife. Perhaps it's thousands of years of women giving birth that allows for their stoic approach to pain. Or maybe they are just tougher than we are.

Anyway, every now and then a man comes along who refuses to go down without a fight, Jim Kohlmeyer to name one.

Jim and his well respected family have served our county well in many capacities. When I was the Posey County Attorney Jim's father, Carl, was one of our three County Commissioners. And Jim's mother, Mildred, served as our Posey County Assessor.

Most recently, just last month in fact, Jim graciously agreed to serve on the Recount Commission it was my duty to convene for the County Clerk's race. Jim knew such jobs are lose/lose propositions and unpaid to boot. I hope the strain of the recount did not make Jim's valiant struggle even harder.

But Jim's main public service was performed through his newspaper, *The Posey County News*. Being a newspaper editor in a small county is like being asked to mediate a family argument every day of your life. Forget about making most people like you. You are lucky if they don't stone you.

Jim was "fair and balanced" with a fine sense of humor, but that did not prevent parents of the next Larry Bird or upset candidates for public office from raining contumely upon Jim from time to time. Small town news reporting ain't bean bag.

As for me, and I know many of you, I will miss him sorely. I am glad you fought to the end, old friend. I expected nothing less.

CHAPTER SIX

JUDGMENT DAYS

HOW ON EARTH DID THAT JUDGE MAKE SUCH A DECISION!

(Week of May 30, 2005)

The past three weeks this column has been about the invasion of Posey County by Confederate soldiers on November 8, 1862. Those articles were offered by me as a Director of the Posey County Historical Society and as part of my personal column, *Gavel Gamut*. I hope you have enjoyed these stories about our interesting local history and that you may wish to help the Historical Society preserve and promote Posey County's rich history. If so, please contact the Society through our Director and Secretary Albert Gibbs at the Black Township Trustee Office, telephone number (812) 838-3851.

And although I might prefer to have the readers assume someone other than myself were responsible for the contents of this and future columns, the thoughts herein are solely mine unless otherwise noted.

Some of you may know that for several years I have served on the faculty of the National Judicial College located in Reno, Nevada. Judges from all 50 states and from many foreign countries attend this institution where America's most sought after product, our system of justice, is taught by judges to judges.

The National Judicial College has asked me to help teach several judges from Palestine in August of 2005. It has been my honor to work with Palestinian judges previously in 1998. I found them to be seeking the same thing we Americans are hoping for, justice.

I found this same hope among other foreign judges when the National Judicial College, at the request of the foreign countries, sent me to Kiev, Ukraine in 2000 and to Moscow and Volgograd, Russia in 2003 to teach their judges about America's legal system.

The Palestinian, Ukrainian, Russian and American judges are remarkably similar in their approach to their duties. Over the years the National Judicial College has identified several factors that are universal to good judicial decision making.

The overarching goal of trial judges whether in Posey County or Palestine is the same: Do justice in the case in front of the judge based on the facts of that unique case and the law that must be applied regardless of who or what is involved.

At the NJC judges are guided in this process to develop a standard approach to judicial decision making that can be modified as needed to the needs of any judge's jurisdiction.

Judges are taught to first analyze the pleadings and identify the issues in contention.

Next, the relevant facts as disclosed by the admissible evidence must be carefully and completely determined.

With a thorough understanding of the issues and the evidence, the judge must research the law to see how the specific legal system's rules, statutes and codifications, regulations, executive orders, and in common law countries such as the United States, case precedents, apply to that evidence and those issues.

Once this initial impression of what is fair, correct and legal is made by the trial judge, if the case is complicated, the NJC suggests the judge withhold making a quick decision while the entire case is ruminated on, often for several days. During this period, the trial judge is encouraged to return to the analysis frequently and with an open mind to the possibility of error by the judge in either fact finding, determination of the law or analysis of issues.

If the case is still unclear to the trial judge, and with notice to and the permission of the parties and their attorneys, the judge may seek input from other judges who have no personal interest or bias in the case. This process allows the trial judge to test the decision against hard analysis from experienced professionals who will not hesitate to point out any errors in the judge's preliminary decision.

This general system of judicial decision making when consistently followed has been found by the NJC to serve trial judges, and more importantly the parties, well regardless of whether in Indiana or Russia.

And, then, perhaps the people who disagree with an outcome in court will not have to wonder, why on Earth did that judge do that?

I WILL, BUT I AM NOT HAPPY

(Week of December 4, 2006)

Andrew Jackson is both famous and infamous for many things. As with many persons, great and small, Jackson is "credited" with statements that others may have wished he had made.

One of the most famous things that President Andrew Jackson never said was, "John Marshall (Chief Justice of the United States Supreme Court) has made his order; now let him enforce it."

In 1832, President Jackson and almost every member of Congress wanted American Indians to be out of sight and out of mind. Removal of Indians from the early United States required that treaties be ignored. One of those treaties involved the Cherokee tribe and white citizens in Georgia.

The Supreme Court ruled in favor of the Cherokees in the case of *Worcester v. Georgia*. Jackson and Congress fumed at this impediment to their plans of expansion. President Jackson railed against the Supreme Court and threatened to ignore its ruling.

Andrew Jackson was an attorney and a judge in Tennessee before he was the military hero of the War of 1812. Jackson believed in, but often complained about, America's system of checks and balances.

Jackson was sorely tempted to abuse the executive power of the presidency to go around the Supreme Court. However, he backed off and approached the Indian removal issue by other, legal albeit devious means.

Such acquiescence in the words of the courts, which have no power except that given to them voluntarily, is a characteristic of our government that is almost uniquely American.

People obey orders of American courts when there is no way the court could force them to do so. Why? It comes down to a matter of belief in our system of government. The Executive Branch executes the laws passed by the Legislative Branch and the Judicial Branch interprets whether certain laws apply to certain factual situations.

We may not like the judge who issues the order. We may disagree with the law the order is based on. And we may know there is little the judge can do if we defy or ignore the order. Yet, generally, we Americans swallow hard and move on.

Somehow we know, either consciously or subconsciously, that we want the system to continue to function for all of us as one of diffused power. We Americans distrust anyone or anything with too much power so we divide and conquer. And in America we rely on our courts to keep the Executive Branch, which has the guns, and the Legislative Branch, which has the power of the purse, in check. But courts must do this with neither police power nor the power to impose taxes. So where do courts get their power? Only from the consent of the governed.

Why do we obey court orders? Because we want to, even when we do not want to.

Next week we may ponder together why American courts are the forum of the powerless. That is, if you are not wealthy or powerful, how and where can you make your voice heard? In other words, why is it we Americans are fond of saying, "I'll see you in court!"?

THE PEOPLE'S FORUM

(Week of December 11, 2006)

If you are still recovering from Thanksgiving surfeit or are now hiding from Christmas shopping, you may have used this column as an aid to an afternoon siesta. If so, through the blissful fog brought on by sunlight outside and a fireplace inside, osmosis may have allowed some of the subject matter to seep in.

Americans and their relationship with their courts have been our recent concern. More specifically, why do we, as individual Americans, look to our courts when we want to protect personal rights and liberties? Why are we described as "A nation of lawyers"?

We often decry our "litigious society" but what we usually are referring to are court cases brought by anybody but ourselves. When we want to have our personal or property rights protected by our courts, we are sure our "resort to the law" is proper.

And why shouldn't we feel that way about our rights? What are our alternatives to a court case when we need our liberty, or our rights or our property protected? Can we, as individuals, get the United States Congress or the Indiana Legislature to enforce our rights? Of course not. Our legislative branch of government must address general needs for large segments of our population.

And can we look to our president or governor to send out the military or National Guard just for one citizen? That would be neither efficient nor constitutional, nor fair. Our executive branch must serve the general weal.

Of course, from a practical view, one person or a small group would not normally have the money or means to make themselves heard and heeded by either the legislative or executive branches of our federal or state government.

So, where can the "little guy" go to get relief from injustice or to get his or her rights protected? Why, an American court. Any citizen can seek redress for grievances through court for the price of a small filing fee.

Yes, it is wise and usually cost efficient to retain an attorney. But, in America, you can represent yourself should you be so inclined.

Every day, all across our great country citizens just like you (and maybe really you) file court cases for about one half the cost of an X-Box. They need not shoot or beat up someone who has wronged them. They need not live in bitterness or impotence when mistreated.

Instead, we in America can ask our fellow citizens to serve on a jury and listen to our complaints. Or we can ask a judge to analyze the facts and the law and tell us if we are entitled to what we seek.

I know, I know. We may not always agree with a jury's verdict or a judge's decision. That is part of the human condition, i.e., both we and our judges are human and subject to fallibility.

Folks, that is not the point. What is important is not that we may not always get everything we want in court, but that we can always go to court and try.

In most countries, the courts are no more accessible to the average citizen than a king is. In America, the poorest and most vulnerable individual can often call "the king" to task by filing a lawsuit.

Ergo, one of our most famous sayings, "I'll see you in court!", reflects much of what makes us different from most other countries.

LAW SCHOOL-YEAR ONE: WHAT'S A HO AX?

(Week of January 19, 2009)

Last week a friend of mine asked me, "What do they teach in law school?" You will note that he diplomatically did not ask, "What did you learn in law school?" I told him what law schools hype as their product is "legal thinking", i.e., "Come here and we will teach you to think as a lawyer."

Now I do not know about you, but when I heard that claim from my law professors, I got less meat from it than from cotton candy. My recurring thought was that if it took three years of agony to gain this one esoteric concept, why bother?

However, since everybody has to be somewhere and I was there, I determined that if lawyers thought so differently, I would try to understand their approach. Here is what I discerned was the essence of legal thinking as taught in law school.

Law School consists of three years. Each year concentrates on one of three principles: (1) consider matters from all sides; (2) try to analogize factual situations; and (3) follow precedent.

My freshman year was spent with professors who thought they were Socrates but who, in fact, were acolytes of the Marquis de Sade. Each class started with a statement of the general idea that we should look carefully at cases from every angle, then the rest of the semester was spent humiliating us into doing so.

Alas, if one of my brothers who went to law school before me had told me the following story before I finished my freshman year instead of the summer afterwards, I could have started with year two.

Anyway, here is my brother, Phil's, explanation of objective analysis:

> "A man comes to see his lawyer about a divorce. He tells the attorney that every time he tries to go upstairs to their bedroom his wife kicks him back down the stairs. The man said, 'I don't think she loves me any more.' The legally trained attorney responded, 'Either that or she just doesn't want you upstairs.'"

Now I know what you are thinking. What does this have to do with a Ho Ax? Well, let's say you were with my judge friend, D. Neil Harris, from Pascagoula, Mississippi, and you were talking about Big Foot. You might wonder if the whole thing is true or simply a Ho Ax as he would say. There it is, try to see a hoax from all angles.

Next week, we will start and complete year two of Law School. That is, we will if you have not already dropped out.

Judge D. Neil Harris
State of Mississippi Chancery Court, 16th District
Photograph by Peg Redwine

REASONING BY ANALOGY – YEAR TWO

(Week of January 26, 2009)

Those few lost souls who landed on level one of last week's law school *Inferno* and have now returned for a chance at level two will recall our topic was objective thinking.

Today we will joyfully immerse ourselves in how this ability to see cases from all sides can lead to deciding a current case by reference to a prior case that has similar facts. Law schools pride themselves on this analogical analysis.

So on day one of year two you might hear the following lecture from some ogre who never practiced law themselves but is confident they know how to teach others to do so.

> "Class, in the 1800's the American whaling industry was in full bloom. During a particular whaling expedition one company of ships had come upon and surrounded a pod of whales and was in the process of harvesting them when another whaling company's ships appeared. Some of the whales escaped the first company's encirclement and were then captured and harvested by the newcomers. The first company sued for loss of the whales. A court decided in favor of the second company on the basis that the whales were feral, wild in nature, and were equally available to all as long as they were not taken from the possession of another."

Then the devilishly devious law professor would say as if cautioning grade-schoolers to remember to have their crayons and scissors handy at all times, "Keep this case in mind."

We, or at least I, would then doze off as our brains glazed over listening to the drone of information about how judges can be led by well-trained lawyers to decide current cases by reference to similar past cases. Then some poor sacrificial lamb would be called upon, in front of the entire class. Let's assume his name is Jim Redwine.

> "Mr. Redwine, at the beginning of the American oil and gas industry one company (One) drilled a gas well but the gas escaped its well and was collected by a rival company (Two) nearby. Company One sues Company Two for the return of the gas. You are the lawyer for Company Two. How do you convince the trial judge to rule for your client?"

There I am, struck dumb in front of all those witnesses, as sweat forms on my brow and panic rises in my throat. Of course, the tender and understanding law professor slowly twists the knife with more vague and arcane questions as my classmates squirm in thanksgiving that they were not called on and in fear they soon would be.

> "Uh, Professor Vlad, would this have anything to do with the crises in the Middle East or O.P.E.C.?" "No, Mr. Redwine, it would not. Do you think any semi-comatose trial judge would be swayed by such a response? I suppose I will have to spoon feed you on this simple matter."

Then with an air of disdain and weary superiority, Professor Vlad the Impaler would "teach" us the second leg of "Thinking as a lawyer should think."

"You see, Mr. Redwine and class, the escaping gas is like the escaping whales, get it?"

My thought was and still is, why not just explain this to law students at the beginning and skip the water boarding? Anyway, you now have year two. Next week we will complete law school by studying the concept of deciding current cases based on earlier court decisions. This is called *stare decisis* or following precedent. See you back at the sweat shop next week.

STARE DECISIS

(Week of February 9, 2009)

Foreign phrases are to law professors as magic elixirs are to snake oil salesmen. For you see, law students do not find out until after law school that some of those who teach law in law schools are only teaching because they were afraid to try practicing law or because they tried and failed. For those types, Latin covers a multitude of sins.

One of the dangers of teaching law students to "think as a lawyer" is that after the first two years they may actually start to do it. And, if so, the third year students may begin to realize that some law professors are as irrelevant to practicing law as is that two day torture, The Bar Examination.

Therefore, in the third year some professors are more likely to obfuscate with Latin. For example, *stare decisis* is the Latin phrase that explains the third leg of "thinking as a lawyer". It means to: stand by the decision or follow earlier court decisions, i.e. follow previously set precedent.

It works like this. Say you were the judge in a case involving an interest in real estate given under a dead person's will. As a normal person you might think all that is required to make sure the dead person's wishes are carried out is to read the will, and most of the time you would be correct. But what if the dead person was trying to save his or her heirs from paying taxes? Why, you might have to look to past cases, the Rule in Shelley's Case from 1581 in England for example, where other judges decided similar issues. And since American law was originally based on English law, the old cases you might look to for "precedent" could go all the way back to the time of the Battle of Hastings in 1066.

Now let's assume instead of being the judge, who is, after all, totally immune personally from any bad effects of his or her decision, that you are one of the heirs of the decedent. How does it make you feel that your judge is looking for an answer in cases that were decided before Columbus stumbled upon America?

Take your family doctor for example. Say you went to your doctor because you had an excruciating stomach ache from appendicitis. If your doctor pulled out a one thousand year old parchment and prescribed bleeding, gold potions and leeches, you might be a little concerned. But American judges are trained to look to history to decide the present case. In fact, if there had been an earlier case with similar law and facts to the one you are involved in as a party, in some cases the trial judge <u>must</u> follow that decision unless it can be distinguished from your case.

Of course, it may turn out that your attorney can convince the trial judge that the Rule in Shelley's Case is as irrelevant as Latin phrases in today's world. On the other hand, your attorney may be a future law professor who has not yet realized he or she cannot and should not be entrusted with real people's lives.

Next week we will update our legal education by reference to the world in which we actually live.

LEARNING LAW

(Week of February 16, 2009)

Perhaps you suffered a similar fate to Peg during the recent inclement weather. She was stuck with me and several past versions of *Gavel Gamut* whose subject was: Learning to Think as a Lawyer. You, of course, did not have the full benefit of the articles as you did not have me to tell you how accurate the articles were and to hear me repeatedly read them aloud.

Be that as it may, you may recall that we broke down law school into: Year One – objective thinking or seeing cases from all sides; Year Two – reasoning by analogy, that is comparing a current case to an earlier case or cases; and Year Three – deciding cases according to *stare decisis* or past precedents, i.e., deciding a current case the same way an earlier judge or judges decided similar cases or distinguishing the earlier cases from our current case. You will note that we had pretty much concluded that law schools were to teaching people to actually practice law as Dante's *Inferno* was to describing heaven.

But unlike Faust, Paradise need not be Lost, law can be taught and, in fact, is learned every day after an attorney graduates from law school and begins working with lawyers, and even judges.

Regardless of your line of work, unless you are a law professor, you probably did not have a clue how to do the job you are now an expert in until you started doing the work under the watchful eye of an experienced mentor. If you were a law student, taught by law professors, and you went straight from being a law student to teaching law students, your inbred training simply carried on.

But let's say you were a nuclear physicist with a PhD. You might go to work for NASA where other physicists would teach you how to put a mouse on Mars. No one would have turned you loose right after college and put you in charge of rocket propulsion. Your mentors and colleagues would have trained you first.

The same is true if you were a cowboy. You might have a doctorate in animal husbandry from Oklahoma State University, but you would not be a real cowboy until experienced cowhands showed you the difference between a soon to be steer and a heifer and taught you how to create the former without injuring the latter.

And the same is true with legal education. Lawyers learn from experienced lawyers and experienced judges. It is a system that has given us about half of our United States Presidents including Abraham Lincoln. It is a good system.

AS THE TWIG IS BENT

(Week of December 22, 2008)

Passion can be a force for good. Divorced parents who feel deeply about their children can harness this passion for the benefit of the children and, per force, themselves. What is most required is a recognition that one's decisions about his or her children may be skewed by this passionate attachment.

If we acknowledge that our own decisions may be irrational due to deep emotions, we can more successfully deal with like actions and reactions from other people. For example, I am well aware that my loyalty to the Indiana Hoosiers is based on hope, not history.

After following the Hoosiers since 1963 and being rewarded with only one Rose Bowl appearance, you might think I would quit falling for, "Wait 'til next year!" Of course, we do have a new coach. We have some good young recruits. We have an expanded football stadium. Heck, I feel pretty good about our chances for next year. Besides that, John Mellencamp is often at the games.

Anyway, our thought processes are often based more on hope or dread than reality. This is strikingly apparent in divorce court. Parents love their children but can lose sight of the love they should retain for their ex-spouse who gave them these wonderful additions to their lives.

One device that counselors use to help divorced and separated parents work together for the benefit of their children is to point out that genetically one's children are exactly one-half one's self and one-half the ex-spouse's.

In other words, many of those characteristics that we find so sterling in our kids only exist because of the other parent. Another reason to recognize these genetic qualities is to help parents deal with any over reaction to traits in children that reflect those of an ex-spouse one is no longer enamored with.

So, how do we use passion to help our children survive, and even thrive, during and after a divorce? We can acknowledge our sometimes irrational actions and reactions are based on emotion, not reality. We can try to be tolerant of the other parent's irrational behavior. And because, unlike football, children's lives cannot be placed on hold until next year, we can accommodate the sometimes overly passionate behavior by the other parent in regards to the children.

How can we do this? First, we should accept our own failings, then allow for those of others. Next we should accept that most parents want what, they think, is best for their children. And, most importantly we must keep the lines of communication open. The telephone was a marvelous invention (although I am not so sure about cell phones).

When you get upset, pick up the phone and call the person you once loved and who gave you the children you now are tempted to fight over. Keep in mind that the irritating behavior we now see as foibles and crochets we once saw as endearing eccentricities. But especially at this time of year so special to us and our children it helps to, as Elizabeth Barrett Browning wrote, "put our passions to use" for the benefit, not the detriment, of our children.

THE CHRISTMAS SPIRIT

(Week of December 8, 2008)

Over ninety percent (90%) of all Americans and virtually one hundred percent (100%) of people in Posey County who profess a religion are Christians. About an equal number of the remainder of Americans who declare a belief are Muslim and Jewish. And the small remaining segment is made up of numerous other faiths. The Christmas Spirit is, in the main, what the season is about in the United States, and this is certainly so in Posey County.

Each of the various Christian sects may define Christmas and how it is celebrated a little differently. But hope, love, joy and generosity are a part of every church's Christmas doctrine.

And because Christmas is rooted in the story of Jesus' birth, children have always been the main focus for most people. We might decry the commercialism of Christmas, but we recognize this is supposed to be the most special time for every child of every Christian family.

However, one thing that is more certain than the arrival of credit card bills in January is the special acrimony that raises its ugly head in court in the weeks leading up to Christmas; Advent indeed.

There is something about the season that should bring out the best in loving parents that can sometimes bring out the worst. One sad statistic that Domestic Relations Courts can foretell with unerring accuracy is a sharp rise in divorced parents fighting over where and how their children will spend the Christmas holidays.

One parent may want the children to spend every second of Christmas Eve and Christmas Day with that parent and that parent's family. Another parent may want to control whether some new significant other can even be in the same house with the children. Perhaps a parent will want to remove the children from the state for the entire holiday. Parents may try to control every aspect of the other parent's lifestyle when the children are with the ex-spouse. Believe me, we have not skimmed the curdled milk off the top of the many permutations of how parents set out to ruin their children's Christmas.

Of course, in most situations, if both parents simply applied their Christian principles to the sharing of their children, these destructive behaviors would disappear. Unfortunately, there are some truly bad parents from whom children must be protected. Fortunately, they are extremely rare. For most situations, children are happier, healthier and more successful when both of their parents and both extended families are there to give love and support.

If you do not mind a little unsolicited legal lecturing and wish to follow along, I plan to write the next few columns about how courts and child rearing experts have attempted to put the Christmas Spirit back into some families' approach to this most important time in their children's lives.

Until next week, Merry Christmas!

SELF-INTEREST

(Week of December 15, 2008)

The Dutch philosopher, Benedict de Spinoza (1632-1677), posited that each human does, and should, strive to advance their own interests. When the interests of two people collide, both people will achieve more of their desires if they compromise. Spinoza believed that this pattern of competing self-interests is the basis of civilization.

Instead of denying our own desires, we should recognize that we are more likely to achieve what we want if we assert our desires while accommodating others.

In Sunday School or when our parents were explaining why we could not have everything our own way, this was called The Golden Rule. If you want justice, you should do justice. If you want all of the toys, you must realize so does the neighbor kid. More importantly, you should learn that if you and the neighbor kid fight over who should get one hundred percent of a toy, the toy may be destroyed by your fighting.

According to Spinoza and virtually every rational human since we began forming groups of humans, this is how societies are built and prosper. Of course, societies and families collapse when people do not compromise and refuse to acknowledge the desires and needs of others.

In other words, self-interest is not a bad thing. It helps motivate us to advance as individuals and groups as long as we accommodate the self-interests of others.

So when parents of minor children no longer live together, it can make their children miserable, especially during Christmas, if one or both of their parents or members of the extended families demand to control one hundred percent of the children's lives.

Indiana and several other states have addressed these issues by promulgating Parenting Time Guidelines. These guidelines can be helpful as an ultimate fall back position, but the children can still be torn, confused, frustrated and angry. The best guideline remains The Golden Rule. If the parents would put themselves in the place of their children or the other parent or the other parent's family, the one size fits all guidelines would not come into play.

As a family court judge who has from time to time seen the destructiveness caused by pride, jealousy, hurt feelings and stubbornness in domestic relations cases, I respectfully suggest that both parents are always happier if their children are happy.

And my experience has been that children have a much happier Christmas if the people they love most, their parents, put the children's interests first.

There is no need to cut the children in half. Recognition that one's own self-interest will be advanced by accommodating the self-interest of others is all that is required.

FOLLOW THE LAW

(Week of April 21, 2008)

As of January, 2008, one of every ninety-nine (99) adult Americans was behind bars. There were 26,983 adults in Indiana's twenty-one (21) prisons. Each prisoner costs Indiana taxpayers $19,202.65 per year.

Approximately sixty-seven percent (67%) of released prisoners are rearrested and fifty-two percent (52%) are re-incarcerated within three years of their release.

These costs do not include figures for lost productivity, welfare to families or new victims from unreformed criminals.

You may wish to check the figures for yourself. If so, see:

> http://in.gov/indcorrection/facts.htm ; http://www.pewcenteronthestates.org;
> and http://prisoncommission.org/report.asp

Over the years, people have frequently cautioned that the law must be followed and even revered. Such a sentiment is emblazoned in bronze on the war memorial statue on the courthouse campus:

> "A patriotism which readily responds to its country's call;
> a deep reverence for its laws; a decent respect for the rights of
> others; a sincere love of justice, truth and country are the
> best safeguards of a Nation's peace."
> **by Posey County native, John Corbin**
> **(July 23, 1908)**

Captain Corbin was one of our numerous Civil War heroes and a community leader of great generosity. Having risked his life to preserve our nation as one of laws, not men, he understood the crucial need to follow the law.

Another hero of that great struggle was Alvin P. Hovey who only ten years before the war helped write Indiana's 1852 Constitution. Both Hovey and Robert Dale Owen of New Harmony voted for Article 1 § 18 of Indiana's Bill of Rights:

> "The penal code shall be founded on the principles of
> reformation, and not of vindictive justice."

When people declare that they want judges to be "strict constructionists", are they calling for the wisdom of Posey County's Founding Fathers? If so, perhaps they want us to turn from hollow vengeance to reformative justice as it is defined by our Constitution.

I do not know about you, but when I see that Indiana spends forty cents on locking people up for every dollar we spend on higher education, I am ready to revisit the wisdom of Corbin, Hovey and Owen.

Over the next few weeks, I plan to write about Posey County's most recent effort to apply the Constitutional principles of Article 1 § 18. You may recall that Judge Almon of the Posey Superior Court and I, along with Prosecuting Attorney Jodi Uebelhack, the Posey County Bar Association and Sheriff Jim Folz, as well as numerous other entities and concerned citizens are looking to implement a Community Corrections project for Posey County.

I hope each citizen of our county will take an interest in this effort. After all, we are the ones who are paying for and are affected by our legal system.

SCHADENFREUDE

(Week of November 19, 2007)

As many in Posey County are of German ancestry, you may be well aware of this handy term that refers to pleasure one feels from another's misfortune. Of course, such reactions are not a Germanic trait but a human one.

We cannot help it. Seeing others in embarrassing situations brings out the worst in us. Most of the time our initial prurient interest is quickly replaced by empathy or at least understanding of the frailty of the human condition. But occasionally even the best of us calls for vengeance, not justice, and surely not mercy.

Posey County's representatives to Indiana's Constitutional Convention of 1850-1852 understood this common tendency to search for the mote in our neighbor's eye. That is why Alvin P. Hovey and Robert Dale Owen helped fashion a Constitution that demanded that:

> "The penal code shall be founded on the principles of
> of reformation, and not of vindictive justice."

One area where virtually every culture has overlapping ideals is the desire to punish others for prohibited behaviors.

Dante Alighieri in his *Divine Comedy* clearly enjoyed placing his personal and political enemies as well as members of other cultures and religions in his view of hell. One reason this work is considered a classic and that it is still read today after seven hundred years is because it touches our basest instincts. It is a well written piece of literature that serves the same purposes of today's *Jerry Springer Show*.

Some systems of criminal justice make vengeance the preferred method of dealing with wrongdoers.

Deuteronomy **19:21** holds:

> "Thine eye shall not pity. It shall be life for life,
> eye for eye, tooth for tooth, hand for hand, foot for foot.

But another approach is:

> "And as you wish that men would do to you, do so to them." (*Luke* **6:30**)

Indiana's Constitution falls squarely within this latter theory of positive reinforcement and understanding.

Instead of "Abandon all hope ye who enter herein", when one gets involved in our state's penal system, reformation, not punishment is the goal.

If you wish to read more about some of Posey County's current and planned for future approaches to complying with the wisdom of behavioral modification by positive stimuli, perhaps we can meet here again.

SELF-FLAGELLATION

(Week of November 26, 2007)

Some Christians in the Thirteenth and Fourteenth Centuries in Europe and some worshippers of Isis in ancient Egypt were among the numerous religious zealots who not only whipped themselves but sometimes even paid professional "flagellators" to whip them. These folks believed the pain purified them by expiating their misdeeds or that their suffering showed loyalty to their deity.

Today we eschew such practices as being based on superstition. However, we still often punish ourselves by spending huge sums of taxpayer monies to build and run jails and prisons because it feels good to punish others.

Of course, we must incarcerate dangerous and violent offenders. Some people just cannot be reformed. And justice for victims sometimes requires punishment for criminals; catharsis is a legitimate goal.

However, for much of today's prison population, the main victim of their illegal behavior is themselves. When society incarcerates such miscreants, we end up punishing ourselves as much as we fail to reform the prisoner.

Recently our Legislature has required that when an Indiana trial judge sentences a felon to prison that the estimated cost of the term be set out in the sentencing order. It is certainly a shock to see the penalty of the defendant visited upon the public in terms of dollars.

And while the law does not require that in juvenile cases the cost of placements be set out, the expense to house young people adjudicated for what would be crimes if they were adults far exceeds the cost to incarcerate adults.

As a law abiding citizen, you may be asking yourself why you should be that concerned about the cost of jailing someone who will not hold a job as you are doing, or about someone who prefers momentary gratification to obeying the law. Well, I will tell you. We simply cannot continue to pay the escalating costs of incarcerating people who are not a threat to others.

A very conservative estimate of the cost of one year in prison for one felon is about $20,000.00. And while such a cost might be worth it if society could be reasonably sure recidivism would be eliminated by removing someone for a year, the statistics belie such a wish.

Perhaps next week we can discuss some alternative approaches for non-violent offenders.

COMMUNITY CORRECTIONS

(Week of December 10, 2007)

The essence of Community Corrections is modification of behavior by means other than long term imprisonment. The goals are the punishment and discouragement of bad behavior and the rewarding and encouragement of good behavior. You have already surmised that the devil is in the details.

Examples of the two extremes of alternative sentences come to us from the ancient Greeks and Jesus. The Greeks, to whom we owe so much of our culture, even came up with sentences that punished beyond death.

Zeus was so upset with Prometheus for giving the blessing of fire to humans that he had him chained to a rock on Mount Caucasus for eternity. There vultures continuously ate at Prometheus's liver that kept regenerating so it could be eaten again. Ergo our expression, "Let him eat his liver."

Zeus, the king of Greek gods, was not one to trifle with. When the human, Sisyphus, attempted to arrogate himself to godlike status, Zeus sentenced him to an eternity of rolling a huge bolder up a high hill. The diabolical element of the sentence was that every time Sisyphus would get the bolder near the top, it would roll all the way back to the bottom.

Jesus on the other hand took a totally hands off approach. When the Jewish Pharisees (*Matthew* 20: 18 and 19) were plotting to condemn Jesus to death, they brought an adulterous woman to him for his views on her proper sentence (*John* 8:3-11). Under Jewish law, she was subject to death by stoning.

But Jesus told the Pharisees, "Let him who is without sin cast the first stone." Then, when the crowd dispersed, he told the woman, "Go, and do not sin again." You can see how this approach to sentencing would require that our judges be paragons of virtue themselves. It will, perhaps, not surprise you that judges often fall short of that criterion.

So, what are we to do if we do not want to condemn people beyond the grave or simply let them go with an admonishment to do the right thing?

Well, that is what our new Posey County Community Corrections Board will be tasked to figure out.

By including a large cross section of our small county, we have an excellent opportunity to devise various approaches to alternative sentencing that will protect and reimburse victims, help make offenders contributors to instead of drainers of our economic base and save large amounts of taxpayer money.

The existing Community Transition laws are designed to allow local communities to develop their own approaches to the inevitable return of convicted offenders. As they are sometime going to be back among us no matter what we do, it is in everyone's best interest to devise alternatives that allow for close supervision once their initial prison terms are served.

As we humans have learned from the times of the ancient Greeks and Jesus, some people are just beyond our powers of redemption and must be kept locked up. However, as most offenders can have their behavior modified by less expensive means, we owe it to ourselves to carefully consider the alternatives.

ALTERNATIVE SENTENCING

(Week of May 26, 2008)

Now that Law Day has been properly celebrated we can return to the topic of Community Corrections. You may have read about Posey County's most recent effort to comply with Article 1 section 18 of the Constitution of Indiana:

> "The penal code shall be
> founded on the principles
> of reformation, and not
> on vindictive justice."

Community Corrections/Alternative Sentencing is hardly a new approach. In 399 BC when Socrates was being tried in Athens on a charge of corrupting the youth by asking them to apply reason instead of blind faith, he set the standard for all judges. Socrates told the judges:

> " A judge's duty is, not
> to make a present of
> justice, but to give judgment;
> and judges are sworn to
> judge according to the laws,
> and not according to
> their own good or pleasure."

> Plato's *Apology Of Socrates*

Under Athenian law, and ours too interestingly enough, upon a person being convicted of a crime, the defendant was given the opportunity to recommend a possible sentence. The range of sentences for the crime Socrates was found guilty of ran the gamut from no punishment up to death.

As Socrates considered himself as providing a great public service by being "the gadfly of the State," Socrates recommended that he receive a reward for his "crimes."

The judges were not amused; they sentenced him to death. So much for alternative sentencing in ancient Greece.

But four hundred years later, Jesus was able to get the death penalty for adultery reduced to nothing by putting the onus on, "he who is without sin to cast the first stone." *Book of John*, Chapter 8.

This complete turn around in community corrections, i.e. from imposing the death penalty when a reward was suggested versus forgiving sin when the law called for the death penalty, pretty much defines the parameters of the issues we are facing with our rapidly expanding population of miscreants.

With a year in prison costing Indiana taxpayers almost $20,000.00 and the prisoner a year of his or her productive life (I am aware there are often non-productive or even destructive behaviors in play) we need to look for solutions. That is the goal of the Posey County Corrections Committee for non-violent offenders. Some folks are just too dangerous for Jesus' turn the other cheek approach to be chanced.

But part of the new program will involve a detailed background check and a risk and needs assessment.

Better restitution for victims, safer streets, and lower costs are the goals. Your Community Corrections Committee has been meeting since March. Next week I will report on our progress.

FACTORS IN SENTENCING

(Week of June 2, 2008)

As the crux of Community Corrections is alternative sentencing, perhaps we should discuss sentencing in general.

The Indiana Legislature, properly, sets the parameters that Indiana judges must abide by in determining sentences for crimes.

Trial judges are, properly, passive. Unlike some countries that follow an inquisitional model, under America's legal system, judges are reactive. Cases are brought to the judges by interested parties, the Prosecuting Attorney for example. Judges then determine what law applies to each case that is filed based on the facts of the case.

In criminal cases, the executive branch of state government is represented by each county's Prosecuting Attorney. Posey County's Prosecuting Attorney is Jodi Uebelhack. Law enforcement officers, usually, and lay people, sometimes, bring complaints to Ms. Uebelhack then she decides what, if any, crime should be charged.

Once a person is charged, a jury or a judge determines guilt or innocence. If a person is found guilty, the judge sets the sentence.

Not only are judges bound by the statutes defining a particular crime and sentence, but the Legislature has promulgated a vast array of sentencing guidelines that a trial judge must follow. Considerable discretion is afforded to sentencing judges in Indiana. However, judges are not allowed to devise whatever sanction may "feel right".

Every crime has particular elements that must be proven beyond a reasonable doubt. Also, every crime has a set range of possible sentences.

In general, a judge must consider the evidence introduced at trial, the offender's background and the range of available sentences pursuant to the applicable statutes. Of course, there are numerous other factors that may need to be considered such as harm to any particular victim and deterrence of future crimes.

Most judges seek consistency, what the public might call fairness, in setting sentences. Similar sentences for similar crimes and similar defendants is the ideal. Naturally, since no two cases have identical facts and no two people have identical backgrounds and character, fairness does not mean that for the violation of the same statute all defendants should receive identical sentences.

So you might wonder, how does a particular judge arrive at a "fair" sentence for the violation of a particular statute by a particular person? One way is for the judge to have a general sentencing philosophy that guides the judge in all sentencing. As for me, the following general goals are what I am trying to achieve with any sentence:

1. Compliance with applicable laws;
2. Similar results for similar people with similar cases;
3. Deterrence of future bad behavior;

4. Encouragement of future good behavior;
5. Punishment of current bad behavior;
6. Rewarding of past good behavior;
7. Punishment of past bad behavior;
8. Rewarding of current good behavior, e.g., no harm to victims or police;
9. Inspiration of confidence in the legal system; and
10. Economic efficacy and efficiency.

Your Community Corrections Committee consists of several members, each of whom has her or his own sentencing philosophy. We plan to try to identify the best parts of all committee members' ideas and then apply them to our county's unique needs and abilities. The process is underway.

PLEA BARGAINING AS ALTERNATIVE SENTENCING

(Week of June 9, 2008)

Should you have followed the column recently you may recall that our topic has been Posey County's Community Corrections Program. The local Committee has been in both plenary and sub-committee meetings for about a month. Progress has been made, but our long journey remains long. Amid the concepts of the program is the use of alternative sentencing to avoid an expensive imprisonment. Of course, public safety is a major concern so persons allowed to participate in Community Corrections types of dispositions must be carefully screened and carefully monitored. This is not a new approach. In my opinion, Posey County's legal system has long taken the view that safety for victims and rehabilitation for offenders are compatible goals. Plea bargaining is a concomitant element of this dual approach.

In plea bargaining, the Posey County Prosecuting Attorney, Jodi Uebelhack, and her Chief Deputy Prosecutor, Kelli Fink, represent the county's interest while a particular defendant's attorney represents him/her. The trial judges, Judge Almon of the Posey Superior Court and I are the neutral arbitrators. The judges, through our probation departments, are fully informed about an offender's background and any possible risk imposed to the public. Judges always retain the authority to accept or reject a particular sentence.

With the prosecutor looking out for the public's interests, the defense attorney making sure the defendant's rights are protected and the judge serving as an objective gatekeeper, huge amounts of time and money are saved in Posey County every month and justice can be administered in a consistent, fair manner.

Our Community Corrections Committee has members from law enforcement, the prosecuting attorney's office, the defense bar, the public, probation and both Posey County courts. Therefore, when criteria are finally established to determine what alternative dispositions will be available for which categories of offenders, all segments of our county will have input. It will not, officially, be "Plea Bargaining" but, in effect, it will have many of the same elements. And, I, for one, believe this will be a good thing for our community.

As the Committee works to establish the guidelines and elements of Posey County's Community Corrections Program, I urge each of you to approach any of us on the Committee and offer your insight and ideas. This is an important endeavor, and it will require collective effort and wisdom.

Committee Members
President: Scott Funkhouser
Secretary: Mark Funkhouser
Judge: Brent Almon
Prosecuting Attorney: Jodi Uebelhack
Sheriff: Jim Folz
Circuit Court Chief Probation Officer: Rodney Fetcher
Director of Posey and Gibson Counties Department of Child Services: Susan Blackburn

County Councilman: Dallas Robinson
Red Cross Director: Walt Brunton
Director Of The John Emhuff Opportunity Center: Jeannie Harshbarger
Southwestern Mental Health Center: Bob Stephens
Ron Neuman
Pat Bartlett
Katherine Hast
Clarence Nelson
Kim Mullen
Jean Hadley, Esquire
Jim Redwine

THE BATTLE FOR AMERICA

(Week of September 11, 2006)

The right to serve on a jury is like the right to vote. We do not get to do either very often and they are both vital to our form of government. Of course, these two building blocks of our democratic republic are also similar in that some citizens choose to never do either.

But, for those of you who do both, and especially to those of you who serve your country while serving on a Posey County jury, thank you.

For, as Attorney George Boldt said when addressing the United States Supreme Court in 1959:

> *"Jury service honorably performed is as important in the defense of our country, its Constitution and laws, and the ideals and standards for which they stand, as the service that is rendered by the soldier on the field of battle in time of war."*

And, since I currently have a son serving our country in battle in Iraq, you may assume, Gentle Reader, that I do not cite this homage to jurors lightly.

Posey County has a proud tradition of jury service beginning with that first Posey County jury in the new state of Indiana who were called to serve by Judge Isaac Blackford, our first circuit court judge. The jury sat on a log and rendered their verdict, "So say we one, so say we all."

Since that first jury trial in 1816, thousands of Posey County citizens have given of their valuable time to help resolve conflicts among their friends and neighbors and to assure that Posey County's legal system remains within the control of those who must rely upon it.

During the twenty-five years that I have been presiding over jury trials in our county, I have had many satisfying experiences. But one of the most interesting to me as a judge, who often worries about whether I have made the best possible decision in cases, is when the jury returns its verdict and looks for some sign from me that they have done the right thing.

There is that gnawing dark side deep within me that, in spite of the better angels of my nature, sometimes cries out: "See, until you were called upon to make these difficult decisions, you thought my job was easy." However, after only a brief moment, this uncharitable thought is overwhelmed by my gratitude to those who accept the solemn duty of judging their fellow human beings.

Of course, I am not allowed to indicate in any way whether I agree with the actual decision of a jury. All I can do is thank them for performing their difficult service.

It is the willingness to listen to the evidence with an open mind and apply the law in a fair manner regardless of personal prejudice that helps keep America worth fighting for, whether on the battlefield or at the polls or in the jury box.

Jurors need not doubt their verdicts nor do they need affirmation from me. As long as jurors would not hesitate to be judged themselves by a juror such as themselves, they have done the right thing, i.e., their duty.

YOUR JURY RIGHTS

(Week of July 23, 2007)

Most of us tend to think of jury service as an obligation of citizenship. We do not want to serve but, for the good of our country, will do so if called. It is a little like how many of us felt about the draft.

On the other hand, if we needed a jury of our peers, we would appreciate our fellow citizens stepping up and taking the oath.

And what most of us see as a responsibility is, also, one of our rights. Each of us is entitled to be fairly considered for jury service. After all, we may wonder about the fairness of the legal system. Or we may believe that we have as much ability to be fair and impartial as anyone else, including any judge.

It has not been so long ago that certain segments of our citizenry were absolutely forbidden to serve on juries.

Even in free Indiana, Negroes were not included in jury panels until near the Twentieth Century. And even after Negro men over twenty-one who had property and voted gained the right to serve, few Negroes ever actually served because peremptory challenges were used to strike them.

As for young people who could die for our country at eighteen but could not serve on juries until they were twenty-one, it took the Vietnam War to convince lawmakers to let them serve.

From our country's founding until 1921, women had no right to vote or serve on juries. Finally, the Nineteenth Amendment to the United States Constitution was ratified in 1920. An interesting piece of Women's Suffrage and the right to serve on a jury is preserved in our historic courthouse. When school children come to tour the courthouse, they are always intrigued to see the "modesty screen" tacked over the front of the jury box. When I explain it was placed there in 1921 to protect the ankles of Posey county ladies from public view, the students, especially the girls, are amazed.

But once again, just because women had to be placed in the jury pool it did not guarantee their right to serve. Peremptory challenges based solely on gender were common.

As recently as 1986 in a line of cases beginning with a case out of Kentucky, *Batson v. Kentucky* (1986), 476 U.S. 79, the United States Supreme Court began to establish that impermissible criteria such as race, gender, religion and national origin could not be used to deny a citizen his or her right to serve on a jury. In 1994, the United States Supreme Court held in an Alabama paternity case where the State removed male jurors to achieve an all female panel:

> "The Equal Protection clause prohibits discrimination in
> jury selection on the basis of gender, or on the assumption
> that an individual will be biased in a particular case solely
> because that person happens to be a woman or a man."
> **J.E.B. v. Alabama** (1994), 511 U.S. 127.

It is a little like Tom Sawyer's famous fence. When we think of jury service as a burden, it does not sound so good. But when we realize what many of us have had to go through to preserve our right to serve, well, sign me up!

I'D CHOOSE A JURY

(Week of August 13, 2007)

If you are unable to resolve a dispute with your neighbor or should you be charged with a crime, you may end up in court. If so, what do you want and what do you expect?

Of course, we all want to win and we want to win on our terms. But what do you expect? Should you be a viewer of T.V. courtrooms, you probably expect to be berated by a pompous sarcastic jerk. You notice they never show any "reality" jury trials, only black-robed tyrants who revel in putting down people who cannot strike back.

In the real world, the right to a trial by a jury of one's peers is the antidote to black-robe fever. If I ever have to go to court for anything but my job, I want a jury. Or at least I treasure my right to ask for a jury trial. Just the thought that I could take my case to my fellow citizens for justice would make me more comfortable with my day in court even if a judge decides the matter.

And, more importantly, just the knowledge that the judge can be bypassed, keeps any judge who might be too full of himself or herself more aware of their proper role.

Two of the best checks on judicial tyranny are the right to free and open partisan elections of judges and the right to a jury trial. Of course, the best check is having judges who understand that the power they may wield is not theirs personally; it belongs to the people who pay their salaries.

But for the past few weeks this space has been concentrating not on elections or judges who may mistakenly think they are divine but upon our sacred right to a trial by our peers. Therefore, I'll just recap where we have been.

First, the column examined the history of our pre-computer jury selection process. Then the roles of the jury commissioners were discussed. Next, our current computer-aided system was addressed. Now, the most important part, actual jury trial service, will be the focus.

Last week, about fifty of our fellow citizens were involved in what is the very best part of America's legal system, a jury trial. After having been randomly selected by the computers from the Posey County Voter Registration and Bureau of Motor Vehicle records, these good citizens responded to a summons to appear at the Courthouse for a trial in Circuit Court.

After being sworn, the whole group, the venire, answered general questions from me and then groups of twelve were examined by the attorneys for the two sides. The attorneys selected a final group of twelve to hear the evidence and decide the guilt or innocence of another of our fellow citizens.

The jury contained Posey County residents at least eighteen years of age who had no knowledge of or personal stake in the case. They were of both genders, varying ages and diverse backgrounds. Not one of them ever raised their voice to anyone else or acted as though they were better than the person on trial.

Almost all of the court cases in Posey County are decided by a judge without a jury. And that's okay by me so long as everybody, especially judges, know that our right to be tried by our fellow citizens is always an option.

HALF-A-LOAF OR A PHYRRIC VICTORY?

(Week of July 24, 2006)

About the time that the New Millennium began, mediation was made mandatory in the Posey Circuit Court. I thought that this was a Twenty-First Century approach to resolving conflicts in our county. Then I came across W.P. Leonard's 1882 publication of the *History and Directory of Posey County* (page 81) where he quoted an eyewitness account of how the Rappites of 1817 decided disputes.

> " '… [D]uring the whole period of their residence in America …there has not been a single lawsuit among them. If a misunderstanding or quarrel happens, it is a rule to settle it before retiring to rest, thus literally obeying the injunction of the apostle: Let not the sun go down upon thy wrath.' "

It may not surprise both of you who read this article that our famous religious community applied a "turn the other cheek" mentality to legal matters. But even our secular frontier justices saw the benefits to "mediation". One of my favorite Posey County cases involved the famous bird painter, John James Audubon, who lived in Henderson, Kentucky from 1810 to 1819. We may think of Audubon as a conservationist due to his marvelous depictions of America's birds. However, he had to first shoot and mount them before he painted them.

So, it should not be a surprise that he, also, engaged in the trade of animal pelts. According to *Leonard's History* (page 33), Audubon made an agreement with a Posey County trapper to provide Audubon with one hundred raccoon skins. The hunter failed to come up with the pelts and Audubon sued him before a Posey County Justice of the Peace, Jack Anthony, whose "court" was near a ferry across the Ohio from Henderson.

Justice Anthony was neither a lawyer nor a judge, but I was duly impressed with his court-mediated solution. When the hunter complained that he could not comply with the contract because his coon dog had been killed, Justice of the Peace Anthony ordered Audubon to loan the hunter Audubon's own coon dog. Then he ordered the hunter to supply the skins.

To seal the deal and assuage any hurt feelings, Justice Anthony then had the local constable, Wat Bryant, to procure a quart of whiskey from a nearby trading boat. Drinks all around "satisfied the parties". Now that's an approach to settling cases we Twenty-First Century judges could learn from.

Next week, if you want a warning, I will tell about one of my brothers who thinks my mediation approach is all wrong. Brother Phil's position is if you are entitled to the whole baby, then, by gum, get the whole baby or die trying.

Such a "resolution" of legal disputes often falls within the ambit of Phyrric victories. Pyrrhus was a king in ancient Greece. In 279 B.C., Pyrrhus's army defeated an army of Romans at the

Battle of Asculum. In the process of winning, the Greeks lost much of their army. King Pyrrhus noted that another such "victory" would do them in.

Still, my brother says, "Compromise is simply surrender without a white flag." Of course, I note that when it comes to "suggestions" from his wife of forty years, he is much more prone to mediate his position. If you are so inclined next week, we will discuss these differing approaches: Mine—fair and reasonable mediation; or Brother Phil's—all out war!

WHOSE CASE IS IT?

(Week of July 31, 2006)

One of my brothers is a lawyer so, as you might expect if you have a brother, he and I occasionally disagree about the relative merits of judges.

About once each season of each year, I will answer a telephone call that begins something like this: "Can you believe what that idiot did to my client's case?" Of course, I know I am in for about ten minutes of a diatribe on the failure of some other judge to make the right decision, i.e., to agree with my brother.

Now this is the brother that I mentioned in this column last week who thinks court ordered mediation is akin to surrender in the face of battle. He is a fighter for justice and, by definition, compromise of a just claim cannot be justice. It may be expedient, but it just ain't right. If your cause is on the side of the angels, then stick to your guns and the devil take the hindmost. [Phil still uses clichés from our small town, 1950's upbringing.]

So after enduring about a solid week of anti-mediation arguments from Phil when Peg and I went to Oklahoma over the Fourth, I was surprised to get a call from him yesterday that opened this way: "Hey, Jim; I got that estate case settled. You know, that one we talked about that I have been working on for three years. We settled it the day before it was set for trial."

I asked him how it came out and he said, "Well, you remember that I advised my clients when they first came to me that I thought the likely outcome would be a splitting of the family proceeds among the relatives, but that a judge or jury might go either way. That is, they could win it all or lose it all. They were upset with their relatives over the deal— you know how these family things can get— so they just wanted their day in court."

"Well, what happened? Why did they end up following your advice after three years?"

"Jim, you just won't believe it. We had one last face-to-face meeting with the other side and their lawyer and a mediator and it all worked out. Their lawyer had apparently advised his clients the same as I had mine, but they, also, wanted it all, or more likely, they just didn't want my clients to get anything. But after the mediator pointed out the merits and the weaknesses of each side's position, the family began to talk like a family again."

"Anyway, when they realized that they still cared about one another and after the attorneys and the mediator warned them that no one ever knows what some crazy judge will actually do in court, they settled it and went away together to have a family dinner. It was just like when we were kids, the boys we fought with were better friends after the fight."

I just couldn't let it alone. After sixty some years you'd think I'd have a clue, but with one's siblings you just want absolute victory. So, I said, "I guess now you see the merits of court ordered mediation." Phil jumped on that like he used to jump on me.

"Court ordered mediation my eye! Why, what that other lawyer and the mediator and I did to get the clients to be reasonable was tell them that the last thing they needed to do was leave their fate in the hands of some judge. We just told them it was their case and they better keep control of it. The only thing the courts did to help was act as a boogey man!"

"Hey, Phil, remember that two foot putt you missed that gave me the match and made me the Redwine Family Fourth of July Golf Champion for 2006?"

PEACEMAKERS

(Week of July 17, 2006)

Abraham Lincoln urged his clients to settle their cases out of court. He, also, urged political compromise right up to the time the South bombed Fort Sumpter. You might question Abe's compromise credentials by raising that Civil War thing. However, as is generally acknowledged, politics is the art of compromise. And, as Karl von Clauswitz said, "War is simply politics prosecuted by other means."

Regardless of these philosophical niceties, Jesus had it just right, "Blessed are the peacemakers." And when you come into a court in Posey County, you will have every opportunity to heed this admonition. For, if the peacemakers are blessed, then the corollary of the Prince of Peace's aphorism must be: Damned are those who encourage conflict.

In most types of cases arising in the Posey Circuit Court, the parties and their attorneys must meet face-to-face and discuss their differences. Frequently the attorneys and I are told, sometimes vociferously, that there is no way the case can be settled so there is no reason to meet. This is particularly prevalent in domestic relationship cases such as divorce or child custody matters.

For years, I have been bemused by the number of spouses and parents who have lived together and produced children together, but who suddenly cannot talk to one another. I suppose it goes back to that old adage that there is no war like a civil war.

Our pride gets in the way and a desire for revenge for wrongs, real and imagined, is sometimes stronger than our ability to be rational. Our self-interest or even the best interests of our children get lost in the primal urge to control others.

But when parties are required to discuss the often-visceral issues such as where a property line between neighbors should be or where the kids should go to school, most people can begin to see the case from both sides.

And, when the parties and their lawyers are unable to come to a fair resolution, a trained and certified mediator is selected who objectively aids the disputants to resolve their own differences.

The advantages to these self-devised solutions are many. People can get on with their lives. They save a great deal of money. They are happier with their own agreements than they would be with a court-imposed outcome. They can go back to being good neighbors or friends or even family once the bitterness and anger subside. They do not have to avoid eye contact or going to church or school meetings where their erstwhile adversaries might be.

As Saint Francis of Assisi admonished himself, "Let there be peace on Earth and let it begin with me."

In short, if an article this long can be called short, the peacemakers are blessed.

MEDIATION AND PLEA BARGAINS

(Week of June 13, 2005)

Our old friend Abraham Lincoln who knew a little about compromise and conflict said:

> "Persuade your neighbors to compromise whenever you can. As
> a peace-maker, the lawyer has a superior opportunity to be a good
> person."

My experience with people who must finally come to or are brought to court supports President Lincoln's advice. People may obey a judge's orders out of fear of possible consequences, but their own agreement will usually be adhered to willingly.

"I'm not going to do it and you can't make me unless you ask me nice." That's a quote from one of my two brothers. He would work like a Trojan if our older brother and sister appealed to his sense of fairness and duty, but he wouldn't do squat if ordered.

People know their own situations, desires and culpability far better than any judge or jury could ever divine from clashing evidence and arguments. What does a person really want? What did a person really do and intend?

If parties, with the help of their attorneys, an experienced mediator or a judge in a less formal setting, work together to resolve their conflicts, society is better off.

It costs Indiana taxpayers about $20,000.00 per year to house an inmate. We know that eventually almost all persons convicted of crimes are released. If we are spending all this effort and money to lock up people, isn't it more productive and safer if when they get out they are not bitter? A fair plea bargain requires that only the guilty are convicted and that they publicly admit their guilt. This allows for more consistent sentencing and better attitudes on the part of victims and defendants.

In civil cases, incarceration is not an issue, but compensation, reconciliation and continuing relationships are often important considerations.

In domestic relation cases, for example, parents are still parents after they are no longer spouses. How much better is it for families and all of us for parents to work out their own arrangements with professional guidance?

And in disputes between business associates, ongoing relationships are more likely to survive a settlement than a trial.

The art of politics is compromise. War is politics by other means. War is bad. Compromise is good.

Ergo, mediation is mandatory and fair plea bargains are approved in the Posey Circuit Court.

"Blessed are the Peacemakers."

THE 94% SOLUTION

(Week of June 15, 2005)

For anyone out there who may have read last week's column on Mediation and Plea Bargains in the Posey Circuit Court this is a continuation of that topic.

I do know that Peg read it because I refused to get off the couch and clean the garage until she did. This week's column may require dinner and a movie.

Regardless of the location of the court, in America about 94 out of every 100 cases of all types are eventually disposed of without a trial. These outcomes include voluntary and involuntary dismissals, settlements and default judgments among others.

Since we know that almost all cases will end without a trial, the goal is to achieve a fair non-trial resolution as quickly as justice allows. This saves the parties involved, and society in general, time, money, emotional damage and lost productivity.

Also, while only about 6% of cases will require a trial, by more efficiently disposing of the other 94%, more time and effort can be devoted to achieving just results in those cases which must be tried in court.

In the Posey Circuit Court, each court reporter has an area of responsibility. For example, Katrina Mann is primarily responsible for processing all probate and criminal felony matters; Becky Rutledge shepherds the domestic relation cases; Kristi Hoffman oversees civil plenary matters; and Ashley Thompson handles claims for court budgets and guilty plea and sentencing transcriptions. Of course, each court reporter has many other duties and they work together to make sure the cases are serviced.

When a new case is filed, the parties are instructed to meet as soon as possible at a pre-pre-trial and attempt to resolve all issues. Many of our cases are settled right then. But, if not, the court reporter sets up mediation for the parties with a certified mediator. This stage eliminates many other controversies before matters between the parties can worsen.

Of course, the parties retain their right to their day (or days) in Court if these efforts are not effective. And by eliminating most cases from the court's docket, the remaining cases can be tried sooner. Agreements are usually good, but justice is not to be sacrificed on the altar of expediency. Some cases must and should be tried. Even well intentioned people cannot always reach a fair resolution on their own. Also, some matters impact other people not directly involved in the case. For example, some controversies concern the public which has a right to be informed and, perhaps, involved. Matters involving environmental concerns, public safety and the expenditure of public funds come to mind.

Because courts can be used to assuage injuries and redress grievances, I feel deeply honored to serve as a judge in our fair county. By the time a case gets to a judge to decide in court, the parties have usually gone through several attempts to resolve it without trial. Maybe they have tried for years to live with a situation as neighbors. Perhaps they have then discussed it themselves. Next, they may ask a friend or a clergyperson to help them alleviate the problem. Someone or all of them may seek advice from their family lawyer. If the attorneys cannot help get the matter resolved, a lawsuit may be filed. Then, after pre-pre-trials, mediation and repeated attempts to settle the case fail to put matters right, the parties go to trial and say, "Hey, judge, help us solve this problem."

Of course, almost all such cases end with people not fully happy as people usually prefer their own solutions. But, at least, they have a decision and can move on. And, after all, that is part of what judges get paid to do. As Alexis de Tocqueville said, "*There is hardly a political* [and many other type] *question in the United States which does not sooner or later turn into a judicial one.*" And that is generally a good thing or at least better than the alternatives.

This 94% solution, <u>i.e.</u> the pre-pre-trial and mediation procedure, has been in place in the Posey Circuit Court for several years now. Its purpose is to help alleviate ill will, save time and money and, perhaps, to help in some way to make our county a more pleasant and productive place to live. For as we all know, ours is a rather small county where one often runs into people or their family and friends the next day after a disagreement has occurred. It is better to make a good faith effort to resolve problems than try to avoid all public places for the next few years.

SACRED HONOR

(Week of December 18, 2006)

The men who revolted against the most powerful nation on earth in 1776 supported their Declaration of Independence with a mutual pledge to each other of their: "Lives, Fortunes and Sacred Honor."

Their honor was as important to them, and to those who relied upon them, as their lives. The guiding principles for graduates of The United States Military Academy are Duty, Honor and Country. Honor was the touchstone of such West Point graduates as Eisenhower, MacArthur, Bradley and Schwartzkof.

"Upon my honor I will do my best to do my duty…." pledge those who pursue the high ideals of scouting.

When we are deciding whether or not to accept the decisions and actions of others we often look first to their reputation for honesty and integrity. When the public is asked to have confidence in the outcome of important controversies, it is usually more a function of the regard in which the participants are held than of the niceties of the various non-human elements.

Most of us have fallen short so often ourselves that we do not expect perfection in others. However, we do require good faith effort and impartial performance of public duty.

That is why when we need people to accept the mantle of difficult public service, such as the recount of a close election for an important public office, we look first to their reputations.

In a democracy, what could be of more importance than public confidence in the outcome of an election? In a small place where "everybody knows your name", what could be of more importance than the reputations of persons who determine such an outcome.

We in Posey County just participated in an election for one of our most important public offices, Posey County Clerk. It must have been important to many of us as it resulted in two extremely nice and competent ladies dividing the votes almost fifty-fifty. No one could fault anyone for wanting a Recount Commission to take a closer look.

Under our law, the Circuit Court Judge is asked to select the three members of such a Recount Commission. I did so.

Now, if you were selecting citizens for such an important, difficult and thankless task whom would you select? Who would be hesitant to say to you, "Are you crazy? Why would I want to spend my Christmas season maybe making at least half the county mad at me?" Who would say yes to such an onerous burden? Whom could you impose upon to work for almost nothing at such a tough job? Why, people who had often given of their time and talent before.

So, just as you would do, I called upon three men who have been well known for many years to be generous and hardworking and fair. Men whom many of you, also, know personally. Men who had absolutely nothing to gain from performing this extremely important public service.

But it was not enough that these men be well known for public service throughout our fair county. This vital duty had to fall upon men to whom honor is more important than partisanship.

These three men who were once again called to serve are Sam Blankenship, Jim Kohlmeyer and Mel Levin.

Enough said, except for THANK YOU!

NOW WHAT?

If you have ever run for elected office and been so unfortunate as to win, you understand what Joseph Campbell meant when he said to Bill Moyers:

> "When someone becomes a judge, or President of the United States, he is no longer that man, he's the representative of an eternal office; he has to sacrifice his personal desires and even life possibilities to the role that he now signifies."

Campbell taught mythology for thirty-eight years at Sarah Lawrence College. As Campbell told Moyers:

> "Mythology teaches you what's behind literature and the arts.... Mythology has a great deal to do with...our initiation ceremonies [such as an inauguration]."

In explaining how myth helps us cohere as a culture and a nation, Campbell told Moyers:

> "When a judge walks into the room, and everybody stands up, they are not standing up for that guy, they are standing up for the robe that he's wearing and the role he is going to play."

Campbell pointed out how a soldier putting on a uniform is performing another mythological ritual where the individual gives up his or her personal life and takes on a life of service.

Of course, there are other such roles, but the significant element of someone going from a candidate to an inaugurated president is a subjugation of personal desires to those of the society he or she serves.

John McCain is a military hero who understands the power of symbolism and mythology. In his concession speech he urged all of his supporters to join him in healing our country.

> "I wish Godspeed to the man who was my former opponent and will be my president."

A good soldier knows the importance of the chain of command and the symbolism of accepting a subordinate role.

Obama's election night speech showed his understanding that he had moved from a candidate to a symbol:

> "This victory alone is not the change we seek—it is only the chance for us to make that change.
>
> …
>
> [T]he true strength of our nation comes not from the might of our arms or the scale of our wealth, but from the enduring power of our ideals…."

As Campbell explained, once we accept the mantle of office, our culture's expectations as contained in our particular mythology prevent turning the office over to personal prejudices and preferences.

See: *The Power of Myth* by Joseph Campbell as told to Bill Moyers (1988).

Posey County, Indiana

1875 Map

CHAPTER SEVEN

BETWEEN THE OHIO AND THE WABASH

LIFE ON THE OHIO

(Week of May 21, 2007)

Samuel Langhorne Clemens spent two and one-half years (1858-1861) as a Mississippi River steamboat pilot after he had learned the newspaper trade. For the young man who took his nom de plume, Mark Twain, from that experience, his time on the river was the happiest of his whole life. His marvelous writings may make us happy, but what made him happy was navigating the river.

To avoid the sawyers, submerged trees that could sink boats, and snags, floating trees, a riverboat pilot had to be alert and adroit. And as the steamboats often traveled at night, the successful pilot had to have the entire river from Cairo, Illinois to New Orleans, Louisiana memorized.

In his book, *Life on the Mississippi*, Twain described the lives of both the river and those who used it. And it is no coincidence that in his classic novels, *Tom Sawyer* and *Huckleberry Finn*, the Mississippi River symbolizes joy and freedom.

For those of us who have the privilege of living on the banks of the Ohio River, when we are feeling sorry for ourselves an hour spent in solitude sensing the beauty and majesty of the river is Mother Nature's home remedy.

As I gaze out the third story windows of our courthouse, the Ohio languidly flows on towards Mark Twain's Mississippi at Cairo. The longest river in North America, the Missouri, pours into the Mississippi by St. Louis. So, when these three mighty waterways join together on their way to the Gulf of Mexico, almost all of the old Northwest Territory and the Louisiana Purchase are represented.

It is not difficult to imagine oneself rafting along with Meriwether Lewis and William Clark in 1804 as they looked up at the high bluff on the north side of the Ohio, i.e. what we call McFaddins Bluff.

And only seven years later our ancestors were amazed when the first steamboat to pass this way came into their view. According to Leffel's *History and Directory of Posey County*, 1882, at pages 105-106:

> "When the steamer (called the New Orleans) came into full view at the head of the bend six miles above McFaddins Bluff, the residents of that place were so frightened that they fled to the woods, supposing that the devil was out on a lark and would do them some injury should he come in reach of them."

Seeing a belching, billowing, churning paddle-wheeler for our early settlers must have been somewhat like seeing a U.F.O. for us.

However, it was not long before steamboats were regularly plying our river and docking at our front door. After all, one could travel downstream on a steamboat at up to sixteen miles per hour. No wonder Samuel L. Clemens was more excited by being a riverboat pilot than a newspaper columnist.

STEAMBOATS REIGNED

(Week of May 28, 2007)

Posey County saw its first steamboat in 1811. And in 1913, according to Leffel's *History of Posey County*, page 187, steamboats remained the king of transportation:

> "The steamboat line on the Ohio River connects Mt. Vernon with all the
> river towns both east and south and brings the markets of Cincinnati
> and Pittsburgh into easy access. Smaller boats connect with the towns
> up the Wabash, making transportation cheaper than by railroad."

According to Leffel, in 1913 we had three steam powered train lines and one electric train line in Posey County. The Illinois Central connected Poseyville, Stewartsville and New Harmony with Evansville. The Evansville & Terre Haute connected Mt. Vernon to Terre Haute. The Louisville & Nashville opened the central part of our county to the county seat then to Evansville. And the electric line ran as a trolley to and from Mt. Vernon and Evansville. Yet this proliferation of rail lines could not best the steamboats for the transportation of goods to and from other markets.

One might have preferred to send his farm products or manufactured goods via semi-tractor-trailer rather than wait the extra time for the steamboats to wend their way to, say, New Orleans. Or one might have opted to send her dress goods over the more expensive but faster rails. Of course, in 1913, Henry Ford's Model T was only five years old and there were no semis or passable roads to drive them on. And as to the railroads, even though they stopped in the major towns of Posey County in 1913, for most farmers and business people time was not as critical to their profits as the cost of transporting them. But by 1920, automobiles, trucks and roads had revolutionized the transportation of goods and people. The United States had been transformed by World War I, 1914-1918. Although we did not enter the war until April of 1917, we had begun to ramp up the building of roads and the manufacturing of vehicles soon after the war began.

World War I did not turn out to be the War to End All Wars, but it did greatly accelerate the dethronement of steamboats as the monarchs of the middle waters.

YOU READ THEM?

(Week of June 11, 2007)

The other night Art Bayer, Jr., called me to say he had read my columns about steamboats on the Ohio and Wabash Rivers. If you know Junior, you know that my first reaction was, "Oh, no. I never expected anyone to actually read the columns. But, if anyone did, I sure hoped it would not be anyone who knew the subject matter. And I really did not need Posey County's number one expert on river transportation to read them!"

Well, such is the life of a newspaper pundit; sometimes you cannot slide by. And not only is Art our Port Authority authority, he is a member of that Greatest Generation. Further, he is one who served in Patton's Third Army in 1944-45. It did not help that Junior called me on D-Day, June the sixth.

When my family and I moved to Posey County from Evansville in 1976, Art Bayer was one of the first to go far out of his way to welcome us to this fine community. While he had nothing to gain from his generosity, we did. His attitude and that of others like him made all the difference to us. But I was not eager to have Junior recognize that this person he had befriended was not exactly up to snuff on his favorite Posey County attributes.

Okay. I girded my loins up about me and asked, "Hey, Junior, how bad were they?" Of course, I really knew I was taking no chances as Art is far too much the gentleman to ask me what he probably wondered, i.e., "Jim, were you ever even on a riverboat?" Instead he simply deflected the artillery rounds by saying, "I have some historical information about the rivers if you'd like to have it." My relief was such that I almost forgot to respond.

So, I walked over to Art's house where he loaned me some extremely interesting charts on boat landings along the Ohio and Wabash dating from just before World War II when we could hear the rumblings from Europe but were still hoping to avoid the inevitable.

The Wabash River is described as, "rising in Grand Reservoir, Mercer County, Ohio, and flowing in a generally westerly direction across the Ohio-Indiana State boundary to Covington, IN, thence generally southwesterly to join the Ohio River about ten miles above Shawneetown, IL (848 miles below Pittsburgh, PA)." The White River is denoted as the principal tributary to the Wabash. And the Wabash is about 475 miles long with an average slope below Lafayette, IN of .63 foot per mile.

I do not know about you, but this was news to me and of interest besides.

Art Bayer and his recently departed wife of 59 years, Marty, represent what made the Greatest Generation the greatest. They started with nothing and with others of their generation brought their home county along with them into the thriving economy we enjoy today. And while they were doing it, they showed the kind of class most of us can only hope to emulate.

As to the surprise revelation that someone other than Peg had actually read the columns, I can only surmise that Art was sucked in by the clever and misleading "steamboating" titles to the articles.

POSEY COUNTY ARTISTS

(Week of February 23, 2009)

Peg and I recently attended an out-of-state gallery showing of contemporary painting. No doubt the work was full of meaning from talented artists. However, I had a hard time appreciating the genius behind globs of paint without definition. Fortunately, Peg, who thoroughly enjoyed making lions and angels out of green circles and orange squares, was there to jab me in the ribs when I started to exclaim, "What the devil is that?"

On the other hand, when Peg became enamored with a particular work, I was able to completely dissuade any possible purchase by reference to the fancy, if almost incomprehensible, brochure on prices.

Those works of art were not nearly as satisfying to me as the sketches by Anne Doane, the photographs by Becky Boggs, the oils by Maggie Rapp and the watercolors by Bob Pote, all of whom live in Posey County. And each one of these talented artists generously contributes their fine work from time to time for worthy causes.

Anne Doane has allowed the Posey County Historical Society to use and reproduce her interesting drawings of Posey County landmarks such as each one of our courthouses and the old Brewery Hills School.

Becky Boggs's excellent photographs of the interior and exterior of our current courthouse give an artist's perception of what makes our history significant and unique. Two of Becky's photographs were selected for the "Courthouses of Indiana" calendar for 2008. This calendar was published by the non-partisan Mike Downs Center for Indiana Politics.

Anne's sketches and Becky's photographs also appear, by generous permission, in my favorite historical novel, *JUDGE LYNCH!*.

Maggie Rapp's oil painting of our 1876, and current, courthouse was selected by the Posey County Bar Association to represent the concept of law in our county. Her beautiful painting now hangs in Indianapolis at the offices of the Indiana State Bar Association. And, thanks to the Posey County Bar Association, the first numbered print of Maggie's lovely painting hangs over my desk at home.

Bob Pote has been painting for over half-a-century. His watercolors are full of light that illuminates the interior of structures as it opens one's mind and senses. Bob has recently contributed his vistas of downtown Mt. Vernon to the River Bend Coalition to help raise funds. Also, due to his generosity, Bob's delightful paintings facing east and west from the roof of our courthouse grace the walls of our 107-year-old converted barn-home. (And, no, I did not raise the original barn!)

And both Bob and Maggie contributed their fine artwork to the 2009 Santa Clothes Club and Albion Fellows Bacon Center fund raising calendar. Maggie's interpretation of the altar in New Harmony's Roofless Church lifts one's spirit and Bob's rendition of an Upton Road barn on a snowy morning puts one's mind at peace.

Thank you Anne, Becky, Maggie and Bob for doing what I only wish I could.

Winter at Upton Road

Mt. Vernon Early Years

Paintings appear by permission of Robert Pote. www.robertpotewatercolor.com

HOMETOWN HISTORY DAY

(Week of November 12, 2007)

I know that both of you who claim to eagerly await the arrival of this column may be disappointed that this week's topic is not the promised scintillating exposition of Community Corrections. Fear not, a plethora of exciting articles on such "specialty courts" will be forthcoming.

However, between last week's column and this one, my wife, Peg, and I had the opportunity to be involved in Hometown History Day held at Austin Funeral Home the afternoon of November 4, 2007. It was the product of several people's ideas and efforts, not mine I regret to say, although Peg provided able technical assistance and sage content control for a game of Posey County History "Jeopardy"!

While I will surely miss several important contributors whom others are urged to write in and recognize, I believe that Linda Young, Merle and Bill Gillenwater, and Pat and Cherie Cron contributed significantly to the planning and execution of what, I hope, will become the impetus for the creation of a Posey County museum. Sam Blankenship and others have called for such a museum for several years. A museum could serve as a focal point for future development and preservation of past accomplishments.

Sunday's numerous contributors of rare, interesting and important items from our county's history included Wayne and Patsy Culley, Sarah Carr, Anne Doane, June Dunning, Becky Higgins, the Moose Lodge, several churches, the Posey County Historical Society and many more that should be named and thanked. Please do so if you have the opportunity.

One of my favorite contributors was Ilse Horacek whose book, *It Was Written*, was given as a valuable door prize. Peg was one of the lucky winners.

Our most recognized Posey County landmark, our 131 year old county courthouse, appeared in many photographs and sketches. Becky Boggs contributed a series of excellent color photographs depicting the outside and inside of the courthouse since its most recent renovation was begun. And Rodney Fetcher used his consummate skill as a video and Power Point expert to create a legal history disc that was quickly claimed as a prize by several people.

Larry Harms displayed a portion of his valuable Civil War collection including a Union uniform that he wore. Larry and his wife live on Seibert Lane in Mt. Vernon. Larry is extremely knowledgeable on Posey County's involvement in the Civil War and he is, also, a Civil War re-enactor.

On a personal note, I was struck by how much Larry, with his full mustache and blue wool Yankee uniform, looked like my family's photographs of my great-great-grandfather who served with the 44th Indiana Volunteers.

And I must thank Larry for his generosity in giving me an original publication of *Confederate Veteran* in which Richard Dale Owen of New Harmony is honored by his former inmates for his humane treatment of southern prisoners of war when he was commander of Camp Morton in Indianapolis. The Rebel side of my ancestry would have been proud.

A true highlight of the afternoon was provided by Posey County's World War II historian, Harold Morgan. Harold lives on Smith Road in Posey County, and his e-mail address is hmorgan@ evansville.net. Harold has a wealth of information about southern Indiana's contribution to the war effort and he held the audience's rapt attention as he spoke.

One of the areas Harold covered was "Rosie the Riveter" workers, the women who did so much to aid in the supplying of the troops. As Harold was talking, local resident, Geraldine McFadin, raised her hand and volunteered that she had worked on the assembly line as a riveter. The crowd gave her a well deserved ovation.

Such important, interesting and perishable historical information as "Rosie-Geraldine" should be preserved. Perhaps more "Hometown History Days" will lead to a Posey County Museum. Without a central repository our valuable and unique history will slowly disappear and be forgotten.

Maybe the generous citizens who initiated and so splendidly carried out this event will be joined in the movement for a county museum by the many others who treasure our history and believe in planning for our future.

MT. VERNON RIVER DAYS

(Week of September 22, 2008)

When I was a kid, my favorite church activities were the covered-dish dinners. Sunday School was okay and my mom and dad were a lot easier to live with if I at least pretended to benefit from the service. But the pitch-ins required no acting; they were always great. It did not occur to me why this was so until this past weekend as I was thinking about the First Annual Mt. Vernon River Days.

The similarities between those satisfying old covered-dish dinners and such events as last week's River Days, New Harmony's Kuntsfest, Poseyville's Autumn Fest and several other county gatherings came clear to me as I watched Peg weed the flower beds.

I got to enjoy the results and did not have to do anything. My grandmother's potato salad, Mom's fried chicken, Mrs. Swiggart's sweet potato casserole and Mrs. Cummings's German chocolate cake still linger in my stomach's memory. I showed up. I ate until I got sick. And I went home. No preparation, no clean-up, no hassle.

Seldom have I enjoyed a *strassenfest* as much as I did River Days. It was well-organized without hidebound restrictions. It was entertaining without demands for one's undivided attention. It was relaxed, varied and rewarding.

As both of you who regularly read this column are undoubtedly aware, these events do not simply spring full grown from the head of Zeus. I did not have to do anything, but a whole host of people did. As it is not possible for me to name all the hard working generous contributors, I will name the 2008 Mt. Vernon River Days Committee and just a few others.

Since I must, due to space restriction, leave many out, please write to the editors of *The Mt. Vernon Democrat, The Mt. Vernon Western Star, The Posey County News, The Carmi Times*, and *The Evansville Courier and Press* and give credit where due. All of these papers helped advertise River Days and make it a success.

First let me thank and commend Jerry and Marsha King and Larry Harms for giving of their time and knowledge in their portrayals of Civil War General Alvin Hovey and his wife, Mary, and Union private John D. Martin. I learned a great deal from each of them and know many others did also.

Next, I will list the members of the Committee and their functional areas: Becky Higgins, Chairperson; Larry Williams, Co-Chairperson/Fundraising; Judy Whitten, Secretary/PR; Sally Denning, Treasurer; Jerry Walden, PR and Kiwanis Car Show; Jesse Montgomery, School Events; Kay Kilgore, Food Booths and Events; Randy Owens, Events and Food Booths/Electrical; David Whitten, Sound/Bandstand; Tom Ertel, Electrical; Don Baier, Logistics; Jerry King, Historical; Sheri Banks, Vintage Photos; Tammy Weatherford, Vintage Photos; Randy Stapp, Lions Club/Fireworks; Mayor John Tucker, City of Mt. Vernon.

I hope we can continue this wonderful event for many years. As for me, I plan to enjoy the benefits immensely, just as I do when Peg weeds the flowers or as I did when the church ladies provided those marvelous covered-dish dinners.

ABRAHAM LINCOLN IN POSEY COUNTY

(Week of March 2, 2009)

On Sunday, February 22, 2009, at the Alexandrian Public Library, the Posey County Historical Society hosted a celebration honoring President Lincoln.

Last Sunday was the 278th anniversary of President Washington's birth (February 22, 1731), and it was just past the 200th anniversary of President Lincoln's (February 12, 1809).

Due to the special significance given to Lincoln's 200th, and because Abraham Lincoln had several direct and many indirect connections to Posey County, the Historical Society wished to particularly honor him. Of course, George Washington and Abraham Lincoln were our greatest presidents. Without Washington there may not have been a United States, and without Lincoln it may have dissolved into, at least, two separate countries.

George Washington never made it to Posey County but several Revolutionary War veterans did. Mt. Vernon, the erstwhile McFaddins Bluff, was named in honor of General Washington.

However, that Abraham Lincoln did come to Posey County on more than one occasion is a well accepted fact. According to Posey County historian, Jerry King, Lincoln may have visited Posey County several times.

Jerry and Marsha King have studied Posey County's rich history for some time. They have a particular interest in Alvin Peterson Hovey and his first wife, Mary nee James Hovey. Sunday, Jerry donned his impressive Civil War uniform as Major General Hovey and Marsha wore her lovely hooped skirt as Mrs. Hovey.

Alvin Hovey and Abraham Lincoln both studied law by reading the same volume of *Blackstone's Commentaries on the Law*. This well known treatise was loaned to both Alvin Hovey and Abraham Lincoln, at separate times, by Judge John Pitcher who lived in both Spencer and Posey Counties. Lincoln studied the work while he and Pitcher lived in Spencer County, and Hovey suffered through this weighty tome when he and Pitcher resided in Posey County.

Another re-enactor at Sunday's celebration, Larry Harms, wore a Union private's regalia and shared his original Civil War artifacts with the audience. One of those artifacts was the actual diary of Private John D. Martin who served with the 25th Indiana Infantry Regiment. Martin came to Posey County from Kentucky to join the northern forces. Martin and Hovey met in Mt. Vernon in July of 1861.

Martin and Hovey fought at Shiloh and numerous other significant battles. They were both true Civil War heroes.

Not only were General and Mrs. Hovey and Private Martin at the library to celebrate Lincoln's birthday, old Abraham himself showed up! Former mayor, Jackson L. Higgins, appeared with stovepipe hat, black suit and beard and gave a rousing rendition of *The Gettysburg Address*. Becky Higgins, as President of the Posey County Historical Society, introduced President Lincoln.

Janet Mann and Beth Dingman provided and served the refreshments, and several other members of the Posey County Historical Society helped with the program. These members included: Linda

Young , Debbie Travers, Don Pierce, Wanda Griess, Ilse Horacek, Bob Webster, Beverly Tucker, Donna Creek and Posey County Bar Association President, Don Baier. Undoubtedly there were others there to whom I apologize in advance for unintentionally omitting.

This celebration was officially recognized by Mayor John Tucker who was in attendance. For, just as in those days when Abraham Lincoln helped dedicate the bridge at Grafton, Posey County still claims the famous Rail Splitter as our own.

Presidents Washington and Lincoln received the honor they both richly deserved from Posey County last Sunday. And, as to Abraham Lincoln, he was not just a national hero, he was well known personally to Posey County. Our county can proudly claim him not just as an icon but, also, as a friend.

THE JAMES GIRLS

(Week of March 16, 2009)

In this 200th year since the birth of Abraham Lincoln (1809-1865) we have been musing about Lincoln's connections to Posey County. As with our own lives in which attenuated coincidences lead to unexpected results, happenstances involving Lincoln led to surprising results in Posey County.

Lincoln lived from 1816-1830 in Perry (later reconfigured into Spencer) County. While there he borrowed books from Judge John Pitcher whose young son, Thomas, hung on Lincoln's pants leg.

Lincoln moved to Illinois with his family and Pitcher moved to Mt. Vernon, Indiana after his first wife died. Pitcher practiced law here and served as a Common Pleas Judge, a sort of justice of the peace. Pitcher, also, loaned the same books Lincoln had studied to Alvin P. Hovey (1821-1891).

In 1849 and 1850, Lincoln rode the law circuit through fourteen counties in Illinois. His frequent companion was his friend and fellow attorney, William Harrow (1822-1872). Harrow moved to Indiana in the 1850's and married Juliette James, who was the daughter of prominent Mt. Vernon banker, Enoch James. Juliette's sister was the lovely Mary James whom Alvin P. Hovey courted desperately. Her father would not allow the marriage until Hovey established his law practice.

Thomas Pitcher was appointed to the United States Military at West Point, New York, from which he graduated in 1845 and then went on to serve with distinction in the Mexican War (1846-1848) during which he was severely wounded. Pitcher rose to the rank of general and served throughout the Civil War. In 1866, he was appointed Superintendent of West Point.

Brothers-in-law Hovey and Harrow both became generals in the Civil War. Harrow had a command at the Battle of Gettysburg where on July 3, 1863 his men helped repel Pickett's Charge which may have been the single most important fight of the war.

Hovey was personally promoted to major general by President Lincoln after Hovey's bravery and brilliance at the pivotal battle of Champion Hill during the siege of Vicksburg. It took Lincoln's position as commander-in-chief to give Hovey this promotion as William T. Sherman took exception to it in a sharply worded communiqué to Lincoln.

Lincoln's future power as president would have seemed a ludicrous possibility if raised to John Pitcher when Lincoln was a poor, uneducated farm boy. Surely Harrow had no thought that his friend who had gone broke running a small store in Illinois and who had lost his first run for public office would be in a position to make Harrow a general.

And not in his wildest fantasies could Alvin P. Hovey, who was a poor, ignorant fifteen year old orphan when he first sought success, have dreamed he would have two direct connections, Pitcher and Harrow, to a president.

And from Posey County's viewpoint, how likely was it that three local Civil War generals would arise from such colliding minor coincidences?

UNEXPECTED CONNECTIONS

(Week of March 9, 2009)

Alvin P. Hovey wanted to fight in the Mexican War (1846-1848). He formed and led a unit of men from Posey County to do so. The war ended before Hovey and his men could take part. Hovey was sorely disappointed by this development.

At about the same time Hovey was trying to enter the war, Dr. William A. Bowles of French Lick, Indiana, was a colonel leading the Second Indiana Regiment. Bowles was popular with his men and other officers until the confusing battle of Buena Vista where the Mexicans overran the Second Indiana.

Part of the Second fell back, they claimed on the order of Colonel Bowles, and the rest of the Second, along with Bowles, fell in with a Mississippi regiment commanded by Jefferson Davis, yes, that Jefferson Davis.

Davis commended Bowles to Commanding General Zachary Taylor for Bowles's gallantry in the battle and Davis and Bowles became life-long friends. Unfortunately, the men of the Second Indiana Regiment who got separated from Bowles and fell back were accused of having fled from the battle. These men never forgave Bowles or Davis for these accusations.

After the Mexican War, William Bowles went back to French Lick and continued to be involved in the practice of medicine and the business he started about 1840. That business was the original French Lick Springs Hotel that Bowles marketed by advocating the medicinal powers of the water from the sulfur springs there.

Alvin Hovey came back to Posey County where he practiced law, participated in Indiana's Constitutional Convention of 1850-1851, served on the Indiana Supreme Court and served as Judge of the Posey Circuit Court. In 1861, he formed a new regiment and fought with distinction in the Civil War (1861-1865).

In 1864, Major General Hovey was appointed military commander, Provost Marshall, of Indiana. In that capacity, he had the authority to control military tribunals that investigated acts of treason.

One William Bowles was accused of fomenting rebellion against the Union by his actions in the Copperhead organization, The Knights of the Golden Circle. Hovey's military tribunal found him guilty and sentenced him to hang.

President Lincoln commuted his sentence to life in prison. Bowles was released after the war and died in French Lick.

Of course, we cannot know if Bowles' connections to the President of the Confederacy contributed to Hovey's suspicions and resentment. Nor can we know if Hovey's disappointment in the Mexican War or his feelings about General and future President Zachary Taylor's praise of Bowles gallantry affected the charges against Bowles twenty years later.

We can safely assume that had Hovey been the one who fought next to Jefferson Davis, the lives of several people could have gone quite differently.

WESTWARD HO!

(Week of August 27, 2007)

I do not know how you normally think of the early white settlers of Posey County, but, in general, I see them as hardy adventurers. However, as to New Harmony in particular I conjure up images of devout adherents to Father George Rapp's visions or free thinking intellectuals applying Robert Owen's views of the Enlightenment.

In other words, I do not usually think of the two main groups of early New Harmony pioneers as pioneers, at least not like I do the rough and tumble group who established the first Ohio River beachhead at McFaddins Bluff.

So it was a reality check for me to read about the group of fortune hunters who left New Harmony on April Fools Day in 1850 for the glitter of California gold. In the *Journal of William Fowler Pritchard: Indiana to California 1850; Return via Nicaragua 1852*, the editors describe the group as consisting of about twenty-one people and more than eight wagons: James Bennett, Mr. and Mrs. Samuel Bolton, William Bolton, Miles Edmonds, William Faulkner, George Hamilton, Jonathon Jackson, Ira Lyon, John Mills, John O'Neal, Mitch O'Neal, Mr. Otzman, Mr. Combs, Mr. Mitchell, Mr. Pullyblank, the leader of the party a Mr. W.J. Sweasey along with his wife and two children, and William F. Pritchard.

Earl and Phil Pritchard who edited William Pritchard's journal mention other accounts of Posey County's involvement in the Gold Rush and conclude that about seventy-eight people from Posey County had their names associated with this particular search for quick wealth out west. Such a number rivals Posey County's losses from the cholera epidemic of about the same time.

In later columns perhaps the names of some of these other gold fever sufferers can be mentioned. As pointed out by the editors of Prichard's journal, it is extremely difficult to accumulate accurate names and numbers from the various accounts of the time. Be that as it may, it is without question that the same spirit that brought Posey County's early settlers here originally burned brightly in the many individuals who helped blaze our country's western expansion during the Gold Rush almost half a century later.

One wonders what affect such a huge drain of some of our most energetic men, ninety percent of gold seekers were adult males, had on our county at the time. Who filled their roles at home and work? How did their families, farms and businesses fare? How did they communicate without cell phones and e-mail? And for those who did make it back to Posey County after a long period of separation, what was left?

Hey, I just ask the questions. Perhaps you can delve into your own family's Posey County history and help answer them. Let me know what you find out.

GOLD FEVER

(Week of August 20, 2007)

Horace (Buddy) Greathouse claims that he has read this column from time to time. He did not say whether he liked it. Regardless, as a member of two of Posey County's earliest families, he cares deeply about our interesting history. So, when he brought me a book about William Fowler Pritchard, Buddy's mother was a Pritchard, he loaned it only on condition of "return it or else."

This journal is an eyewitness account of Mr. Pritchard's travels from Posey County to the California gold fields and back (1850-1852). If you want to know what such an arduous adventure was like, I highly recommend this account compiled by the father and son team of Earl and Phil Pritchard: ISBN 0-87770-569-0; published by Ye Galleon Press in 1995.

William F. Pritchard and his wife, Florence (MacDonagh) Pritchard, immigrated from England to New Harmony before the gold strike at Sutter's Mill in 1848. Although Florence and William had five young sons and Florence was pregnant, William caught gold fever and left New Harmony on April Fools Day in 1850 in search of his fortune. He kept the journal of his great adventure in six notebooks written in pencil. The editors had to make assumptions about the meaning of several of Mr. Pritchard's entries.

Pritchard traveled from New Harmony to Sacramento almost entirely on foot. The trek out took him through Illinois, Missouri, Nebraska, Wyoming, Idaho, Nevada, and halfway across California. He arrived in Sacramento on September 27, 1850.

As the journey out by land was so dangerous and difficult, he returned via ship from San Francisco to San Juan del Sur then overland to San Juan del Norte, Nicaragua. Then he took a steamship to New Orleans. From New Orleans he caught a steam-powered riverboat up the Mississippi to the Ohio at Mt. Vernon. From Mt. Vernon, he walked the remaining fourteen miles back to New Harmony. The return trip began August 11, 1852. He arrived home about one month later. Pritchard wrote that his roundtrip was a distance of five thousand miles.

In reading Mr. Pritchard's eyewitness account of the Great American West in 1850, I was impressed with the matter-of-fact way he coped with the lack of Holiday Inns and McDonalds'. He spent a great deal of the trip sleeping in the open, eating snakes and frogs and drinking brackish water.

If you want to travel along some with Mr. Pritchard the next few weeks, we can examine the non-movie version of westward expansion. We all respect what many of our ancestors did for us in building America. But when we get a glimpse of what an amazing ordeal some of them endured, it makes us glad to accept the benefits of their adventurous spirit from a distance.

One of my favorite parts of the observations of Horace Greathouse's great grandfather is his acceptance of the hardships of his freely chosen adventure with humor and grace.

Although he probably would not have started on the trip had he known in advance how hard it would be:

<u>Entry for September 12, 1850</u>

"I was very unwell but still had to walk as the roads were
very bad, being deep sand…. The road was strewn with dead
animals, wagons, cooking stoves, water barrels, harness, guns,
clothes, tents abounded, and broken-down cattle left to die.
The destruction of property is unparalleled in history except
in wartime…. Many people escape without anything at all,
glad to save their lives…. There are many deaths here….
There has been a great deal of sickness here (the desert)
by the number of graves there are here: the bad water.
I have seen sights on this route that would make the
stoutest heart quake…. I would not come through
again for all the wealth of California." (See page 53 of journal)

On the other hand, maybe there will be gold over that next mountain.

PIONEERS' PROGRESS

(Week of September 17, 2007)

The National Judicial College is in Reno, Nevada, which is eighty miles from Sacramento, California. I have been both a student and instructor at the National Judicial College since 1986. To get to Reno, I drive about one hour to Evansville, then fly via Chicago to Reno. I usually have to get up about 5:00 o'clock a.m., and I am registering at the college by the afternoon of the same day. I get neither cold nor hungry.

Our Posey County gold feverers suffered untold hardships for six months to make the same trip in 1850. Every time I fly over the Nevada desert, I marvel at the mental and physical toughness it required for our ancestors to cross it on foot or in covered wagons or horseback.

In reading the journals of William Fowler Pritchard and James Bennett it appears they were constantly reminded of the price they might pay for their dreams. Both men made numerous entries about the Forty-Niners who failed.

As of May 1, 1850 seven hundred sixty-five wagons had passed St. Joseph, Missouri. With a presumed average of six people per wagon, Fowler and Bennett were included with about 4,590 travelers. They noted several new graves almost every day after they left Missouri. And they lost two of their own party, Mrs. Samuel Bolton and William Faulkner.

In addition to those who lost their lives in search of gold, after our Posey County party reached Nebraska, they were constantly being passed by pioneers who had given up and were returning "to the states".

As I am flying over the old Oregon Trail, I often think about the difference between my trips out west and those of the pioneers and wonder if they ever wished they were like the birds who could fly over the desert. The Gordon Lightfoot song, *Early Morning Rain* sometimes drones along in my head:

> ♫Hear the mighty engines roar, see the silver bird on high
> She's away and westward bound far above the clouds she'll fly
> There the morning rain don't fall and the sun always shines
> She'll be flying over my home in about three hours time.♫

Three hours versus six months. You know that just as the ancient Greeks imagined the wings of Icarus and Pegasus, the flying horse, and the Romans worshiped Mercury, the winged messenger of the gods, the early pioneers must have dreamed of faster, safer, easier means of travel and communication.

I think we all should be glad they endured the hardships then so we do not have to now.

James Bennett preserved his impressions of the passage over the Nevada desert.

(September 11, 1850)

"In the first five miles, the distance traveled by daylight, we counted the dead carcasses of sixty-four oxen and fifty-five horses and mules ... The destruction of property here is immense. For forty miles the road is strewn with abandoned wagons and sometimes the whole of their contents except provisions. Whole corrals, numbering five or six wagons, were found deserted and the place literally covered with dead cattle; many of them still tied to the wheels of the wagons. The whole air throughout the desert was tainted with the smell of carrion."

ALL THAT GLITTERS

(Week of September 10, 2007)

Unless you are Horace Greathouse or his cousin, Martha Leigh, or June Dunning or my wife, Peg, I can claim five readers. I know Peg suffers through every column because she does not like to hear a grown man whine.

And Buddy Greathouse, Martha Leigh and June Dunning were sucked in at least once due to their interest in Posey County Forty Niners.

After Martha read my first column about her early relatives, she loaned me her copy of **Overland Journey to California,** **ISBN 0-87770-403-1**, published in 1987. This is the re-printed version of the **Journal of James Bennett:**

> *"Whose Party left New Harmony in 1850 and crossed plains*
> *and mountains until the Golden West was reached."*

This personal journey was written over the six months it took Bennett to go from New Harmony to Sacramento, California (April 1, 1850 – October 1, 1850). James Bennett's company was part of the same group of hardy Posey County gold seekers that included William Fowler Pritchard who wrote his own account of the adventure.

James Bennett's journal was originally published by **The New Harmony Times** in 1906, thirty-seven years after Bennett's death. According to the editor of the *Times,*

> *"The plunge into the western wilderness was here (New Harmony)*
> *to commence and many were the misgivings as old friend held old*
> *friend's hand and relative saw their kith and kin departing on a*
> *voyage beset with unknown terrors."*

The greatest fears of the Forty Niners were of the unknown in general and of Native Americans in particular. Although during the whole trip out and back not once did our intrepid fortune hunters meet hostile Indians, before they left Posey County they were much in doubt.

Our adventurers did note the indigenous American culture as they ♫*clumbed the wide prairies and crossed the high peaks*♫. And it appears that it was not only American Indians who had habits our early settlers found strange.

On Saturday, June 22, 1850 Bennett came upon an encampment of about one hundred Sioux Indians near Scotts Bluffs, Nebraska. There were thirteen lodges and huts where the main tribe lived. But about three hundred yards away two Frenchmen lived with their Indian wives and children.

> *"They were having a dog feast. Near their campfire was the*
> *head of a large mastiff; a bleeding evidence of the fact."*

Mr. Bennett's journal ends when the party reached "the gold mines". He did not account for his luck, good or bad. Perhaps our Posey County gold fever sufferers could have benefited from the wisdom of Larry Gatlin's song, *All the Gold in California*:

> ♫ *So if you're dreaming about California,*
>
> *. . . .*
>
> *Trying to be a hero, winding up a zero*
>
> *Can scar a man forever, right down to his soul*
>
> *. . .*
>
> *Cause everything that glitters is not gold.* ♫

CALIFORNIA HERE WE COME

(Week of September 3, 2007)

June Dunning and I have served together on the board of the Posey County Historical Society for years; I really do not recall how many. June is, also, one of the Alexandrian Library's best resources. And when it comes to combining a knowledge of Posey County history with the ability to find information at the library, there is no one like June.

Now, I have always liked June. And that was true before she told me last week she had actually read my column on New Harmony's gold fever sufferers. However, it did dispose me ever so slightly more in her favor.

Of course, it was probably June's genteel way of nudging me in the right direction when she provided a file folder full of interesting information on Posey County's Forty-Niners. I did note in our conversations about my earlier columns that she abstained from evaluating my column's worth.

Anyway, thank you, June, for the historical data on a party of Posey County's first gold seekers who left Posey County for Sutter's Mill on the tenth of May, 1849. This was hardly one year after gold had been discovered.

According to the account of Milton Black as related to his son-in-law, George W. Kimball, Black along with fellow Posey County citizens Frederick Phillips, Adrian and James Hinkley, Samuel Bradley, John Welborn, Gilbert Smith and John Wright decided to, "try our fortunes" in California.

These eight adventurers joined their three covered wagons with a train of thirty-six others near St. Joseph, Missouri. Their supplies consisted of picks and shovels, hard tack and hope. The wagons held six men each and were pulled by as many as five yoke of oxen. There were no women or children in their train.

As they plodded towards the west, sometimes they made as little as a mile or two and sometimes as much as fifty miles in one day. They reached the summit of the Rocky Mountains on July 4, 1849 where they celebrated our country's birthday with a giant snow ball fight.

The men occasionally ran into Native Americans who not once were hostile but almost always wanted to barter and trade for various goods such as kettles.

Our hardy miners struck gold in the Bear River where they panned enough "powder" to buy their winter supplies. Then they moved on to the thriving tent city of Sacramento where on the north fork of the American River they worked hard but made little.

While we are not informed by Mr. Black as to the extent of his fortune, he told his son-in-law that when he decided to return to Posey County, "I felt pretty well satisfied with the earnings I had saved to carry home with me."

Perhaps we can delve into the fortunes, or lack thereof, of some of our other Posey County Forty Niners later.

END OF THE TRAIL

(Week of September 24, 2007)

If you have suffered through these recent columns about the sufferings of our seventy-eight Posey County Forty-Niners, you may wish you could trade places with them. However, we have now come to the end of their great adventure with little knowledge of how much gold made it back to Posey County. Did any of them strike it rich in California?

The only people who admit to having read the previous stories say the same thing to me, "Show me the money!" I guess we are not so different from our gold fever suffering ancestors from 1850. The hardships may have been hard and even in some cases, fatal. But just as they were focused on buried treasure, we care most about any unearthed bonanzas.

Well, Gentle Reader, I'll tell you. I believe we have been dealing with a generation of pioneers who did not believe in blowing their own horns. The journals of William Fowler Pritchard and James Bennett and the accounts of Milton Black concerning forays to Sutter's Mill by Posey Countians, concentrate on the journey, not the destination. Perhaps the old adage is correct, "It is one's life journey, not our final destination that really matters."

So, if any of our early settlers struck it rich, they kept it to themselves. The folks from the 1850's must have been much like the generation that survived the Great Depression. Complaining was considered weakness and bragging was considered sinful.

Perhaps there is someone out there who has information on the fortunes of our fortune hunters. If so, please share it with me and I may start the wagon train up again.

For now, thanks to Horace Greathouse, Martha Leigh and June Dunning for sharing your research on Posey County's Forty Niners. Let me know when you want your books and articles back.

HERE COMES THE SUN!

(Week of January 2, 2006)

On December 21st at about 12:30 p.m. the sun began to return. I am ready. The winter solstice marks the point in the earth's orbit around the sun where the tilt of the earth produces the shortest amount of sunlight in a day.

"Solstice" comes from a combination of the Latin words *sol* (sun) and *sistere* (to cause to stand). It is as if the sun is at the bottom of a circle and starts toward the top. At least it seems that way to us.

All I know is I like longer days and lots of sunshine. Two of my favorite days are the winter solstice and the summer solstice, the day with the most hours of sunlight.

As winter begins, I appreciate each small increase in the returning light. And around June 21st each year I try to squeeze every moment of sunshine from the days. Of course, the day after the summer solstice is a bit of a downer.

The Beatles song *Here Comes the Sun* by George Harrison captures why we humans have celebrated the return of the sun for thousands of years:

> ♫ Here comes the sun, here comes the sun
> And I say it's all right
> Little darlin' it's been a long cold lonely winter
> Little darlin' it feels like years since it's been here
> Here comes the sun, Here comes the sun
> Little darlin' the smiles returning to their faces♫

It doesn't take a psychologist such as my dear sister Jane, whom you may have met in an earlier column, to tell us how depressed one can get when the skies are gray. We understand why people resort to artificial lights and even chemicals to replace sunshine.

When the National Judicial College sent me to Russia to teach Russian judges in December, 2003, my wife, Peg, and I were struck by the lack of any sunshine in Moscow or Volgograd and the amount of alcohol we saw consumed. After a few days there we understood! It was grim.

Russia and specially the Russian people were great, but the Russian winter could make even Pollyanna depressed. We appreciated why they say Russia's best generals include December, January, February and March. Ask Napoleon and Hitler!

It was a wonderful experience but it sure helped us to cope with the relatively short and mild winters of southern Indiana. I remind myself of my good fortune when our gray days intrude too heavily.

And sometimes, such as now, I dig through my files and re-read one of my favorite comic strips about New Year's Resolutions and depression.

It is from *Peanuts* and involves Charlie Brown all sappily positive telling Lucy of his plans for a good new year. Then he makes the mistake of asking Lucy about her resolutions.

Lucy tells Charlie she doesn't make New Year's Resolutions but just plans to rue her fate and curse the darkness.

Charlie crumples his carefully prepared list and mopes away.

Well, instead of dwelling on my mistakes of the past, when the winter solstice comes along it helps me to look to the future. And, if the sun will cooperate, I can do it.

As John Denver sang: ♫Sunshine almost always makes me high♫.

BACK HOME AGAIN IN INDIANA

(Week of July 11, 2005)

Our Hoosier state has music deep in its soul.
I really like Paul Dresser's chorus:

> "Oh, the moonlight's fair tonight along the Wabash,
>   From the fields there comes the breath of new mown hay,
>   Through the sycamores the candle lights are gleaming,
>   On the banks of the Wabash, far away."

And, *Back Home In Indiana* by James Hanley and Ballard MacDonald fits Dresser's *On the Banks of the Wabash, Far Away* as well as an early Posey County settler's hand hewn mortise and tenon:

> "Back home again in Indiana,
>   And it seems that I can see
>   A gleaming candlelight
>   Still shining bright
>   Through the sycamores, for me
>
>   The new-mown hay
>   Sends all its fragrance
>   From the fields I used to roam
>   When I dream about the moonlight
>   On the Wabash
>   Then I long for my Indiana home."

Of course *The Wabash Cannonball* is about a railroad train, but no one can hear it without conjuring up an image of Indiana:

> "Well now listen to the jingle
>   To the rumble and the roar
>   As she glides along the woodland
>   Through the hills and by the shore
>   Hear the mighty rush of the engine
>   And the Lonesome hoboes call
>   No changes can be taken
>   On the Wabash Cannonball."

247

Not even our sister state to the west would disagree that the Wabash River and references to it belong to Indiana. They can claim part of Abraham Lincoln, but they get none of the Wabash.

Making a switch in tracks I ask you to think of one college fight song to represent all college fight songs. You thought of Notre Dame, didn't you?

Yep, even those of us who are neither Irish alumni nor Catholic, hum along to:

> "Cheer, cheer for Old Notre Dame
> Wake up the echoes cheering her name,
> Send the volley cheer on high
> Shake down the thunder from the sky."

At least, it is a Hoosier institution, that school with the Golden Dome and the Touchdown Jesus, that stands for college football throughout the nation.

We Indiana University types may root against those bullies from South Bend, but we probably know Notre Dame's fight song better than our own.

There is a great deal more music with its roots in Indiana, but as the Jackson 5 from Gary, Indiana sang:

> "Every soul that passes by
> This song's to you from the Jackson 5
> I'm comin' home it's plain to see
> I still got Indiana soul in me."

A GLIMPSE OF STOCKING

(Week of August 8, 2005)

Indiana's own Cole Porter wrote the musical *Anything Goes* in 1934. The title song will occasionally rumble through my brain when I take the Bench in our 129 year old courthouse. Why you might ask? Or perhaps you might suggest that my brain can ill afford to be divided between two tasks.

Be that as it may, when I gaze across the courtroom at the historic jury box where so many of you have served and where so many important decisions have been made, my mind will sometimes hum to itself:

> ♫ In Olden Days a glimpse of stocking
> Was looked on as something shocking
> But now goodness knows,
> Anything goes!♫

We are back to your question, why? Well, I will tell you. The beautiful oak jury box that was so carefully crafted as a symbol of our great democracy was installed in 1892, about 15 years after the "new" courthouse opened. More to the point of your insistent question, it was installed about 28 years before women got the right to vote.

Ergo, since Posey County then drew its jurors solely from the list of registered voters, only adult male voters, "of good repute for intelligence, fairness and integrity," could serve on juries. And, as all men of that day wore trousers, the short front railing of the jury box revealed nothing of prurient interest.

However, after 1920, thanks to the efforts of our erstwhile protagonist, Frances "Mad Fanny" Wright, and many others, women were afforded the same opportunity as men to serve the American judicial system. Some of you may be unsure of the benefits of this development.

But I digress from your nagging concern about Cole Porter and my dual tasking. Here's your answer. Our county forefathers, they were all men at that time, decided to tack a "modesty shield" over the front railing of our original jury box. This was done so that ladies might cross their legs while serving on a jury without concern for exposing their ankles. With some of the outfits of today they would have had to erect a wall.

Regardless, one of the pleasures of my job is speaking with our young people who frequently come to the courthouse on field trips. All of the children, but particularly the girls, are amazed when I point out the modesty screen and tell them that for about the first 150 years of American democracy women had no right to vote.

My mother was born in 1913. She told me of her mother's pride the first time she could vote. Grandmother never missed a chance to vote. And one of her great pleasures was canceling out my grandfather's vote. Grandmother was the only member of my family who would admit to voting

Republican. As she always said, "If it was good enough for Honest Abe, it should be good enough for anybody." Well, maybe.

Anyway, why don't you stop by and I will show you our antique jury box. It's good to preserve these reminders.

Posey County Circuit Court Jury Box
Photograph by Becky Boggs, Nature Photographer, Mt. Vernon, Indiana
wvgardengirl@insightbb.com

CHAPTER EIGHT

DEMOCRACY IN ACTION

A POSEY COUNTY OWENITE SUCCEEDED WHERE A U.S. PRESIDENT COULD NOT

(Week of June 19, 2006)

Dorothy Challman died last October at age 98. She used to write newspaper columns that I greatly enjoyed. Dorothy would publish her scimitar-like positions without apology.

Her son, Steve, inherited his mother's keen discernment, but with a little more Teflon-like subtlety. I find both approaches to my liking.

As had his mother, Steve has a deep interest in history and political science. He recently gave me a copy of the February, 2006 edition of *Old News*. I had never heard of this publication from Landisville, Pennsylvania, but enjoyed the content, look and feel of the folio-type magazine.

Steve pointed out the article concerning the Smithsonian Institution and its co-parentage by our sixth president, John Quincy Adams, and Posey County favorite son, Robert Dale Owen.

"Quincy's" father, the second president, John Adams, was never able to bend his stiff Massachusetts neck and form coalitions. So too, Quincy was unable to humble himself to marshal support for the establishment of his ideal of a national educational center.

Then, after his defeat by Andrew Jackson in 1828, John Quincy Adams was elected to the House of Representatives where he served from 1830 until his death in 1848. As a member of Congress, he continued to push for a national museum, but could not win over his colleagues until manna from heaven or, at least England, miraculously appeared.

The one-half million dollars that Englishman, James Smithson, gave to America in 1835, via his will, was the impetus that the former president used to push for a national museum. Through no fault of Adams, due to financial chicanery, the original endowment was squandered away. However, Adams managed to preserve the interest payments as a start-up fund.

Adams put in bill after bill to use the fund as Smithson's will instructed. But his inability to get any such bill passed frustrated him at every turn.

Then Posey County's Robert Dale Owen introduced a bill in 1846 that, with Adams's strong support, was passed into law.

Owen's bill provided for a governing board, a site search, and a building to be designed to include , "…[a] museum, an art gallery, a chemical laboratory, lecture rooms, a school, a library and a facility to publish inexpensive pamphlets for mass distribution."

Similar to our own local treasure, The Working Men's Institute in New Harmony, Robert Dale Owen envisioned this national archive and living institution as a place for "[d]iffusion of useful knowledge to the common man."

Owen's personal ideal of practical education for all was the bedrock of the Smithsonian Institution's charter.

John Quincy Adams had similar dreams for America, but Robert Dale Owen made it happen. This, alone, should be legacy enough for anyone. But it barely scratched the surface of Posey

County's freethinking Robert Dale Owen. If you are out of Sominex, you can join me for the next few weeks as we examine more of this unassuming intellectual giant's fearless contributions.

ROBERT DALE OWEN: THE LESS GOVERNMENT THE BETTER; ALVIN PETERSON HOVEY: GIVE THE PEOPLE WHAT THEY WANT

(Week of June 26, 2006)

Robert Dale Owen and Alvin Peterson Hovey were Posey County's representatives to Indiana's Constitutional Convention of 1850-1852. The Convention was called to re-write Indiana's original Constitution of 1816.

There were several reasons why we needed a new constitution but the main cause was the financial impact of our involvement in the Wabash and Erie Canal project. Avoidance of another fiscal debacle was a primary goal of the Convention.

However, the great social issue of Ante-Bellum Indiana was slavery, particularly Negro migration into free Indiana from slave holding states. The Convention delegates were charged with drafting a new constitution that would be adopted by the citizens. And one of the burning issues throughout our state was the "Negro Problem".

Owen had already represented our area in the Indiana Legislature from 1836-1838 and in Congress from 1843-1847. He had long been an advocate for general practical education as well as for equal rights for women. And he and Frances (Mad Fanny) Wright had attempted to help abolish slavery through their community of Nashoba in Tennessee.

As a wealthy aristocrat, Owen could have easily avoided these thorny problems, but he chose to get involved and stay involved. He put his fortune, his reputation and his social status at risk to champion these causes.

Robert Dale Owen was not one who believed we should rely on our government to effect change. He called for a government that would enable its citizens to bring about social justice.

In the Constitutional Convention of 1850-1851, he was attacked by the delegate from Tippecanoe, Mr. Clark, who tried to paint Owen as anti-government for his approach to the issue of civil rights for African Americans.

Owen responded:

> "He (Clark) says that he does not, as I seem to do, regard Government as an evil, and that he does not wish to escape, as I seem to desire, from the expressed will of the people [on the issue of Negro rights in Indiana].
>
> Now, I should be very glad to believe that all laws that are passed do really embody the will of the people; but I do not believe it.
>
> ...

As regards the proposition that government is an evil....
My proposition is this, that the best government, so [long as] it
attains the legitimate object of government, is that which governs
the least."

Robert Dale Owen and Alvin Petersen Hovey approached the great divisions over how Indiana's Constitution should deal with the "Negro Problem" from diametrically opposed positions.

Owen saw his delegate's role as an architect with long-range goals for Indiana. He understood that most Hoosiers were against full citizenship or even civil rights for Negroes. But he saw it as his duty to lead in the direction he saw as right.

Hovey saw his role as a delegate to represent the majority view of the people who elected him to the Convention. Hovey responded to Owen's larger schemes with a hint of sarcasm:

"Some gentlemen (Owen) talk about reforms that are in advance
of the present age, and expect to reap many laurels for their great
political discoveries. Let me say to such, that those who are up
with the age...will demonstrate their wisdom by molding their
reforms to suit the people as they are, and not as they may be."

Perhaps, Gentle Reader, you may come down on Owen's side or Hovey's when it comes to making law. What with the Fourth of July coming up next week, if you have not already despaired of ever getting to the end of one of these columns, we may delve further into the political philosophies of these two Posey County Founding Fathers.

LEAD, FOLLOW OR COMPLAIN

(Week of July 3, 2006)

Posey County has had several well-known public servants whose contributions to society reach far beyond our parochial interests. Three of our historical figures whom I find especially noteworthy in this regard are Robert Dale Owen, Alvin Peterson Hovey and Frances Wright.

As we celebrate our country's birthday, a description of the differing approaches of these three to social change might be interesting (at least to me).

Hovey tended to approach socio-economic issues as a representative of the people. He sought to lead from the center. Still, Hovey did not lack for either political or military courage. Hovey was a major general in the Civil War during which he served under Ulysses S. Grant at Vicksburg.

Frances Wright was more towards the opposite end of the continuum from Hovey. She appears to have believed that the majority simply meant the greater number of people, not the greater wisdom.

Robert Dale Owen had Wright's visionary outlook and Hovey's respect for the opinions of others. Owen neither denigrated the world's Cassandras nor venerated its Quislings. Cassandra was the figure from Greek mythology who had the gift of prophecy but the curse of being ignored. Quisling was a Norwegian politician who, during World War II, collaborated with the Nazis. Quisling has become a synonym for a leader who will do anything to accommodate whoever has the most power.

When a visionary such as Frances Wright would make dire predictions based on mankind's foibles, Owen respected the message instead of being put off by the messenger. Owen respected the possibility that the majority's opinion might be valid, but he, also, had the courage to speak and act against popular opinion if he believed the majority to be wrong.

Each of these three Posey County founders was deeply involved in the issue of Negro and women's rights. And though each vigorously opposed slavery, Wright, Hovey and Owen approached the volatile matter of civil rights for African Americans differently.

Hovey courageously fought a war to free blacks from bondage. However, as one of Posey County's delegates to Indiana's Constitutional Convention of 1850-51, Hovey opposed civil rights for Negroes and took a more paternalistic attitude towards women than Owen. Of course, Hovey and Wright were in different time warps on the roles of women.

As a woman in the Nineteenth Century, Frances Wright did not have the right to vote, much less serve in public office. But she placed her personal fortune, her health and her reputation on the line by publicly and vigorously demanding equal rights for blacks and women. Unfortunately, Wright's arrogance and disdain for the views of others resulted in the great majority of the people she needed to convince dismissing her as "Mad Fanny".

Owen, also, invested a great deal of his assets and public status in the cause of both women and Negroes. But Owen was more circumspect in appealing to "the better angels" of the public's nature on these issues.

Looking back on those Fourth of July celebrations involving Frances Wright, Robert Dale Owen and Alvin Peterson Hovey from about 1828 to 1892, we might be a little smug about our humanitarian impulses. Of course, a few years from now our descendants may treat us in the same way.

Wright, Owen and Hovey were each products and captives of their birth and times. Perhaps we can learn from our brilliant ancestors without being awed or condescending.

Happy birthday to us, and thank you Fanny, Alvin and Robert Dale.

GOVERNMENT BY THE PEOPLE

(Week of December 17, 2007)

New Harmony, Indiana has less than one thousand residents. In November, 2007, thirteen of them offered to serve their fellow citizens as members of the Town Council. If you include Clerk/ Treasurer, Karla Atkins, and the other two members of the New Harmony Election Board, Sue Krozel and Gayle Williams, and Recount Commissioners, Donna Kohlmeyer, Jim Alsop and Bill Wilson, nineteen people who live in New Harmony were trying to help govern their town.

When one considers that there are only about sixteen contenders to be President of the three hundred million citizens of the United States, New Harmony shines forth as a beacon of self-government.

As there were only five available council seats, eight candidates were not able to serve their community on the council. However, they can, and I predict will, continue to offer their many talents to help make their town an even better place to live.

I am not sure why America gets so many people to help keep our towns safe, clean, interesting and fun to live in. I am sure that it is not the paltry sums of money we pay them nor is it the abuse we often heap upon them.

I am, also, not sure how we get public servants such as the members of my staff to work long hours and implement innovative solutions to the tough problems of election recounts, but I thank Rodney Fetcher, John Emhuff, Kristie Hoffman and Katrina Mann for doing so. My other staff members: Ashley Thompson; Becky Rutledge; Jason Simmons; Shawnna Rigsby; and Michelle Fortune, had to take up the slack in other areas so that the unexpected and emergency needs of the recount could be addressed.

Sam Blankenship, who has served Posey County in each of the election recounts from 1984 to this one in 2007 where he, once again, volunteered his talent, time and considerable knowledge of voting systems, deserves special thanks.

And Sheriff Jim Folz was personally present throughout the recount to provide security while the County Election Board consisting of Donna Butler, Ron Bennett and Don Oeth offered logistical support and advice.

In these times of apathy and movements toward more centralized government, it is good to experience responsible self-government at the local level. As we are all too aware, it may be tempting to trade our rights in for convenience, but power abhors a vacuum. Responsibility shirked leads to self-government lost.

Thanks, New Harmony, for the civics lesson and the reminder.

Oh, and if you are wondering which of the following thirteen candidates won, they all did and so did their town because they refused to sit on the sidelines: Kenyon Bailey; William M. Cox; Donald Ray Gibbs; John E. Tron; Linda Warrum; David Campbell; Joe Straw; Roger Wade; Joe Morris; Marvin A. McDurmon; Ronald Eimer; Gregory A. Cox; and Ralph D. Hardy.

REMEMBER THE LADIES

(Week of July 18, 2005)

When John Adams went off to Philadelphia in 1776 to help in the birth of our country, he left Abigail behind in Massachusetts to rear their children and run their farm. And while Abigail fully supported the revolution against the British, she did not shirk her duty in the Battle of the Sexes.

Abigail wrote to remind John that while he was struggling for "The Rights of Man" he should:

> "...[R]emember the Ladies, and be more generous and favorable to them than your ancestors. Do not put such unlimited power into the hands of the Husbands. Remember all Men would be tyrants if they could."

And if this appeal to fairness and reason did not melt the hearts and convince the minds of the original Philadelphia 76ers, perhaps Abigail's stern warning would:

> "If particular care and attention is not paid to the Ladies we are determined to foment a Rebellion and will not hold ourselves bound by any Laws in which we have no voice or representation."

I suspect John was more than a little concerned when he returned home. Those Yankee winters can be cold!

As the wife of our second president and the mother of our sixth, John Quincy Adams, Abigail wielded great influence on such matters as women's rights and the eventual abolition of slavery. She called for the education of women and Negroes. She even enrolled a young Black man in school in spite of fierce opposition.

Of course, Abigail was saddled with day to day chores of caring for her family even as she engaged these great issues. She was the first First Lady to live in the White House (which was not nearly finished when she moved in). She had to make do and did so, even hanging laundry on makeshift clotheslines inside the empty rooms. For, as most women, Abigail, also, had at least two jobs.

Another Lady who should be remembered is Dolly Madison who was married to "that great little giant" James Madison who was most responsible for drafting our Constitution.

As First Lady in 1814, she braved the British assault on our capital and refused to leave the White House without George Washington's portrait and many valuable governmental documents.

Dolly Madison and Abigail Adams are among the many women who make it impossible to forget "The Ladies" and what they have meant to our country.

If you have nothing to do for ten minutes next week and are so inclined, check in and we can discuss my favorite Posey County lady (say revolutionary if you wish) from the 19th Century. She was known as Mad Fanny!

MAD FANNY

(1795-1852)
(Week of July 25, 2005)

Was Frances Wright crazy or just marching to her own drummer?

One of Posey County's brightest had a highly developed intolerance for social injustice and a star crossed, though very interesting, personal life.

Brilliant, wealthy and Scottish, Fanny was a perfect fit for her fellow Scot, Robert Owen's, New Harmony commune built on principles of the Enlightenment.

As a teenager she authored a play and when she was twenty-three she and her younger sister, Camilla, traveled from Scotland to New York City to see another of her plays publicly performed.

Lafayette, the great hero of the American Revolution, and Fanny had a four-year relationship at his home in France just before she joined the New Harmony community.

Fanny's years with the great Revolutionary helped mold the young woman's egalitarian ideology and intensify her passion for justice.

Fanny had become interested in the United States while still a child in Scotland. She found the new social experiment of democracy fascinating. She studied and wrote about America frequently before permanently settling here in 1825.

Fanny and Camilla accompanied Lafayette on his triumphal return to America. Congress had invited him and his son, George, (named for George Washington) to return after 50 years to thank and honor the Marquis for his crucial role in the War.

This was a perfect opportunity to cool their relationship and for Fanny to dive headlong into her self-ordained mission to save humanity, particularly women and slaves.

Upon arriving in New Harmony she won at least one convert's heart and mind when she simply overwhelmed the Founder's son, Robert Dale Owen.

The twenty-three year old Robert Dale Owen was captivated immediately and completely by the beautiful and worldly twenty-nine year old Fanny. Robert Dale and Fanny proceeded together to implement Fanny's theories of true democracy.

Of course, there were many people who believed in equal rights for women and freedom for slaves. However, most of them approached these gurgling volcanoes with caution; not Frances Wright!

As the contemporary but more traditional Catherine Beecher said of her:

> "Who can look without disgust and abhorrence upon such a one as Fanny Wright…mingling with men in stormy debate and standing up with bare-faced impudence to lecture to a public assembly."

Frances Wright was, perhaps, the most influential person in bringing women into the world of public lecturing on matters of substance. In fact, she may have been one of the first women in America to publicly address an assemblage of both women and men. This occurred on July 4, 1828 in our own New Harmony, Indiana.

There is so much more to this fascinating person that one column will not suffice. Her views on marriage, organized religion, slavery and several other volatile issues would be controversial today. Imagine the reaction 150 years ago.

However, what probably did more to brand her "The Red Harlot" and "Mad Fanny" were her ultimate solutions to marriage and slavery. Frances Wright sank her soul and her fortune into her settlement of Nashoba and its system of freeing slaves through education and miscegenation. And she publicly stated her support for ending marriage and replacing it with a system of universal education and cenogamy (I had to look it up too). And, as this is a family newspaper, we will leave it that way!

A REBEL IN SOUTHWESTERN INDIANA

(Week of March 10, 2008)

Celia Morris's book, *Fanny Wright – Rebel in America*, is about the only treatise on Frances Wright that I have found. One book for such a brilliant and original thinker is not enough. Perhaps you, Gentle Reader, will know of other in depth treatments concerning Mad Fanny. And, you may recall that I have written about this fascinating person before. I most likely will do so again.

"Mad Fanny" the "Red Harlot" and numerous other derogatory epithets were hurled in derision at Frances Wright who was born in Scotland on September 6, 1795 and died in Cincinnati, Ohio on December 13, 1852.

According to Morris's book, Fanny managed to know and gain, at a minimum, the admiration of Lafayette, Thomas Jefferson, Jeremy Bentham, Robert Owen, Robert Dale Owen, William Maclure and so many more of the great men of America and Europe as to make one wonder if she was, indeed, only one woman.

Apparently, Ms. Wright refused to accept the traditional role that women of her times were assigned. She had the temerity to think and act as she wished. As an orphaned young single woman with a modest fortune, she became enamored with the new country of the United States and its claimed creed of equality of opportunity.

She wrote plays and articles lauding America's egalitarian principles. But when she crossed the Atlantic Ocean to see the great experiment in action, she was disillusioned with slavery and the low status of women and, as she saw it, the role religion played in maintaining both.

With the direct involvement of Robert Dale Owen, the indirect support of Lafayette and the encouragement of Thomas Jefferson, Fanny planned to create a communal sanctuary where slaves could work to earn their freedom and women could contribute as equals with men. An important element for Fanny was the absence of any religious influence.

She bought almost two thousand (2,000) acres along the Wolf River about fifteen miles from Memphis, Tennessee and started to buy slaves whom she had live and work at her Nashoba. She illegally educated them and taught them trades. Her grand plan was to have them earn enough money to reimburse her for their costs so she could buy other slaves who could then earn their freedom.

Alas, Mad Fanny refused to recognize how complicated it would be to change the entire culture of The Peculiar Institution. She, also, failed to see that her own hubris would be one of the greatest impediments to her dream.

And it did not help that The Red Harlot, so called because of her strawberry blond hair and her calls for total cenogamy, sharing of mates, allowed miscegenation among her staff and slaves at Nashoba.

You are correct if you surmise that such "forward thinking" was severely chastised during those Ante Bellum days in Tennessee. Later we might be able to see somewhat more clearly why Mad Fanny's utopian plan crashed on the shoals of reality.

YA GOTTA GET THERE

(Week of March 3, 2008)

One reason the Founding Fathers took six months slowly crafting our Constitution was that once they got to Philadelphia it was just too much trouble to leave.

Today, legislation can be piecemealed because our Representatives and Senators can leave Washington, D.C. and return home in a few hours. And who can blame them for wanting out of there? But such stopping and starting does contribute to laws that resemble Christmas trees, that is, all baubles, bangles and flashing lights with presents for us all around. Of course, the presents are picked out by strangers and paid for with our money and are often of no value to us.

Anyway, I did not want to talk about Washington. I want to talk about travel in the first half of the 18th Century. It was not for sissies. No roads, mud, no McDonalds, well, you get the idea. So the rivers were the highways for our ancestors. The rivers did not have to be repaved and they were free. And they were why Lafayette and Frances Wright visited Shawneetown, Illinois and why Frances Wright and Robert Dale Owen lived in New Harmony, Indiana. The Mississippi, Ohio and Wabash rivers are the reasons the towns of New Orleans, Shawneetown, Mt. Vernon and New Harmony were settled.

And the fact that the nascent settlement of Chicago was not on a major waterway was why the bank in Shawneetown refused to take a risk on buying Chicago's bonds.

If you happen to read last week's column, you may be wondering, or you may not care, what any of this has to do with Mad Fanny Wright and her dreams of freeing Negroes and women? Well, what I often wonder is why so many brilliant and imaginative people gravitated to our area? You, Gentle Reader, probably long ago figured out it was the rivers.

Father George Rapp may have had a vision that guided him to Harmonie, but he could have never got here from Pennsylvania without the Ohio and Wabash rivers. And Frances Wright and Robert Dale Owen may have dreamed of a Utopia in Tennessee where slaves could work to earn their freedom, but the reason that Nashoba was on the Wolf River by Memphis is because the rivers made it accessible.

Now I know we have not, as yet, done much investigation of Mad Fanny's grand plans, but as I keep saying, ya gotta get there first.

FROM SHAWNEETOWN TO NEW HARMONY

(Week of February 25, 2008)

The 1960's are to my generation what Hannah Montana is to the current one, all consuming to us and unfathomable to everyone else.

Our heroes include traditional ones as with every generation, but we have a proclivity for the offbeat dreamer. You are correct if you read that as weirdoes.

For example, when M.I.T. mathematician turned folk singer, Tom Lehrer, read the 1964 obituary of Alma Schindler Gropius Mahler Werfel, he was moved by her slight regard for such conventions as wedding vows. He wrote a satirical song about her.

In like manner, one of my favorite southern Indiana unconventional historical figures is Frances (Mad Fanny) Wright who attached herself at age twenty-six to the great French hero of our Revolution, Marie Joseph Paul Y'ves Roche Gilbert du Motier, Marquis de Lafayette (yeah, that is one person) when he was in his sixties. Their relationship lasted four years until Lafayette was invited by our Congress to return to America for a triumphal final lap.

But his family feared that Lafayette was becoming that saddest of caricatures, a great hero turned old fool. So when Fanny accompanied Lafayette on his tour of America in 1824-25, Lafayette's son, George, encouraged her to peal off with twenty-three year old Robert Dale Owen of New Harmony when Lafayette's entourage stopped at the bustling and vibrant Shawneetown, Illinois on May 7-8, 1825.

According to Wikipedia, Shawneetown and Washington D.C. are the only towns chartered by the United States Congress. And when Lewis and Clark stopped there in early November, 1803, it literally put Shawneetown on the map.

When Lafayette and Fanny's steamboat came up the Mississippi River from New Orleans to Cairo and then on to Shawneetown on the Ohio River, it was met by Moses Rawlings who owned the fine hotel there. Lafayette's party may have also been met by Governor Edward Coles of Illinois and a contingent from New Harmony, Indiana headed by Robert Owen and his sons, Robert Dale and David.

Lafayette and Fanny, along with Fanny's younger sister, Camilla, had already spent time at Monticello with Jefferson and made the rounds in Washington D.C.

After a gala reception in Shawneetown, Lafayette continued on his promenade through America while Frances Wright and Robert Dale Owen dreamed of eliminating the institutions of slavery, marriage and religion: not what one might see as modest goals, but certainly the kind of stuff that catches the attention of people from the last half of the last century.

HUBRIS

(Week of March 17, 2008)

Adlai Stevenson ran for the presidency twice, 1952 and 1956. He had the bad luck to run against the well liked Ike Eisenhower both times. General Eisenhower was a West Point graduate who led the Allies to victory in Europe. But not even Ike thought of himself as an intellectual. On the other hand, Stevenson was known as an "egghead".

One of my favorite stories about Ike was the rumor that because he had been in the Army his entire adult life until he ran for president, the first time he voted in an election was when he voted for himself.

And one of my favorite stories about Stevenson was told to me by my good friend, Sam Blankenship. According to Sam, when the intellectual ran against the war hero, one of Stevenson's aides was trying to boost his morale when the polls showed Ike was way ahead. The aide told Stevenson, "Do not despair, Senator, you are bound to get the thinking man's vote." Stevenson dryly responded, "That may be so, but we need a majority."

This recognition of reality eluded our old friend Frances Wright. Fanny saw herself as the crusading heroine who was unappreciated and misunderstood by the ignorant masses.

In a letter to Mary Shelley of *Frankenstein* fame, Ms. Wright gives us a window into why she was unable to muster support for her plans to free slaves and women:

> "I have made the hard earth my bed,
> the saddle of my horse my pillow, and
> I have staked my life and fortune
> on an experiment having in view
> moral liberty and human improvement [Nashoba].
> Many of course think me mad…."
>
> *Fanny Wright, Rebel in America*
> by Celia Morris @ p. 152

Those other older friends of ours, the marvelous ancient Greeks, understood all too well how human pride often prevents those of genius from succeeding. In fact, hubris comes from the Greek root, *hybris:*

> "Wanton insolence or arrogance resulting from excessive pride."

Mad Fanny would have been well served if she could have known Adlai Stevenson. He may not have won the presidency but he knew one had to build a consensus to get difficult things accomplished.

Another promising person who might have benefited from less arrogance and more coalition building was the erstwhile Governor of New York, Eliot Spitzer. When one chooses to frequently live in certain houses, one should probably not overzealously cast stones at others.

As Mad Fanny probably realized too late, the "my way or the highway", is not the best way. But then again, Fanny remains a heroic, if tragic, champion of freedom and equality. And she did much of her great work right here.

A WARNING TO WRITERS

(Week of March 31, 2008)

I write these columns with two abiding assumptions: (1) nobody but Peg is likely to read them; and (2) because of assumption number one (1), I can pretty much rattle off anything I want without fear of contradiction.

Of course, usually both premises are sound. But when one writes about Posey County history in Posey County, sometimes both (1) and (2) fail me. Such was the case when I wrote about Posey County's most intriguing distaff member of Robert Owen's great experiment, Frances (Mad Fanny) Wright.

Would you believe it? I first heard from Linda Warrum who pointed out that Fanny was an education reformer who advocated many of the same theories espoused in B.F. Skinner's *Beyond Freedom and Dignity*. Skinner wrote his work in 1971, about one hundred and twenty years after Frances died. But his calls for an atheistic society where children were raised by a community, not just their parents, were quite similar to Wright's theory of education. She advocated that children should be raised separate from their parents during their early years. [See Volume I of the *History of Women Suffrage* by Stanton, Anthony & Gage (1881)] This excerpt was taken from the website of Antiquarian Book Sellers' Association of America.

Linda, also, furnished me with information from the Frances Wright – Thomas Jefferson Wikipedia site where Wright's relationships and friendships with Jeremy Bentham, Mary Shelley, Robert Owen, Lafayette and Thomas Jefferson were mentioned.

Here she is described by a female detractor as:

> "In person she was masculine, measuring at least 5 feet 11 inches,
> and wearing her hair… in close curls, her large blue eyes and
> blonde aspect were thoroughly English, and she always seemed
> to wear the wrong attire.
>
> …
>
> To ladies she never spoke…the Frenchmen told many instances
> of her masculine proclivities."

The bedrock reason for Frances Wright's plan to end slavery in America by having slaves earn their freedom then shipping them to Haiti is explained:

> "The prejudice whether absurd or the contrary against a mixture
> of the two colors is so deeply rooted in the American mind
> that emancipation without expatriation…seems impossible."

On the subject of Mad Fanny's grand plan to free slaves, Beth McFadin Higgins loaned me her copy of Goodspeed's, *History of Posey County, Indiana* (1886), where at pages 393-394 the experiment is described.

> "Frances Wright was a woman of extraordinary talent as
> a lecturer and author...and the founder of Nashoba....
> The object of this society was the amelioration of the
> condition of the poor and the freedom of the slave,
> 'on a just and equitable basis.'"

Well, Gentle Reader, I know you will be saddened to know we are out of space for this week. But in the next two weeks I will quote from material furnished to me by Mad Fanny fans, Charles Gaston and Nancy Magnuson. And to think that I thought I had discovered her....

A CLOSER LOOK

(Week of April 7, 2008)

When Nancy Magnuson, college librarian, popped up on my email, I assumed Indiana University had finally tracked me down for that over due book from forty years ago. I should be so lucky!

Instead it was the worst of circumstances; the college librarian had actually read my column on Frances Wright in which I asserted that I had read only one book on Mad Fanny. Well, let me tell you, Ms. Magnuson was not only a college librarian at Goucher College in Baltimore, in the free state of Maryland, but her family has two hundred years of Posey County roots. I knew I was in trouble.

Nancy led me to: http://www.worldcat.org where one hundred and seventy two items about Frances Wright are listed. She instructed me to put in: su:Wright, Frances, and when I did I found way too much information. I prefer to write from plausible deniability. Now, at least as far as Fanny Wright is concerned, I may become a victim of factual content. Thanks a lot, Nancy!

Well Gentle Reader, let's you and I ignore such things as research and, "return to those thrilling days of yesteryear", that is, before I knew of more than one book.

Let me first refer you to http://www.secularhumanism.org/hall-of-fame/wright where the Council for Secular Humanism describes Mad Fanny's supposed madness, i.e., her out-of-step idealism in the areas of civil rights for Negroes and women. And since I am confident you read and carefully preserved my column on Ms. Wright in which I cited Celia Morris's book *Fanny Wright-Rebel in America* (1984), you will have access to an in-depth study of this fascinating resident of New Harmony during the Owenite years.

To give you an insight as to why Mad Fanny's commune of Nashoba (Memphis, Tennessee-1825) did not attract many volunteers or contributors I offer Fanny's own prospectus as set out on p. 153:

"Everyone would have equal rights, no matter the color of their skin, no matter what their sex, no matter what their material goods. Moral pleasure would be their only compensation for badly thatched cabins, hard beds, and simple fare. The dirtiest work would have the greatest social value, and together they would discover how human beings ought properly to live."

Now, who could turn down such an opportunity? Of course, those of you who have enjoyed the rigors of military basic training will easily relate to such attractive pleasures.

Okay, Nancy, are you happy? You made me read another book. Next week we might see how Posey County's "Rebel", Mad Fanny, and that rebellious new country of America are related.

AN AMERICAN IN POSEY COUNTY

(Week of April 14, 2008)

Charles Gaston of New Harmony took the time to copy several pages (175-181) from George Browning Lockwood's, *The New Harmony Communities,* and send the information on Frances Wright to me. Thank you, Charles.

In his cover letter to me, Charles used the same term to describe Mad Fanny that I often use and that Celia Morris used in her book, *Fanny Wright-Rebel in America.* I usually think of this often exasperating person as a rebel.

But after reading Lockwood's description of Frances Wright, I was struck by the similarities between Fanny and the way I sometimes think of America. According to this account, she was an eccentric woman who did not fit into any "social map" or "domestic form". She had, "a strong… mind and character." Fanny was: "[A]n advocate of universal suffrage without regard to color or sex… She was a radical alike in politics, morals and religion. She had a strong, logical mind, a courageous independence of thought, and a zealous wish to benefit her fellow creatures…To carry out her convictions she was ready to make great sacrifices, personal and pecuniary."

When I read Mad Fanny described this way, she did not seem all that mad. Although her efforts to abolish slavery and win equal rights for Negroes and women caused Frances Wright to be scorned, ridiculed, broke, and eventually marginalized, she gave all she could give in the pursuit of justice. Somehow that reminds me of how I think of America and what I want America to be.

Now, why did she fail? Mr. Lockwood offers insight on this issue also: "[Her] courage was not tempered with prudence… an inordinate estimate of her own mental powers, and obstinate adherence to opinions once adopted, detracted seriously from the influence which her talents and eloquence might have exerted."

I want to thank those of you who have contributed to these articles on Frances Wright and those of you who have taken time to read them. For now, I plan to give Mad Fanny a rest.

CHAPTER NINE

LAW PUT TO USE

GREASING THE AXLES

(Week of October 30, 2006)

Posey County was founded by some pretty astute people who understood human nature. When I read our county's interesting history I am frequently impressed by the intelligence and resourcefulness of our pioneer leaders.

When our county was first being organized in anticipation of Indiana's statehood in 1816, our first county seat was located in Blackford, which was about a mile north of present day Caborn.

In 1815, our County Commissioners, who had been appointed by a special act of the "General Assembly of the Indiana Territory", selected three hundred twenty (320) acres to be sold off in lots to raise money to pay for our first courthouse, $125.00, and our first jail, $565.00.

The sale of these lots was held in June, 1815. The sale was conducted at the home of William Hutchinson. Mr. Hutchinson allowed his home to be used as the office of the County Commissioners. Mr. Hutchinson, also, was commissioned to conduct the sale of the lots. Among the approved costs of the sale was a claim for $6.00 for the whiskey Mr. Hutchinson freely furnished to the prospective land buyers.

As there was a small group of bidders, and whiskey in 1815 cost 25 cents per gallon, the county did quite well at our first public fundraiser.

Blackford served as our county seat for about one year before statehood and one more year afterwards, 1815 to 1817. Then our founding fathers moved it to the new and planned community of Springfield.

To pay for our new jail, $458.00, and our new courthouse, $4,500.00, you can guess what proven plan of public financing was used. Of course, our county had grown in population so we needed more "supplies."

One Thomas E. Casselberry conducted the sale of the lots, which went for $100.00 if on the Springfield public square and $12.00 if not. Our County Commissioners approved Mr. Casselberry's expense of $7.00 for whiskey.

Posey County raised enough money from the sale of the public lands to pay for the $6,000.00 we had expended on our public buildings.

Our early County Commissioners may well have been Bible students who applied the Good Book's lessons to county government. For as one finds in **Proverbs 31:7**:

"Let them drink and forget their poverty."

Or as my favorite Biblical author, **Ecclesiastes**, says at Chapter 10, verse 19:

"Bread is made for laughter and wine gladdens life and money answers everything."

Now, as a judge and, ergo, a separate branch of government from our county's executive and fiscal bodies, I am not in any way suggesting that when our annual county auctions of abandoned or tax delinquent properties are held that spirits be furnished.

Our separation of powers leaves such matters beyond the scope of the judiciary.

(Much of the information in this article was taken from Leffel's *History of Posey County,* **published in 1913.)**

A FIRM FOUNDATION

(Week of May 22, 2006)

Anne Doane's recent articles about Posey County's courthouses are interesting and informative. They, also, portray the wisdom of our county leaders who knew that the only reason that governments exist is to provide services to the governed.

The provision of services in the present and planning for the citizenry's future needs are the primary duties of our leaders.

Posey County began the provision of court services in 1815 at the home of Absalom Duckworth. As our county and American society changed, our county officials did not shirk their duty to meet the need for new and renovated courthouses.

As Anne Doane's excellent articles show, each iteration of county offices met new and greater needs and required more extensive and expensive facilities. Log courthouses were functional when our citizens lived in log homes. But as our population grew and our economy became more complex, logs had to be replaced by bricks and stone.

Nostalgia, inertia, wishing, fear of criticism and unwise penury could have kept Posey County's seat of government in Mr. Duckworth's home for 200 years. Fortunately for those of us living in Posey County after 1815, our leaders have stood up to these negative forces and done their duty.

You may know that as early as 1993, I and others publicly advocated for the provision of a governmental center located on the banks of our beautiful Ohio River. We suggested that we preserve our historic courthouse as a repository of our rich history but that we invest our public money in a new governmental center.

We live in a democracy where our three branches of government balance and check one another. The majority of the other branches chose to buy and renovate the Hovey House (1995), to renovate the Coliseum (1998); and to renovate our Courthouse for actual court services (2006).

While this approach differed from what I and some others preferred, I still commend our county leaders for planning for the provision of services to our citizens while preserving our heritage. This approach could well carry Posey County far into our current century as long as we maintain our facilities.

Just as Anne Doane's history of our county's several courthouses was being published, the contractors working on the most recent courthouse renovation struck a stone foundation and brick cistern buried for 130 years.

One of the photographs you see was taken by my Chief Probation Officer, Rodney Fetcher. It shows what is probably the foundation of our "new" courthouse in 1825 and its cistern used to collect rainwater.

In 1876, after our favorite son, Alvin Peterson Hovey, laid the cornerstone of our current courthouse, workers filled this old cistern with dirt and building debris. They then covered up the foundation of the 1825 courthouse.

The other image is a drawing of our 1825 courthouse made in 1833 by artist Karl Bodmer. I wish to thank Sherry Graves and Frank Smith of the New Harmony Working Men's Institute and the Joslyn Art Museum for sharing this painting.

I do not know how you feel about the firm foundation our founders laid for our county, but as for me, I thank them for their vision and hope that our descendants will feel the same way about us.

POSEY COUNTY'S FIRST COURTHOUSE
1816-1817

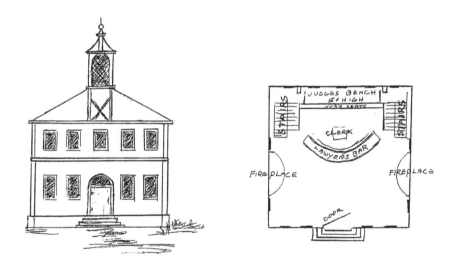

POSEY COUNTY'S SECOND COURTHOUSE IN SPRINGFIELD, INDIANA
1817-1825

Sketches courtesy of Anne Doane

Photograph by Rodney Fetcher on May 11, 2006, at the existing Posey County Courthouse during renovation.
It is believed to be the foundation and cistern of the 1825 courthouse

First Courthouse at Mt. Vernon, Indiana, 1825-1876.
Painting by Karl Bodmer (1834) by permission of The Joslyn Art Museum, Omaha, Nebraska

Sara Manifold of *The Mt. Vernon Democrat* asked me if I was aware of any ghost stories in Posey County. She thought that since I was probably here when Posey County was founded I might have some information in that regard. Here is my response.

THE HAUNTED COURTHOUSE (?)

(Week of November 3, 2008)

"I saw it in the room in the southwest corner of the basement. It passed right beside me as I was going through the old files. It was a dark form that was inside the room with me as it went between two aisles of file folders. I ran right up to the Clerk's Office on the first floor and told the women there, 'Do you know you have a ghost?' The women said, 'Oh, yeah, we know. We have felt its presence several times. We call him, George.'"

That was the account I received October 19, 2008 from a man whose work requires him to from time to time search through the records in the catacombs of our one hundred and thirty-two year old courthouse. In checking with our County Clerk, Donna Butler, she and her deputy, Mary Stillwagoner, told me they had felt an eerie presence in the basement numerous times. The man swore me to secrecy as to his identity as he claims to have a wife who already thinks he is batty. His wife must be a lot like Peg.

My own court reporter, Katrina Mann, who is as sensible and intelligent as any human can be, told me she did her best to only go into the file room in the basement's southwest corner when she absolutely had to, and never after hours when she is working alone. And Katrina's fellow court reporter, Kristie Hoffman, who has served the Posey Circuit Court for over twenty years tells me she refused for months to go back to the file room in the southwest corner of the basement after hearing noises and feeling an evil presence there.

One of the advantages of being judge is that I never have to do any real work myself. The clerks, court reporters, bailiff and probation officers bring me files while I remain above the basement's nether world. I do get to determine what issues are to be discussed from those files. I define the issues for our poltergeist séance as follows: Are there such things as ghosts? And, if so, do one or more such goblins consider the southwest corner of the courthouse basement to be their domain? Let's take these thorny matters on one at a time.

As to whether ghosts exist, let me boldly state that I haven't a clue. I have never seen one but, then, I have never seen the Chicago Cubs win a World Series either. Yet, I believe, they may have won one a hundred years ago.

So let us move on to issue two. If the courthouse has a ghost, who or what might it be and why is it unhappy with people invading its space? Let me suggest just a few possibilities.

JOHN ANDERSON AND/OR ZACK SNYDER

In 1883, nineteen year old Anderson and twenty year old Snyder murdered nineteen year old James Vanweyer by slashing his throat and drowning him in the Ohio just east of Mt. Vernon. Being new to the crime game, they readily confessed their heinous acts and sought mercy from the legal system. They were hanged together just two blocks from the courtroom where the death penalty was imposed.

It is possible they might still be a little upset with the outcome of their honesty in admitting their sins. As they say, confession may be good for the soul, but for these candidates for "specterhood", not so much for the body.

OLD DANIEL HARRISON

In 1878, fifty-one year old Daniel Harrison was charged with murder and lodged in the county jailhouse that was then on our courthouse campus. A mob broke into the jail and cut Harrison to pieces then dumped his parts into the jail's privy. They probably remain there yet today.

Old Dan's bones may be rattling around waiting for justice.

JIM GOOD, WILLIAM CHAMBERS, JEFF HOPKINS AND EDWARD WARNER

These four young men were dragged from our jail October 12, 1878 and lynched on the courthouse campus. Perhaps they still seek to have their day in court.

JUDGE GOODLET

Judge Goodlet never forgave Posey County for voting him off the Bench in 1832. He was particularly angry at the man who beat him, Judge Samuel Hall. He tried to kill Judge Hall in the Posey Circuit Courtroom. Maybe Judge Goodlett is still trying to take back his judgeship. I will try to stay alert.

"INTROSPECTERATION"

And speaking of myself and courthouse ghosts, there are some of my so called friends who allege that the whole purpose behind digging up the southwestern portion of the courthouse campus during the renovation and replacing the ancient, leaking sewage pipes in that infamous room in the basement was to give me a permanent resting place. I can only hope to return to haunt such wags myself.

CONCLUSION

So there you have it Gentle Readers of Halloween lore. You now have another reason to avoid jury duty in the Posey Circuit Court.

HELP!

(Week of March 24, 2008)

Usually when someone says to me that they need hip boots in my court, it is some lawyer who has been left unimpressed by my legal analysis. But whoever ventured into the catacombs of our one hundred and thirty-two year old courthouse last Wednesday morning had two options, sink or swim. Well, Kristie Hoffman, my long-time court reporter, took a third course of action. She first tested her sailor's vocabulary then cried and screamed.

Kristie works from seven a.m. to three p.m. She called me at home at two seconds after seven: "Judge, you'd better get down here immediately before I *#*#! There's water everywhere and it's getting deeper by the minute. Get down here right now!"

After working for Kristie for over twenty years, I have learned to simply follow orders until the crisis of the moment subsides. "Okay, Kristie, would it be okay if I finish taking my daily orders from Peg first?" By the way Gentle Reader, what happened to, "It's a man's world."?

When I got to the courthouse, somewhat attired for both court and a job excavating the English Chunnel, I found Jim Tron and his crew of Fly Thompson, John Brown, Mike Deves, Rick Vaughn, Todd Redman, Tony Rich, Jeremy Morrison and Jeremy Brock up to their knees in the two feet of water that was lapping at my historical court records dating back to 1815.

Other than my years as judge, I have not experienced hell on earth. However, seeing Jim and his men bent over wielding shovels, picks, hoses and pumps with their arms and legs covered with grey mud under the arched ceiling of the old dungeon, gave me a pretty good preview of the ultimate destination to which some of my customers have directed me.

And the water was pouring in faster than the hardworking galley slaves could bail it out. This time I had to agree with Kristie's dire warnings, things were indeed at a desperate pass.

But out of nowhere help arrived as if in a Saturday morning black and white western. My probation officers, Shawnna Rigsby and Jason Simmons appeared with brooms, mops and, in Shawnna's case, a pirate's bandana wrapped around her head. My highly organized bailiff, John Emhuff, offered his services including procuring new plastic storage containers to replace the wet boxes in an effort to help preserve our records. Court Reporters, Katrina Mann and the much maligned Kristie, as well as Probation Officer Michelle Fortune kept the regular business of the court on schedule without a break in service. Katrina and Kristie, also, planned for the implementation of a replacement system for maintaining our evidence.

My other two court reporters, Becky Rutledge and Ashley Thompson, with rubber boots so new they looked like their mommies had sent them out to play in the rain, moved boxes, files and irreplaceable evidence from hundreds of cases. County Commissioners Jim Alsop and Scott Moye quickly sized up the emergency and acted with alacrity, while Sheriff Jim Folz both personally and with his deputies provided security at a time his office was stretched thin by other high water emergencies. However, one of the deputies, Mark Heinrich, is Jim's son-in-law so he may not have been a true volunteer.

Rodney Shephard and his industrial cleaning crew of Jim Hughes, Bob Largent, Bob Sharber, John Bethel and Dan Bratcher helped clean the floor coverings that were installed in the recent renovation.

Sharon Carr worked like a Trojan to haul, clean, drain, you name it, for almost twenty-four straight hours. And thanks to Charley Chambliss and Rodney Fetcher, our very expensive and irreplaceable county computer terminals and electronic data were saved and up and running again within a few hours.

Well, I am sure there are others who deserve credit and I apologize if I omitted someone. As judge and as Jim Redwine, I sincerely thank all who helped. It felt like an old barn raising. It felt great!

WHERE'S THE PONY?

(Week of December 25, 2006)

I have always liked Christmas. Before I started school, I liked Christmas because my older brothers and sister were home playing with me instead of being in school.

After I started school, I liked Christmas because I got out of school.

Now I like Christmas because my grandchildren are home, thankfully their homes, for me to play with.

Although I grew up where white Christmases were rare, we had a few. Since I have been a southern Indiana Hoosier, we have had about one white Christmas every ten years. I like white Christmases.

Peg and I like to snow ski so perforce we must like snow. We prefer it on mountains but the Ohio River bank is about as high above sea level as we can hope for in Posey County.

What a nice combination: I like Christmas and I like snow. To have both Christmas and snow is the ultimate holiday experience.

Of course, the usual term is ♫I'm dreaming of a <u>white </u>Christmas♫, not a snowy Christmas. So in places such as Posey County where snow is rare on Christmas Day, people may have to settle for other, non-frozen white stuff to set the holiday mood.

And thanks to our feathered friends, there is a definite "white" Christmas around our newly renovated historic courthouse.

Should you need legal services at our courthouse, I suggest that you resist the natural urge to make "snowballs" of the large and pervasive accumulation of ♫a blanket of white, laid out like diamonds in the-**noise**-of the night. ♫

That white covering from lawn to tree branches to walks to parking lot to windows to roof is not what it seems. Should you be on the village square right after a light rain, you will know that smell is not from frankincense or myrrh.

On the other hand, as I am an eternal optimist, especially during the Christmas season, when I step in a dollop of horse droppings I expect a pony is near.

Ergo, I now am looking for a very large and very active Big Bird!

CHANGES

(Week of December 26, 2005)

I like change. Some of my court staff, particularly Katrina Sue Mann, who has been in charge for 28 years, hate it. This combination can be volatile; such as now as we move the Posey Circuit Court, Circuit Court Clerk and Election Office to our temporary digs.

Should you have need of any of these services you will find us at 327 Main Street in Mt. Vernon. The telephone numbers, faxes, emails and regular mails remain the same.

And, should you need to see me, you will have to survive the gauntlet of five of my staff who will be between me and the World for the next year as the Courthouse is being renovated.

Kindly Dr. John Emhuff is my bailiff. Contact with him if you are on jury duty will be a pleasure. Unless, of course, you want to be excused.

After John though you must deal with the court reporters: Katrina; Synda Waters; Becky Rutledge; or Kristie Hoffman.

Before the move, you couldn't have found four more pleasant and competent public servants. But now, with their computers, phones and fax machine not working, it's as if crossing Main Street was more like crossing the River Styx to Hades.

"Abandon All Hope Ye Who Enter Herein!"

It all seems so gay to me. The hustle and bustle at Christmas time is just enhanced by boxing up thousands of documents and books as well as antique furniture.

And speaking of antique furniture, if you pass by the front windows of the temporary courthouse, you will see furniture from 1817, 1825, 1876 and 1892 on display.

As the men from Shetler Moving were bringing in my huge oak desk I was helping, actually just directing, them. I'm not sure what he meant but one of those young wags asked me if that was my first desk?

Anyway, change has always appealed to me. When I told my staff, including my four Probation Officers, what an opportunity for adventure this move is, Katrina retorted, "That's because you don't have to do anything!" I thought that was unkind.

Speaking of the Probation Department, anything to change the subject, my Chief Probation Officer, Rodney Fetcher, and my Bailiff, John Emhuff, have worked sun up to beyond sundown on this move. The rest of the staff and even one of their spouses, Heath Rigsby, have also endured much and worked hard.

Shawnna Rigsby, Michelle Fortune and Jason Simmons who comprise the rest of the Probation Deartment have a great deal of important responsibilities to carry out even in normal times.

They are protecting the public and servicing victims and persons charged with offenses under very trying circumstances.

Richard Simmons and Sharon Carr who maintain the courthouse and Charley Chambliss who does our IT work have gone way beyond the call of duty.

And, of course, David Angermeier's Clerk and Election Office and particularly his Chief Deputy, Mary Hess, have had the same challenges and have done yeoman's work.

To all of these people I have but two words:

THANK YOU!

ANTS OR GRASSHOPPERS

(Week of November 6, 2006)

Aesop who was born a slave in Greece in 620 B.C. became one of his country's most influential free citizens. His wisdom, often expressed through his fables, helped Greece's leaders plan for the country's needs. This planning over several years led to the Golden Age of Greece.

A recurring theme of Aesop was that the future was going to come regardless, so ignoring it and simply living for the present was a recipe for disaster.

Posey County has been blessed over the years with many people who understood that the world was not going to end when they did. Therefore, their duty as responsible citizens was to plan for the future as previous good citizens before them had.

That is why we in Posey County today enjoy excellent schools, good roads and public facilities such as our 130-year old courthouse, the War Memorial Coliseum built in 1927 and renovated in 1998 and the historic Hovey House we renovated in 1996 and now use for the Prosecuting Attorney's office and meetings of the Posey County Council and Board of Commissioners.

Our county leaders decided, starting about 1995, to renovate the three historic buildings on the public square in Mt. Vernon. While I applauded the preservation of our links with our past, I and others such as Commissioner Martin Ray Redman suggested in 1993 that we maintain our existing public buildings while we planned for a comprehensive facility that would be functional in the 21st Century with its requirements for modern technology, accommodation for persons with special needs and security concerns. A majority of our county's elected leaders chose a different approach. That is the essence of democracy.

Democracy's best feature is that it pools the thoughts of many people on issues important to many people. One person's ideas may be of value, but, if so, the input of others is more likely to be of the most value.

Now that we have the Hovey House, the Coliseum and the Courthouse in usable condition for our citizens who are seeking public services, I suggest that we must maintain these edifices while we plan for our county's future needs.

Just as Aesop's ant slowly but steadily prepared for the future while the profligate grasshopper put nothing away, if we start now incrementally saving a reasonable amount, we could help our future citizens be prepared.

According to a comprehensive study of government planning done by a branch of the University of Missouri, the best approach is for a public entity to have plans for the short term (up to 6 years), the middle range (5 or 6 to 10 to 12 years) and the long term (more than 20 years). As our county is just completing several capital improvement renovations that will probably provide usable facilities for several years, we should start now to plan for when the use of these current facilities is no longer in the public's best interest. Of course, due to constantly changing federal and state mandates, that inevitable day may come before the useful life of our present buildings has run its natural course.

If so, it is even more imperative that we do not leave our descendants with empty coffers and crisis management.

In this regard I wish to thank the leaders of Mt. Vernon for having the vision to look to our beautiful Ohio River front for future development. This week the removal of the old grain elevator began. It may take a year or two to complete the project, but a great beginning has been made.

This major move toward tomorrow and the street improvement project in Poseyville along with such items as the beautiful and historic renovation of the Granary in New Harmony and the State's modernization of Highway 69 between State Highway 62 and Interstate 64 are the kinds of long term investment in ourselves that can lead to an even better place for us and those who come after us.

BACK HOME AGAIN

(Week of November 13, 2006)

Should you wish to drop by Moll's Furniture Store at 327 Main Street in Mt. Vernon to do any court business, don't; we have moved back home.

As of Monday, November 13, 2006 the Posey Circuit Court (including Probation Office), the Circuit Court Clerk and the Election Office will no longer be in our temporary quarters.

After almost twelve months in our temporary digs, we will transition back to our renovated historic courthouse on the town square. Please come see the results of a year's labors.

During what could have been a mad house of lost files, and unprovided public services, the staffs of the Posey Circuit Court, Clerk's and Election Office have shown how to roll with the punches and keep on their toes.

Put yourselves in the position of public servants who must ensure that vital legal services are not denied regardless of circumstances. In Indiana, our Constitution requires that courts remain open at all times, that is, Indiana does not have court just certain times of the year.

Think of the court reporters, probation officers and bailiff who have had to graciously respond to inquiries for information and help in filing or responding to cases. Frequently these matters are tough on the people involved and they may, understandably, be nervous or intimidated. It is even worse when the court, itself, is in flux.

Katrina Mann, Kristie Hoffman, Becky Rutledge and Ashley Thompson are the court reporters. Rodney Fetcher, Michelle Fortune, Jason Simmons and Shawnna Rigsby are the probation officers. And our bailiff is John Emhuff. Each member of the staff has had many challenges to face as a result of this upheaval. They have served the public well throughout.

Special thanks from all of us is due to Chief Probation Officer Rodney Fetcher and bailiff John Emhuff. Each of them has contributed countless unpaid hours and untold effort to help preserve and make usable our beautiful courthouse. When you see your "new" 130- year-old edifice, please remember to tell Rod and John thank you!

And Terry Newton, Peyronin's foreman, who oversaw the job, deserves credit for going above and beyond his contractual obligations. His hard work, expertise and cooperative spirit are represented throughout the courthouse. But please give special thought to Terry "Fig" Newton when you see the wonders he has wrought in the courtroom.

David Angermeier, the Court Clerk, and his staff of Jane Murphy, Mary Hess, and Mary Stillwagoner, along with Shelly Nelson and Martha Horton in the Election Office, have been as uprooted as the Court these last several months. It has been a pleasure working with every one of them throughout.

Well, the time has come. When you read this, if anyone does, we will all be up and running in the courthouse whose cornerstone was laid July 04, 1876 by our most famous citizen, Alvin P. Hovey. I think he would approve.

HEY, THERE'S A RIVER OUT THERE

(Week of November 20, 2006)

On December 19, 2005, the Courthouse renovation began. On November 13, 2006, those of us privileged to work in this 130-year-old edifice of living Posey County history moved back into it.

How quickly one can forget the pain of childbirth (especially if one is the father) or moving.

We left falling plaster, backed up sewers, and a myriad of other impediments to serving the public. Our county's most representative public building had a misleading veneer that covered a neglected and crumbling interior. But you ought to see it now. Just as a newborn may somehow remind one of the baby's ancestors, the courthouse still feels connected to our heritage as it calls forth the needs of the 21st Century.

At least it will when the telephones and computers are working. Right now the public is being served the old fashioned way, with sweat and Yankee ingenuity.

When I first became a Posey County Judge in 1981, push button phones were the leading edge of our I.T. revolution. Court decisions written out long hand on legal pads and legal research done by hunting down then reading dusty law books were the only options we had.

Then we began to modernize. We went to local area networks and on-line electronic research. Soon the old, yellow legal pads were retired and replaced with high-tech.

Ah, life was good. But as with life in general, we all know that the crest we may be currently enjoying is likely to crash into some harsh shore.

Our shore came into view November 13th. The phones do not work, the computers are in revolt and our furniture has not arrived. On the other hand, I have become reacquainted with the same long, yellow legal pads I used almost forty years ago in law school. You know what? They still work.

Another effect of not having a computer screen to look at is one must look somewhere else. I was pleasantly surprised to find, as I gazed out my third floor window, that the Ohio River is still there. As I watched a tugboat maneuver a coal barge along the channel, I realized that when our courthouse was first built in 1876, then Judge William F. Parrett, Jr., probably stood in this same spot gazing in wonderment at the Ohio.

Judge Parrett and Alvin P. Hovey and other august members of the Posey County Bar were surely proud of this new center of justice. And just as they did not have their reverie interfered with by today's all intrusive modern conveniences, with our technology currently reduced to 1876 standards, neither do I. You know, I may just step out of my quiet chambers and tell the phone and computer guys to cool it.

Mt. Vernon River View
Painting appears by permission of Robert Pote. www.robertpotewatercolor.com

LAW DAY 2006

(Week of April 24, 2006)

In 1958, President Eisenhower declared that the United States would celebrate The Rule of Law each May to counter the Communist celebration of military might.

For almost fifty years, America's legal profession has sponsored mock trials and other celebrations in honor of America's system of justice.

In Posey County, the Bar Association has worked with schools throughout our county to help inform students about the benefits of deciding conflicts peaceably and fairly.

This will be the twenty-third consecutive year that Posey County's three high schools have presented a mock trial. Each of those twenty-three years, Mr. Rick Johnson of New Harmony and Mr. Mike Kuhn of North Posey have given of their time and talent to help their students prepare their roles.

First Mr. Charles Martin, then Mr. Steve Britt and now Ms. Ann Shank of Mt. Vernon have worked with the Bar to help their students benefit from a hands-on learning experience in the courts.

With approximately one hundred students either actively participating or observing these exercises, over two thousand Posey County High School students have served as judges, juries, attorneys, parties, witnesses, or observers in a Posey County Courtroom.

This year the mock trial will be held in the temporary quarters of the Posey Circuit Court, which is severely limited in space. Hopefully, by next May, we will be back in our renovated courthouse. But for 2006, it will be a tight squeeze.

Each year an original case is written based, loosely, on some news event. For 2006, the case involves a civil suit for damages arising out of the delivery of cookies by Boy and Girl Scouts. Because the student jurors may read this column, I will not be able to be more specific.

The roles in the mock trial rotate every year. This year, North Posey will provide the court personnel, i.e., the judge, jury, court reporter, bailiff and clerk. Kelly Clem will be the student judge.

Mt. Vernon will present the side of two elderly plaintiffs, Bertha and Barry Oldman, and their witnesses. The Plaintiffs will be represented by student attorneys, Kathryn Lee and Matt Upshaw.

New Harmony will present the side of the Defendants, Alice and Alec Smart, and their witnesses. Ann Wenzel and Jon Hibrader will be the student attorneys who represent the Defendants.

Some of the student attorneys and judges have gone on to careers in law. And the school administrations and school boards of all of our schools have always been extremely supportive of the Posey County Bar Association's efforts to help instill in our future leaders a deep respect and desire for justice. And our students have many times shown a flair for the dramatic as well as the ability to turn these mock trials into excellent learning experiences as well as a lot of fun.

LIFE AFTER HIGH SCHOOL?

(Week of April 30, 2007)

Is there life after high school? That was the question posed by author Ralph Keyes in his 1976 book of the same name.

The students from our three high schools who participated in the annual Law Day mock trial know the answer can be, "yes!"

When they see graduates from New Harmony, North Posey and Mt. Vernon high schools who now help govern our county, they have direct evidence that our schools offer a solid foundation for future achievement.

And when they see graduates from other area high schools who have gone on to be teachers and even the Chief Justice of Indiana, they know that their own goals can be achieved.

We may sometimes doubt the value of our hometown experiences because of their familiarity or because we often only read or hear about famous people through the media.

But when students have the opportunity to see for themselves the accomplishments of people who were not that long ago the same insecure self-doubting high schoolers they are today, they can realize the possibilities for themselves.

That is especially true when the leaders of today attended the very same schools and had the same doubts that the current students do.

For about a quarter of a century now, our three high schools and the Posey County Bar Association have used the Law Day mock trial to help give our students a view of some of what is possible for them. And some of the students who have participated in these exercises have gone on to careers in education, law, government and business.

High school truly has been a commencement for the successful and happy careers of these students.

NOMOLOGY

(Week of May 7, 2007)

On Law Day, Tuesday, May 1st, the students from our three county high schools engaged in the science and art of law making, i.e., nomology. With the guidance of their teachers, Ms. Shank, Mr. Britt, Mr. Kuhn and Mr. Johnson, and with the encouragement and cooperation of each of the school systems, the students had a hands-on civics experience.

Once again, Posey County's educational system has produced students with imagination and industry who provided enjoyment to the large audience that included news media, families of the participants, members of the Posey County Bar Association, and even the Chief Justice of Indiana, Randall Shepard, and his law clerk, Amanda Feltman.

So many people from the schools, the Bar, law enforcement and the courts contribute to the success of this annual event that it is not possible to fairly give everyone the thanks they are due.

However, starting with Chief Justice Shepard and Ms. Feltman who had to fly from Indianapolis and back to celebrate America's legal and educational systems with us, thank you.

Sheriff Jim Folz and Lt. Dennis Marshall of the Indiana State Police planned for the landing of the state police helicopter and Sheriff Folz, along with deputy sheriffs, Ed Thompson and Dan Montgomery, Mt. Vernon Chief of Police, Grant Beloat, and Indiana State Police officers, Frank Smith and Gregg Wagner, gave of their time and expertise in providing security.

The helicopter landing zone was outlined by members of the Mt. Vernon Fire Department, including Chief Charles Reese and firefighters, Roger Waters and Dave Idler, who brought a fire truck and equipment to ensure a safe landing.

Our historic and newly renovated courthouse was shown to its best advantage thanks to the efforts of the hardworking maintenance crew, Richard Simmons and Sharon Carr. Dick and Sharon, also, moved lots of furniture, removed trash and hung several irreplaceable items from Posey County's rich history in the impressive Alvin Hovey and Thomas Posey memorial conference rooms that were established through the efforts of Posey Circuit Court Chief Probation Officer, Rodney Fetcher. And I need to personally thank, I think, Posey Circuit Court Probation Officer, Shawnna Newton Rigsby, for including my photograph with the other old judges in the display in the Hovey room.

Sherri Banks and Rodney Cox of the Four Seasons Motel and Conference Center provided excellent accommodations for our formal luncheon and did so on very short notice.

And Chef Shawn Dimmick and server Donna Gassier of Western Hills Country Club prepared and served a marvelous meal.

The *Posey County News*, the *Mt. Vernon Democrat* and the *Evansville Courier and Press* provided thorough early notice to the public and coverage of the actual Law Day addresses and Mock Trial.

The members of the Posey County Bar Association sponsor and are deeply involved in our Law Day celebration. As attorneys and judges, the Bar has always acknowledged the wonderful social climate in which we in Posey County have the good fortune to practice law and preside over the courts.

And all of the participants and attendees of Posey County's Law Day for this past quarter of a century have recognized and applauded the quiet, hardworking, efficient and courteous staff of the Posey Circuit Court. They are terrific!

Finally, on a somber note, it was sad that after twenty-three years of enthusiastic support of this important celebration, my good friend, Jim Kohlmeyer, of the *Posey County News* was not here to join in the festivities that he always enjoyed. He is truly missed. Even though he would have chided me for using "That horse choking word!", nomology.

WHY LAW DAY?

(Week of May 12, 2008)

Those of us who grew up with the Mickey Mouse Club and bomb shelters remember when the Soviet Union celebrated May 1st with a show of military might. One of the benefits of growing up on the Oklahoma prairie was there were already "bomb shelters" before there were atomic bombs. Mother Nature's tornadoes were reason enough to have concrete reinforced bunkers.

That great war hero, President Dwight David Eisenhower, helped establish Law Day as our American response to the old USSR's bellicosity. They used bombs, we used laws. They were an oligarchy, we were a democratic republic. They had the KGB; we have the Bill Of Rights. They had the Politburo; we have three separate and equal branches of government. History has proven that "law" triumphed, and although May Day has returned to a celebration of spring, we in America continue to reinforce our reliance on law. After all, history also teaches that, "eternal vigilance is the price" of both liberty and equality of opportunity.

Some recent events have reinforced our commitment to the Rule of Law. First, we had an interesting and exciting election primary, and second, our three high schools and the Posey County Bar Association celebrated Law Day on Monday, May 12 in the Posey Circuit Court.

The Bar hosted the event that included honored guests, Indiana State Bar Association President, Douglas Church, and his daughter, Julia Kozicki. Ms. Kozicki represented the State Bar's Special Committee on Courthouse Art. Local artist, Maggie Rapp, was commissioned by the Posey County Bar Association to paint our historic courthouse. Her painting was presented to President Church to be hung in the offices of the Indiana State Bar Association in Indianapolis.

Judge Brent Almon of the Posey Superior Court and Judge Donald Baier, Posey County Bar Association President, spoke to the audience of students, teachers, attorneys, county officials and guests.

Then the Silver Anniversary Mock Trial was presented by the students.

Thank you all for participating in this important reaffirmation of our democracy and a special thank you to the staff of the Posey Circuit Court for all of their hard work in helping to put on this event.

LAW DAY WINNERS

(Week of May 19, 2008)

The Posey County Bar Association donated an original painting of our historic courthouse to the Indiana State Bar Association. This work of New Harmony artist Maggie Rapp will take its rightful place among representative pictures from Indiana's ninety-one other counties. Much of our county's interesting and important history occurred in or is chronicled in our one hundred and thirty two year old courthouse.

Of course, not all of our courthouse's history is interesting or important. For example, I have been part of our courthouse's fixtures since January 1, 1983. To either commemorate my tenure, or, perhaps, to gently remind me of my mortality, the Posey County Bar Association honored me with my own beautifully framed print of Maggie's painting. Regardless of the catalyst for this marvelous gift, I am sincerely grateful and wish to thank each of the members of our Bar Association. It means a great deal to me and to Peg. It was a special Law Day.

Law Day is properly celebrated in the spring. You are aware that Law Day is America's response to the old USSR's saber rattling on May Day. From the beginning of the Communist Party's usurpation of the age old festival of rebirth, many countries have resented having their ancient traditions tromped upon by the Soviets' ostentatious display of military power.

As the featured speaker at this year's Law Day State Bar President Douglas Church said:

> "In contrast to Thomas Hobbes's description of human existence as, 'solitary, poor, nasty, brutish and short,' the life of Anglo Saxon jurisprudence as practiced in America helps guarantee right over might."
> (*The Leviathan* @ chapters 13 and 14; written in 1651)

This is the essence of Law Day and the main lesson that the Posey County Bar Association and our three county high schools hope that our bright and energetic students learn from the annual Mock Trial.

Russia continues to growl as if it were a she bear protecting her cubs. Whether it is the USSR, Russia, or any country that opts for might over right or power over the rites of spring and rebirth, our students today will need to be prepared to meet rashness with reason and licentiousness with law.

From my observation of our students' performances during the Mock Trial, we need have no worries. Ergo, they and we are all winners.

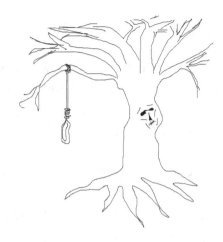

CHAPTER TEN

JUDGE LYNCH!

WHERE THERE'S A WILL

(Week of March 12, 2007)

William Shakespeare probably thought that the fictional will he wrote for *Julius Caesar* [Act III, sc. ii] would be the most famous one he would ever write. He was wrong. Shakespeare's personal will has lived long after him and is quoted more often than most of his great literature. Why you might ask? Because Shakespeare's Last Will and Testament left his, "second best bed to his wife."

For almost four hundred years scholars and sidewalk psychiatrists have mused over what this clause in the Bard's will signifies. Did he not love his wife? Did he have a mistress to whom he left his best bed? Did the greatest wordsmith in the world simply write a bad will?

If Shakespeare had died today, the "Drive By Media" would milk the great man's last wishes for far more than fifteen minutes.

One thing that even the most neophyte law student is taught in law school about what the legal biz calls "Future Interests" is to resist leaving in ink what you should not say even in private.

This sound advice reverberates in my mind from time to time when I am brought a Last Will and Testament that contains a clause that the now dead person was too ashamed or too sensible to say while alive.

Another thing I have learned from trying to fix my own automobile or my own plumbing is that saving a few shekels at the start of a project is poor compensation for needing to hire a professional to fix my mistakes. So is it with lay people who write their own wills. Often they will take terms of legal art that they do not understand and plug them into their personal documents. Later, after their deaths, of course, their heirs and beneficiaries are left to clean up the malapropisms.

It is somewhat like that current television commercial where a lay person is holding a butter knife while his surgeon is instructing him over the phone to, "make an incision between the fourth and fifth abdominal muscles."

On the other hand, sometimes the results of non-professional drafting of wills can lead to interesting dilemmas.

Such was the case in an early Posey County will that was brought to my attention by attorney, Marc Hawley. Mr. Hawley's firm helps provide title insurance for real estate and as part of a title search on some property in the Upton area, just north and west of Mt. Vernon, he found a will dated March 1, 1817.

This will was executed by a man who died two weeks later. This early Posey County resident was concerned about the welfare of his young daughter, Almina. He tried to encourage her from the grave to wait until she was eighteen to get married. His will instructed that if she did, she was to receive $500.00. Interestingly, in the same paragraph by which he tried to encourage Almina to wait to marry, he tried to help ensure that she would be a sought after bride. He instructed the executors of his estate to immediately pay Almina the $500.00, "...together with all the interes prophet emoluments (sic)" (interest, profits and emoluments), should she marry before she turned eighteen.

But that is not the clause of the will that truly surprised me. No, what caused me to re-read this old Posey County, Indiana, document was its paragraph number thirteen in which the dying man gave his slave, Stephen, to his executors who were, also, his brothers.

Who would have thought that in *free* Indiana, a legally filed document would so casually mention slavery? Perhaps the issue of which side of the Mason-Dixon Line some of our early Posey County residents came down on, at least emotionally, was not completely settled in 1817. If you are not completely absorbed in March Madness, we might look into this issue more in depth the next few weeks.

THE SLAVE (?) STEPHEN

(Week of March 19, 2007)

You were probably as surprised as I was at the discovery that in 1817 slavery existed in Posey County. Evidence of this was found in a will that was recorded on March 17, 1817. We know that when Indiana was admitted to the Union in 1816 that it came in as a free state with a constitutional prohibition against slavery. And we know how in the Civil War (1861-1866) Posey County provided many soldiers, including three generals, in the struggle to end slavery in America.

But in the beginning of the 19th Century, much of the law on slavery was unsettled. There were still many unanswered issues. For example, if a person who was already living in Indiana before 1816 owned slaves, were the slaves freed by the new constitution? Did the Northwest Ordinance that was authored by Thomas Jefferson and which governed the territory that included the future state of Indiana carry over to the new state? If so, since slavery was forbidden by the Northwest Ordinance, was slavery illegal in the area that became Posey County?

Of course, Jefferson himself owned slaves, some of whom he only freed after his death by his will. Why should our early Posey County resident be judged any differently?

And that most admired of all Americans, the Father of Our Country, George Washington, and our first First Lady, Martha Washington, only freed their 300 plus slaves via George's will and only after Martha's death.

There seems to have been ample precedent for Mr. Joseph Kennedy of our fair county to believe he had the legal right to own Stephen in 1817.

In fact, some Biblical scholars of that time pointed to the Old Testament where the ancient Hebrews even had written procedures for selling their own children into slavery. (*Exodus* 21:7-- 21:11.)

Suffice it to say, we must afford people the right to live in their own times and not judge them as if they lived today.

On the other hand, just three years after Mr. Kennedy's death, the Indiana Supreme Court decided several of these thorny slavery issues. In 1820, our highest court heard the Knox County case of *Lasselle v. State*, an anti-slavery decision in which Justice Isaac Blackford took part.

Isaac Blackford was the first judge of the Posey Circuit Court before he was appointed to the Indiana Supreme Court on September 10, 1817.

Justice Blackford set the standard for Indiana judges at all levels. And on the issue of slavery, he led the curve. Perhaps Judge Blackford can help guide us to a resolution of Stephen's status as we try to navigate these sticky wickets in the next few weeks leading up to our nation's celebration of the rule of law that will take place on Law Day which is May 1st.

WHAT'S IN A NAME?

(Week of March 26, 2007)

If you have followed our recent analyses of the 1817 will of Mr. Joseph Kennedy of our fair county, you may recall that he left his slave, Stephen, to his brothers, Samuel and David Kennedy.

According to paragraphs thirteen and fourteen, Stephen was to be hired out for four years with Samuel and David to each receive half of his earnings. Then, if Samuel and David were satisfied with Stephen's work, Stephen was to be freed.

This method of freeing slaves via one's will was a common device when our country was new. Many slaveholders such as Thomas Jefferson who may have owned his own children by the slave Sally Hemmings and George and Martha Washington who may have owned Martha's own half-sister, Ann Dandridge, ordered their slaves released upon the owner's death.

We may look back and wonder how such things could happen. But a few years from now our descendents may try to judge our actions by the future's standards. We might, also, be found wanting.

Anyway, back to the case in front of us. What did these four years of continued slavery mean to Stephen in March of 1817?

Mr. Joseph Kennedy must have had every confidence that his two brothers would deal fairly with Stephen and free him after four years. By the terms of the will, Samuel and David were the sole determiners of whether Stephen's service was adequate for his manumission. Now, you and I, and probably Stephen too, might be a little concerned to have our freedom hanging on such a tenuous thread. However, Stephen had no say; he was property, not a person in much of 1817 America.

But help was on the way for Stephen and it came in 1820 from the Indiana Supreme Court that included former Posey Circuit Judge Isaac Blackford.

Justice Blackford had been Posey County's first circuit judge and later served on the Indiana Supreme Court longer than any other person (1817-1853). Blackford was vociferous in his anti-slavery views. He and his colleagues on the Indiana Supreme Court left no doubt about the law in Indiana on slavery when they decided a famous case that started out in the old Northwest Territory and involved an American Indian tribe, a leading businessman in Vincennes with the unusual name of Hyacinthe Lasselle and a slave named Polly.

Next week, if you care to follow along, we will see how the case from Knox County decided by our Supreme Court in 1820 gave a clear and ringing answer to what many had thought were debatable issues concerning slavery in Indiana.

FROM BOY TO MAN

(Week of April 2, 2007)

Joseph Kennedy thought he was being generous to the person he called "my Negro slave Stephen" when he wrote his will. Mr. Kennedy set forth a plan whereby Stephen might earn his freedom after Kennedy's death through four years of unpaid labor that was "agreeable" to Mr. Kennedy's heirs.

But the 1817 Posey County slaveholder was attempting to give freedom to one already free under Indiana law. As set forth in the 1820 Indiana Supreme Court case of *Lasselle v. State*, Indiana's 1816 Constitution prohibited slavery in any form, i.e. either through ownership or indentured service.

Hyacinthe Lasselle was a well-to-do tavern keeper in Vincennes, Indiana, who prior to 1820 had purchased a woman named Polly from a tribe of American Indians who inhabited the Northwest Territory.

Although slavery was prohibited in any part of the Northwest Territory, as Indians were not afforded the rights of American citizens, Mr. Lasselle's attorneys argued that they were not bound by United States laws. The Indians had captured Polly's Negro mother before the passage of the Northwest Ordinance of 1787. And Lasselle's attorneys further argued that even though Polly was born after 1787, since she was born to a slave, by law Polly was also a slave.

The Circuit Court Judge in Knox County agreed with Lasselle's position and decided that Polly was, in fact, and by Indiana and federal law, the duly paid for property of Mr. Lasselle.

Polly's attorneys appealed the trial court's decision to the Indiana Supreme Court. By the time Polly's case came before the Supreme Court, Posey County's first Circuit Court Judge, Isaac Blackford, was a member of the high court.

Justice Blackford and his colleagues decided that Indiana's 1816 Constitution was all the authority needed to guarantee Polly's, and ergo Stephen's, freedom. The Court held that according to Indiana's Constitution:

> "There shall be neither slavery nor involuntary servitude
> in this State…. [T]he framers of our constitution
> intended a total and entire prohibition of slavery in this
> state."

Our Supreme Court declared that the will of the people of Indiana as expressed in our 1816 Constitution could not be more clear:

> "Slavery can have no existence in the State of Indiana."

Although in 1820, the "Negro issues" appeared to be clearly settled in Indiana, as we may find, later developments muddied these waters.

Some of the information in this and related Gavel Gamut articles was taken from an article written by Sandra Boyd Williams for the *Indiana Law Review*, Volume 30, No. 1, page 305, published in 1997.

THE DOOMED BOYS: PART 1

(Week of February 19, 2007)

Nineteen-year-old James Vanweyer had left his widowed mother in Webster County, Kentucky, in the summer of 1883 and traveled to Posey County to work on the farm of Thomas Watson.

After helping Mr. Watson to harvest corn, Vanweyer was paid $30.00. He made his first stop at Niedert's Tavern in Mt. Vernon on August 9th where he was separated from almost half of his money buying drinks for people he met that night.

On August 10th, Vanweyer asked Mr. Lowenhaupt, one of the owners of Rosenbaum's General Store at 315 Main Street in Mt. Vernon, to hold in the store safe the $18.00 he had managed to save from the freeloaders.

Early the next morning, Vanweyer withdrew his money and went down to the hominy mill located by the iron bridge over McFaddin Creek. As he was sitting there, John Anderson and Zack Snyder, who had met Vanweyer the night before at Niedert's, walked up to him and asked him to go swimming in the Ohio River with them.

Young Jim Vanweyer must have been very naïve to fall for the story that Anderson and Snyder had just happened upon Vanweyer on their way to a swim. After all, he had met them for the first time just the night before. And, while in their company, he had lost almost half of his summer's earnings.

As the three young men approached the river, Anderson and Snyder tried to coax Vanweyer into the water. They stripped and waded in but Vanweyer just sat on a log and watched.

After about fifteen minutes of urging Vanweyer to join them, the two gave up and got out. They dressed, then Snyder said to Anderson that Anderson and Vanweyer should box to see who was the better fighter.

Vanweyer and Anderson began to spar, and Snyder sneaked up behind Vanweyer and hit him in the back of the head with a club two or three times. Anderson and Vanweyer fell to the ground clinching and began rolling on the riverbank. As Anderson held Vanweyer, Snyder grabbed Vanweyer by the throat and began choking him.

Both Anderson and Snyder stated that the "dull iron handled pocket knife" used to ultimately subdue Vanweyer belonged to Anderson. However, as with almost all joint defendant crimes, each accused the other of being the one who actually wielded the knife.

John Anderson's mother confronted John and Zack Snyder when they came to Anderson's home for supper that evening. She was immediately suspicious of their muddy clothing and overall disheveled appearance. But they told her they had done nothing wrong. Their cover story was that they had just gotten muddy while swimming.

The next evening about 11:00 o'clock p.m., Mrs. Anderson confronted the nineteen-year-old John again, this time while his father lay drunk on a pillow between the kitchen and the smokehouse of the Anderson home.

She was crying and told John that she had "run the cards [Tarot cards], and every time she did so she saw death and trouble." Young John broke down and told his poor mother what she most feared to hear.

Next week, we can take up with John's confession and his mother's advice to him.

AN INVITATION TO A HANGING

(Week of February 26, 2007)

Confession may be good for the soul but, perhaps, not so much for the body, at least as it worked out for young John Anderson and Zack Snyder in 1883.

Anderson's hardworking mother struggled to support the family by raising and selling chickens as her alcoholic husband drank up the profits. Mrs. Anderson's experience with both her husband and their son, John, had led her to expect the worst. When John and his ne'er do well friend, Zack Snyder, came home muddy and nervous she knew they had been up to no good.

But when she heard that her deadbeat son had been buying drinks at one of Posey County's houses of ill repute, her suspicions were totally aroused. The soiled doves who occupied Maude's place in Mt. Vernon may have had "hearts of gold", but they were a cash only business. And Mrs. Anderson knew that any money John had to spend was of dubious origin.

So Mrs. Anderson, who must have fancied herself to be a shrewd detective, confronted her son when he returned from a night of revelry with Katie at Maude's establishment.

John might have been a young tough about town but he folded immediately when his mother accused him of mayhem.

"We killed him [James Vanweyer] for his money." John's mother advised him to confess his awful crime to the authorities. Both John Anderson and Zack Snyder gave all the gory details to Posey County Sheriff Ed Hayes. Each claimed the other had been the one to slash young Vanweyer's throat, but both admitted holding him under the waters of the Ohio River until he ceased to struggle.

Although Zack Snyder admitted his role in the sordid affair, he pled not guilty and in September, only one month after the killing, submitted his fate to twelve men tried and true: James Campbell (Foreman), Henry Benner, Michael Reumner, Harrison Barrett, Truman Johnson, Louis Wilson, Ferdinand Grebe, John Ziegler, Alonzo Allen, Thomas Allman, Robert Kight and Clarence Thomas.

After a thorough two-day trial, the jury rendered its verdict: "We, the Jury, find Zack Snyder Guilty of Murder in the First Degree and that he suffer death."

Upon learning of the jury's approach to the case with Snyder, John Anderson opted to plead guilty and throw himself upon the tender mercies of Judge William F. Parrett, Jr., of the Posey Circuit Court. This strategy unfolded in October, 1883.

John Anderson's court-appointed attorneys, each of whom was paid $100.00, presented Anderson before Judge Parrett in the same courtroom we still use one hundred and twenty-four years later.

Attorneys J.G. Owens and M.W. Pearse pled for mercy, but equal justice was Judge Parrett's ruling. John Anderson received the same fate as Zack Snyder: to be hanged by the neck until dead.

The Judge ordered Sheriff Hayes to build a private scaffold at the "new" jail, now the Riverview Manor Boys Group Home, and to carry out the Court's judgment on both Snyder and Anderson on January 25, 1884 in the presence of an invited audience. Sheriff Hayes issued special tickets to an audience approved by Judge Parrett. The tickets contained drawings of both young men and the admonition that the tickets would be void if there was any attempt to use them by a non-approved attendee.

As frequently occurs when one is faced with the prospect of impending doom, Snyder and Anderson both sought forgiveness and redemption while awaiting their fate. Perhaps they prayed for a miracle of deliverance.

Surely each of their minds was "greatly concentrated" when the J. C. Woody Company began to erect the double gallows right outside the walls of their cell on January 14, 1884. Daily cares suddenly became less significant.

And how did our local community respond to the possibility of Posey County's only legal execution? Well, "all I know is what I read in *The Western Star* newspaper of 1884." I'll share that next week.

Admit Bearer to Assist in the Execution
OF
JOHN ANDERSON AND ZACK SNYDER,
——TO BE HANGED AT——
Mt. Vernon, Ind., Friday, January 25th, 1884.

Sheriff

This Ticket will be Taken up if Presented by any other than the one to whom it was issued.

THE WAGES OF SIN

(Week of March 5, 2007)

Last month, Posey County Sheriff Jim Folz gave me copies of the 1883 Death Warrants for John Anderson and Zack Snyder.

You may have read that Mssrs. Anderson and Snyder confessed to murdering James Vanweyer in order to steal his hard earned wages.

A few years ago, Posey County historian, Ilse Horacek, brought me a copy of an article that appeared in the Posey County *Western Star* newspaper on January 25, 1884. That was the fateful day that Posey Circuit Court Judge William Parrett, Jr., had set for then Sheriff Edward Hayes to hang both young men at what is now the Riverview Manor Boys Group Home (the old jail).

As reported in the *Western Star*, "Sheriff Hayes performed his duty without flinching." And to their credit, "Both walked to the scaffold like men, and in a firm tone stated that they were prepared to die."

I surmise that after sitting in jail for several months awaiting the fall of the Sword of Damocles, hanging might well have been a relief. This is especially true as the sheriff was ordered to build the gallows right outside the defendants' jail cells. Every cut of the saw and every fall of a hammer must have penetrated the sinew of the condemned men.

When I first read the account of how these unfortunate criminals had to endure the erection of their gallows beside their cells, it brought to mind William Faulkner's classic short story, *As I Lay Dying*. I wondered if Faulkner had heard about our only legal hanging before he wrote his story. The dying Addie Bundren's son, Cash, would measure his mother through her bedroom window as she watched him construct her coffin. Is it any wonder she sought relief in her memories?

As for Anderson and Snyder, the *Western Star* reported, "The pounding and hammering, which was distinctly heard upon the inside of the jail excited them considerably."

But the good folks of Posey County sought to ease the crossing over of the murderers. Both prisoners spent a great deal of their time in prayer with the assistance of Reverand Asbury of the M.E. Church and Reverand Wulzen of the German M.E. Church.

Also, a choir of young Christian ladies sang hymns outside the jail cells the night before the executions.

However, the editor of the *Western Star* kept the significance of the public message well in mind:

> "The tragedy of today has a terrible significance for
> those pursuing the same career of depravity as was
> followed by Anderson and Snyder.

•••

Young men reflect! If you have adopted idleness as a
profession, you cannot avoid its concomitant, CRIME!"

As reported by the *Western Star*, "The Last of the Doomed Boys" took place when the drop
sprung at 11:45 a.m. January 25, 1884. The bodies were left dangling for thirteen minutes.

NO STATUTE OF LIMITATIONS

(Week of October 6, 2005)

On Monday, October 07, 1878 ..."[T]hree white girls living very quietly in a retired and lonely part of the city were outraged by negroes." So said the front page of the *The Mt. Vernon Dollar Democrat* published October 17, 1878.

The New Harmony Register of Friday, October 11, 1878 reported that Deputy Sheriff Cyrus O. Thomas had been killed Thursday, October 10, 1878 while trying to arrest a Negro who had been indicted by a Posey County Grand Jury for the "outrage".

The Western Star, another Posey County weekly newspaper, lead its Thursday, October 17, 1878 front page with the banner headline "**Judge Lynch Holds Court**."

Officer Thomas who had been, ..."[a] prominent candidate for sheriff", was described as brave, noble and generous. His death had been avenged by 300 of Posey County's "best citizens" and the bodies of ..."four Negroes were suspended from the large locust tree on the Courthouse Square until after Thomas's funeral."

The term Judge Lynch is an oxymoron. To judge is to apply settled law to particular facts using established procedures. To lynch is to kill a human being without any safeguards or due process of law.

William Lynch who lived in Virginia from 1742-1820 acted as a sort of Judge Roy Bean. He set up his own court and made up his own rules. His name became the metonymy (the representative term) for mob rule. For the newspaper to describe such an event as justice dispensed by "Judge Lynch" was a well understood literary device in America when lynchings were more recognizable. It was usually applied to an *ultra vires* (illegal) action that the majority of a community publicly condemned but privately sanctioned. Such was the case in Posey County in October 1878.

I first learned of the newspaper reports of the death of Captain C.O. Thomas and the circumstances which led up to it and the lynchings which grew out of it from my friend Ilse Horacek on March 14, 1990. Ilse is one of Posey County's best writers and historians. I had spoken to the Posey County Coterie Literary Society in the Circuit Court Courtroom about the incident which I had found briefly mentioned in W.P. Leonard's *History and Directory of Posey County*. Afterwards, Ilse gave me a copy of one of the articles from 1878. My memory of our conversation from 1990 is that Ilse told me she has a particular interest in C.O. Thomas and the surrounding happenings as her husband's family is related to Officer Thomas. Some accounts refer to him as O.C. Thomas and others as O.S. Thomas.

The lynchings occurred right outside what was then our brand new courthouse. I am reminded of it whenever I walk across the courthouse campus. And in October each year the events of 1878 feel as though they just occurred.

If you wish to follow along we might relive some of those days. And if you have an old family Bible or diary or letters or other information about the outrage of the white girls or Officer Thomas's death or the lynchings we could, perhaps, be fairer to the memory of all involved if you would contact me. As we used to say when some other boy would threaten, "I'll see you after school!", I am not that hard to find.

A particular artifact that another of my friends, Posey County Historian Glenn Curtis, told me he saw in the barber shop a few years ago was hawked for sale in October, 1878 in *The Mt. Vernon Dollar Democrat*:

> "Mr. Jones, our artist, took photographs of the four
> Negroes lynched by the vigilants [sic] last Friday night.
> It is an excellent representation of the tragic scene.
> Mr. Jones has copies for sale."

Perhaps one of you may have access to such a photograph or other evidence and together we can investigate what occurred that other October 127 years ago. Let's talk again next week.

MT. VERNON'S BELLEVILLE, OCTOBER, 1878

(Week of October 17, 2005)

The *Mt. Vernon Dollar Democrat* described the women alleged to be the victims of the rape of October 1878, as, "[T]hree white girls living very quietly in a retired and lonely part of the city." The "girls" lived in an area of Mt. Vernon then known as Belleville.

This area was generally located just north of the Ohio River and south of what was then First Street (now Water Street). This part of Posey County provided much of the flavor for its reputation as a good place for a good time for Ohio River boatmen and others.

The three belles were the named victims of the rapes by Edward Hill, William Chambers, Jim Good, Jeff Hopkins, Ed Warner and "three other Negroes". The crimes were alleged to have occurred October 07, 1878. These men were indicted by a Posey County Grand Jury on October 08, 1878.

Chambers, Warner, Good and Hopkins were charged with raping Jennie Summers. Ed Warner, Jeff Hopkins and "three other Negroes" were indicted for the rape of Rosa Hughes. Ed Hill and "other unnamed Negroes" were charged with raping Emma Davis.

According to newspaper accounts the men gained entrance to the women's home by presenting a false note ostensibly from a "white gentleman". On being admitted the eight proceeded to sexually assault the women while threatening them with a knife and pistol.

Court records from 1878 are still stored in our historic courthouse. The holographic court accounts are devoid of detail but pregnant with character. The penmanship is a work of art and the terminology used often camouflages an ironic sense of humor in our ancestors.

These records are contained in what we judges call Order Books because they are a permanent account of the judge's court orders.

In the Order Books of 1877 and 1878 is mention of some of the men indicted for the rapes in October 1878. There were charges for theft and assault. Jim Good had been convicted of a prior sexual assault and William Chambers had been suspected but not convicted of murdering his white prostitute lover, Annie McCool. Jeff Hopkins had been tried and acquitted of an earlier unrelated murder.

And Rosa Hughes, Emma Davis and Jennie Summers appeared regularly in court for prostitution. They were usually fined five dollars and told to go forth and sin no more.

Of course, some of these men who were indicted, four of whom were later lynched, had no record of prior legal difficulties. And, those with court records still deserved due process of law and the presumption of innocence.

And as to the "working girls", their manner of surviving did not preclude them from the protection of the law nor did it mean they could not be victims of rape.

As with many cases in court today, the fog of the facts requires a reservation of judgment and a diligent inquiry.

With your help we might be able to come to some fair conclusions about the alleged rapes, the death of Deputy Sheriff Oscar C. Thomas and the lynchings on the courthouse campus in October 1878.

It is, also, possible we might find that our history from October 1878 has relevant lessons for our lives in Posey County in October 2005.

Next week we will get into the Coroner's Inquest of Officer Thomas's death. Please remember, if you have discovered any information about these incidents, I am not immune from hearing the entire case.

EYEWITNESS TESTIMONY FROM OCTOBER 1878

(Week of October 24, 2005)

Should you have wandered across this column on your way to something important the past two weeks you may recall we have been ♪lost in the 70's♪, the 1870's.

Our put upon "white girls living very quietly," our brave Captain Cyrus O. Thomas and our Negro lynch victims are still our concern.

I thought some references to the contemporary (1878) eyewitness accounts might aid those of you who may have information about the events of October, 1878. Perhaps you could search your family memorabilia and share your information.

Ilse Horacek, Jerry King, Linda Young, and Glenn Curtis have generously helped me in researching these incidents. I want to be accurate. You, too, may be able to help shed light on these puzzling moments of Posey County history. If so, please give me a call.

Before we get to the Coroner's Inquest into the death of Deputy Sheriff Thomas and the lynchings of James Good, Jeff Hopkins, William Chambers and Edward Warner, some general observations about the reliability of eyewitness testimony may be in order.

Elizabeth F. Loftus is one of modern America's foremost authorities on eyewitness testimony. She is a professor of forensic psychology at the University of California. Loftus has conducted numerous experiments on eyewitness accounts of events. Among her conclusions is that eyewitness testimony is not only subject to factors such as personal prejudice, personal interest, physical and mental incapacity to observe and understand what we think we have seen, fear, excitement, lighting, length of observation, suggestions by others and many other factors, but it often is unshakable even when wrong.

In other words, our eyewitness testimony from October 1878 should be evaluated carefully just as you would do if you were to decide cases in court today.

Be that as it may, it is all we have to go on as all the circumstantial and physical evidence is now unavailable. So let's do the best we can with what we can glean from the 127 year old documentation of these first hand observations. And please note that you and I will only have space and time for a cursory exposition of these accounts.

Three eyewitnesses and two medical doctors testified at the Coroner's Inquest into C.O. Thomas's death. Daniel Harrison, Sr., the man accused by the Grand Jury of shooting Officer Thomas, gave his account of the incident to a newspaper editor, John C. Leffel, just before Harrison was killed by a lynch mob.

Harrison claimed that he had been shot first that early morning of October 11, 1878. He, also, claimed that on Wednesday, October 09, 1878 his son, Daniel Harrison Jr., had been taken from his home and lynched. Harrison, Sr., told Leffel that on October 10, 1878 three white men came to his home on First Street (Water Street) looking for another of his sons, John. According to Harrison, Sr., Henry Jones, William Combs and George Daniels came into the home at supper time on October 10. Jones put a pistol to Harrison's head and said "I'm going to kill you tonight." The three white men then searched the home.

Harrison, Sr. told Leffel that, "I don't know if my boys ravished the girls. I had nothing to do with it....I am married, have eight children, and I am 51 years old. Take me out and hang me I have no more to say."

Due to the events of October 09 and 10, Harrison had been sleeping with a loaded shotgun which he fired after he had been shot. He claimed he did not know the men were law officers.

Harrison was shot either through a window to his home (Harrison's version) or by the law officers after Harrison had shot O.C. Thomas (officers' version).

Harrison ran from his home but turned himself in later. He was locked up in the County jail which then was on the east side of the courthouse. He was later assaulted by a lynch mob and cut into pieces that were thrown into the jailhouse privy.

At the Coroner's Inquest, officers Charles Baker, Edward Hayes, and William Russell testified that they had gone with Deputy Sheriff C.O. Thomas to Daniel Harrison, Sr.'s home on First Street looking to arrest Edward Hill who was one of the men indicted for the alleged assaults on the prostitutes. They walked the few blocks from the jail and got to Harrison's house about 2:00 a.m.

Baker and Hayes were armed and went to the back of the house. Thomas and Russell had no weapons. They went to the front.

Hayes stated Thomas died instantly which agreed with the medical opinions of Dr.'s Edwin Spencer and Simon Pearse who performed the autopsy on Thomas.

Baker and Russell testified that Thomas lived for about one half hour after the shooting and made statements about who shot him.

Russell testified that immediately after he heard shots fired he went to Thomas who told him: "Bill, I am shot, they have killed me. Don't let the Negro get away."

Next week we will review the statements made by the "[T]hree white girls living quietly in a retired and lonely part of the city." Their establishment was one of several called "Red Ribbon" houses by our German ancestors. It was within three blocks of the courthouse and four blocks of Daniel Harrison's home.

Their eyewitness accounts of the alleged sexual assaults were, also, published on the front page of John C. Leffel's *Western Star* newspaper in rather lurid detail.

SHE SAID; HE SAID; THEY'RE DEAD

(Week of October 31, 2005)

I.

SHE SAID

The "three white girls living very quietly in a retired and lonely part of the city" were Jennie Summers, Emma Davis and Rosa Hughes. They lived on Water Street in the "Belleville" section of Mt. Vernon in a "red ribbon" house.

Each woman related her account of the incident occurring Monday, October 7, 1878 to John C. Leffel, editor of the *The Western Star* newspaper. He printed their versions in the October 17 edition of his paper.

Jennie Summers stated that "about 11:00 pm some person stepped to the door and knocked. He said he had a note for us from a white gentleman". When she opened the door, Jim Good, Jeff Hopkins, Bill Chambers, Ed Warner and Ed Hill rushed through the door with revolvers in their hands. The intruders immediately blew out the lights.

Hopkins and Warner "threw Summers down and ravished her for half an hour." Then Good and Chambers "went through the same procedure".

Summers told the newspaper that there were eight Negroes and she was positive of the identity of the four who raped her plus Daniel Harrison (a.k.a. Harris), Jr., who did not accost her. Summers did not recognize the other three.

Emma Davis told Leffel that she was "thrown down and ravished" by Ed Hill who then hid her behind a door and protected her from being attacked by any of the others.

Rosa Hughes stated that Ed Warner was the "first one who ravished me." After he did this, he "took sick", went to the door and vomited.

Hughes said that she did not know the identity of the other three Negroes that ravished her, but with revolvers drawn, "they made me get down on all-fours and remain in that position until they each in turn were satisfied".

On Tuesday, October 8, 1878 a Posey County Grand Jury was convened and indictments for rape were returned against Jim Good, Edward Hill, William Chambers, Jeff Hopkins, Ed Warner and three other "unnamed Negroes".

When on October 11, Deputy Sheriff Cyrus O. Thomas and three other officers went to the home of Daniel Harrison, Sr. looking to arrest Edward Hill, Thomas was killed by a shotgun blast.

After Harrison, Sr. turned himself in to the authorities, he said he had been shot first and that he did not know the men outside his home were lawmen. Harrison, Sr. claimed his son Dan, Jr. had been taken away and lynched on Wednesday, October 9 by white men with guns. Harrison Sr. was killed by the lynch mob on October 12, 1878. He was 51 years old with a wife and eight children. He owned a farm and two houses in Mt. Vernon.

II.

HE SAID

Editor John Leffel took statements from the lynching victims just before they were hanged from the locust trees on our courthouse campus on October 12, 1878.

Jim Good said, "I'm going to tell the truth before God and Man." He said he was not guilty and that he could prove where he was the night of October 7.

Good said he did not "ravish the girls" nor did he know who did. He stated he used to lead a gambler's life but was now a married man with three children and was about 38 years old.

Good was lynched a few minutes after this statement.

Jeff Hopkins related an alibi for the evening of October 7. He claimed he was innocent and could prove it. He said he was married, had five children and was 42 years old. According to the front page account in *The Western Star*, Hopkins, Good, Chambers and Warner were marched out of the jail with their hands tied. "One man walked on the right of each Negro while four men walked on the left holding the ropes in their hands and leading them to the public square."

When the four men were at the locust trees, "Ropes were quickly thrown over the limbs, and a dozen willing hands had them soon drawn four feet from the ground."

Leffel did not publish an account of any statement made by Ed Warner. Leffel did witness Warner's lynching and indicated Warner was the third one hanged. He survived about three minutes.

William Chambers told Leffel he was innocent and related his whereabouts on October 7. But as he was giving his account, "the rope attached to his neck was quickly thrown over a limb, and he was hung before he had time to finish his story."

III.

THEY'RE DEAD

Officer Cyrus O. Thomas was shot and killed while performing his duty.

Daniel Harrison, Jr. was killed by a mob. He may have been thrown into the furnace of a train's steam engine.

John Harrison may have been killed and his body stuffed into a hollow tree.

Daniel Harrison, Sr. was shot twice on October 11, 1878 then, while in the Posey County Jail, he was cut into pieces and thrown into the jail's privy.

Jim Good, William Chambers, Jeff Hopkins and Edward Warner were lynched on our courthouse square.

Edward Hill's final outcome is unknown, at least to me.

IV.

OBLIVION

Editor John C. Leffel suggested in his newspaper on October 17, 1878 that Posey County should just "let the appropriately dark pall of oblivion cover the whole transaction." And, for most of the past 127 years that's what has occurred.

Next week we (or at least I) will examine the legal system's role in the events of October 1878.

THE LAW'S DELAY

(Week of November 7, 2005)

Hamlet's uncle murdered Hamlet's father, married Hamlet's mother and stole Hamlet's kingdom. Hamlet was not amused. He, also, was indecisive. Hamlet vacillated between action and relying on the law for justice. He finally chose to take matters into his own hands, but, thereby, doomed himself and others.

Of course, there are reasons for allowing the law to handle society's problems. Facts can be developed. Charges can be put to the proof. Properly guided juries and judges can make objective decisions. Penalties can be fit to the crimes and the criminal.

Hamlet personally took revenge and bypassed these time-tested safeguards. Disaster resulted to Hamlet, to his family and friends, and to his country of Denmark where there was, indeed, something rotten.

Posey County was subjected to similar choices in October 1878. Unfortunately, we made similar mistakes.

Gentle Reader, please note that almost all of the information in these articles about a bygone time was taken from newspaper accounts that were often incomplete and sometimes contradictory. I have had to fill the logical lacunas and factual hiatuses with some surmises. Of course, if you know of better sources, I am open to correction.

When "three white women living in a quiet and lonely part of Mt. Vernon" claimed they had been raped by several African-American men on Monday, October 7, 1878 a Posey County Grand Jury quickly returned indictments against Daniel Harrison, Jr., John Harrison, Jim Good, Jeff Hopkins, Edward Warner, William Chambers, and Edward Hill.

On Tuesday, October 8, 1878 three white vigilantes took Daniel Harrison, Jr., from his father's home and lynched him or threw him into the furnace of a railroad steam engine. On October 9, 1878 these same men returned to the Harrison home looking for John Harrison. They put a revolver to Daniel Harrison, Sr.'s, head and threatened to kill him. The men did not find John Harrison at the Harrison home, but did later dispose of him by putting his body into a hollow tree just east of Mt. Vernon.

Four white lawmen went to the Harrison home at 2:00 o'clock a.m., on Thursday, October 10, 1878 to arrest Edward Hill, who was rumored to be hiding at the Harrison home. At the time the lawmen arrived, Daniel Harrison, Sr., was home in bed, fully dressed and sleeping with a loaded shotgun due to the earlier instances at his home. During a melee at the home, Deputy Sheriff Cyrus O. Thomas was shot and killed, and Harrison, Sr., was charged with the shooting. Harrison, Sr., who had been shot during the melee, turned himself in that same October 10th morning. He was lodged in the Posey County Jail which was then located on the campus of our present courthouse.

Also, Jeff Hopkins, Jim Good, Edward Warner, and William Chambers had been taken into custody and were incarcerated with Daniel Harrison, Sr., in the Posey County Jail.

On the front page of Posey County's *Western Star* newspaper edition of October 10, 1878 editors, John C. Leffel and S.D. McReynolds, stated:

> "Jeff Hopkins, Jim Good, … and … other Negroes…forced
> an entrance into a house of ill-fame on First Street, Monday night,
> and raped the inmates there. …Jim Good is not as good as his name,
> this being the second time he has been guilty of this crime. …The girls
> raped were all white. A little hanging would do Jim Good a great deal
> of good."

Editor Leffel attended the jail break-in and the summary executions that took place two days after his article appeared. Much of the information in this article came from his accounts.

In the early morning hours of October 12, 1878 a mob broke into the jail, cut Daniel Harrison, Sr., into pieces and threw his body into the jail's privy. Jim Good, Jeff Hopkins, Edward Warner, and William Chambers were dragged out of the jail and hanged from the locust trees ringing the courthouse. The four bodies were left hanging on the square until after the funeral of Cyrus O. Thomas, which took place the afternoon of October 12, 1878.

It was not unusual, especially in the south, for Negro lynch victims to be left hanging for an extended period of time as a "warning" to others who may have, also, "deserved hanging" but who had not been caught.

In 1939, Billie Holiday first performed the song "Strange Fruit", which was her paean to all those black people who had been lynched.

> ♪*Southern trees bear a strange fruit,*
> *Blood on the leaves and blood at the root,*
> *Black body swinging in the Southern breeze,*
> *Strange fruit hanging from the poplar trees.*
>
> *Pastoral scene of the gallant South,*
> *The bulging eyes and the twisted mouth,*
> *Scene of magnolia sweet and fresh,*
> *And the sudden smell of burning flesh!*
>
> *Here is a fruit for the crows to pluck,*
> *For the rain to gather, for the wind to suck,*
> *For the sun to rot, for a tree to drop,*
> *Here is a strange and bitter crop.* ♪

By leaving the young men hanging on our public square all day, it would have been practically impossible for our law enforcement and judicial communities to be unaware of the lynchings.

However, even though the Posey County Prosecuting Attorney, the Judge and, in fact, most of southern Indiana knew the men indicted for the rapes of the women and the murder of Officer Thomas had been killed in1878, the legal system kept up a charade that the cases were going to be tried. Every term of court from 1878 to 1881, the cases were called, then "set over to the next term."

During these three years, no action was taken against the people involved in the deaths of Daniel Harrison, Sr., Daniel Harrison, Jr., John Harrison, Jim Good, Jeff Hopkins, Edward Warner, and William Chambers. In 1881, the Prosecutor, without fanfare, dismissed the indictments against the dead rape defendants. I have not been able to determine the ultimate fate of Edward Hill.

This was not our legal system's finest hour. Of course, injustice is not the sole province of days gone by. Today, "lynchings" are usually more procedural than literal and can involve letting the guilty go free as well as convicting the innocent. Or they may involve imposing Draconian or effete punishment instead of justice.

I am reminded of what Supreme Court Justice Clarence Thomas said about his confirmation hearings: "This is simply a high class lynching." And I recall a recent case in another Southern Indiana county where a young black man was sentenced for non-payment of child support and for assaulting a white police officer who had intervened in a domestic dispute. At the sentencing hearing, the police department filled the courtroom with uniformed officers. Was the judge improperly influenced? Probably not even that judge knows for sure. After twenty-five years of imposing sentences, I can attest that it is not easy to exclude all extraneous factors. Court decisions are already hard enough. Justice is ill served by outside attempts to pressure court proceedings.

Hamlet would have been well advised to let the law, even with its many unsatisfactory outcomes, handle affairs in Denmark.

Usually Shakespeare's characters personify lessons for all of us.

As for now, the month of October has come and gone again and the spectres that haunt my mind as I walk across the courthouse lawn are less demanding. And though justice may have been delayed one hundred twenty-seven years, perhaps with your help it will not be completely denied.

Taken from The Police Gazette (1878),
edited by Gene Smith & Jayne Barry Smith

Peg and Jim Redwine at JPeg Ranch Pond
Photograph by Jane Redwine Bartlett

ABOUT THE AUTHOR

It was a dark and stormy night outside the tiny log cabin on the Osage Indian Nation. A.C. Redwine could only hold his wife's hand and pray as Clarice struggled to give life to her beloved son. It was the best of times; World War II was half over. It was the worst of times; World War II was only half over.

All right, with apologies to Edward Bulwer-Lytton and Charles Dickens, the actual "about" follows:

Born:	1943 in Pawhuska, Osage County, Oklahoma (in a hospital);
Reside:	JPeg Ranch, neither hat nor cattle, in New Harmony, Posey County, Indiana, with wife, Peg, a dog, and two cats;
Immediate Family:	Wife, Peg, son, Jim who is married to Gina, two daughters, Heather and her husband Tony, Nikki and her husband Doug and seven grandchildren: Alec, Kerstin, Adrian, Paxton, Jonathan, Nick and Elyse;
Employment:	1981-present, Posey County and Circuit Court Judge;
Education:	Indiana University, 1968; I.U. School of Law (Bloomington), summer of 1970; Indiana Graduate Judges College, 1997;
Judicial Teaching:	**National Judicial College faculty member;** Has taught judges from Palestine, Ukraine, Russia, Jordan, Bahrain and America for the NJC since 1998;
Hobbies:	Snow skiing, golf, writing and mowing lots of grass. Used to work with boxers but quit in 2001 because it hurt and made him tired; and
First Book:	The historical novel, **JUDGE LYNCH!**, published July 2008; ISBN: 978-1-4343-9402-6 (sc) ISBN: 978-1-4343-9403-3 (hc).